MW01252875

PSYCHOLOGY RESEARCH PROGRESS

PSYCHOLOGICAL WELL-BEING

CULTURAL INFLUENCES, MEASUREMENT STRATEGIES AND HEALTH IMPLICATIONS

PSYCHOLOGY RESEARCH PROGRESS

Additional books in this series can be found on Nova's website
under the Series tab.

Additional e-books in this series can be found on Nova's website
under the e-book tab.

PSYCHOLOGICAL WELL-BEING

CULTURAL INFLUENCES, MEASUREMENT STRATEGIES AND HEALTH IMPLICATIONS

RAFAEL BOWERS
EDITOR

publishers
New York

GUELPH HUMBER LIBRARY
205 Humber College Blvd
Toronto, ON   M9W 5L7

Copyright © 2016 by Nova Science Publishers, Inc.

All rights reserved. No part of this book may be reproduced, stored in a retrieval system or transmitted in any form or by any means: electronic, electrostatic, magnetic, tape, mechanical photocopying, recording or otherwise without the written permission of the Publisher.

We have partnered with Copyright Clearance Center to make it easy for you to obtain permissions to reuse content from this publication. Simply navigate to this publication's page on Nova's website and locate the "Get Permission" button below the title description. This button is linked directly to the title's permission page on copyright.com. Alternatively, you can visit copyright.com and search by title, ISBN, or ISSN.

For further questions about using the service on copyright.com, please contact:
Copyright Clearance Center
Phone: +1-(978) 750-8400   Fax: +1-(978) 750-4470   E-mail: info@copyright.com.

NOTICE TO THE READER
The Publisher has taken reasonable care in the preparation of this book, but makes no expressed or implied warranty of any kind and assumes no responsibility for any errors or omissions. No liability is assumed for incidental or consequential damages in connection with or arising out of information contained in this book. The Publisher shall not be liable for any special, consequential, or exemplary damages resulting, in whole or in part, from the readers' use of, or reliance upon, this material. Any parts of this book based on government reports are so indicated and copyright is claimed for those parts to the extent applicable to compilations of such works.

Independent verification should be sought for any data, advice or recommendations contained in this book. In addition, no responsibility is assumed by the publisher for any injury and/or damage to persons or property arising from any methods, products, instructions, ideas or otherwise contained in this publication.

This publication is designed to provide accurate and authoritative information with regard to the subject matter covered herein. It is sold with the clear understanding that the Publisher is not engaged in rendering legal or any other professional services. If legal or any other expert assistance is required, the services of a competent person should be sought. FROM A DECLARATION OF PARTICIPANTS JOINTLY ADOPTED BY A COMMITTEE OF THE AMERICAN BAR ASSOCIATION AND A COMMITTEE OF PUBLISHERS.

Additional color graphics may be available in the e-book version of this book.

Library of Congress Cataloging-in-Publication Data

ISBN: 978-1-63484-354-6

Published by Nova Science Publishers, Inc. † New York

DUGLAH HUMBER LIBRARY
205 Humber College Blvd
Toronto, ON   M9W 5L7

CONTENTS

PREFACE

Psychological well-being can be influenced by several factors. This book provides research and reviews cultural influences of well-being, as well as discusses measurement strategies and health implications. Chapter One studies immigrants' psychological well-being by investigating their motivation, preference of tourist activities, and emotional experiences during their visit to their homeland. Chapter Two proposes the creation and validation of theories and measures on positive psychological constructs that can be integrated into a tool that aims at what might be called a desirable and credible global psychology. Chapter Three examines the relationship between language, identity and behavioral acculturation and well-being among non-western skilled migrants in a western host society. Chapter Four discusses well-being, health status and culture. Chapter Five analyzes emotional intelligence in adolescents. Chapter Six provides a study of the psychological well-being of Chinese immigrant adolescents. Chapter Seven explains variables related to psychological well-being, and discuss the importance of psychological well-being in the field of psychological counseling and guidance. Chapter Eight examines the predictive role of marital relations and communication styles in psychological well-being within a model proposed by Ryff. The final chapter studies the psychological health among frail older adults with chronic pain.

Chapter 1 - Literature review suggests that homeland tourism benefits immigrants' psychological well-being. However, immigrants' homeland visit behavior in relation to their psychological well-being is still unclear due to lack of empirical research. This study attempts to study immigrants' psychological well-being by investigating their motivation, preference of tourist activities, and emotional experiences during their visit to homeland. This study takes place in Macao and targets the Chinese immigrants from Asian regions. The statistical results reveal three major dimensions of travel motives, namely, attractiveness of the place, connect to the past, and socialize with people. These travel motives have significant effect on respondents' preference of tourist activities and emotional experiences, revealing immigrants' behavior during their homeland visit and how homeland visit contributes to immigrants' positive feelings and improvement in psychological well-being.

The value of homeland tourism should be taken into account for the management of immigrants' travel satisfaction and psychological well-being. The managerial implications for destination managers and are discussed.

Chapter 2 - In this chapter, the reiterated need for creating psychological knowledge and measurement instruments that are universal in character is postulated. This effort would inevitably be based on the simultaneous and/or continuous study of different cultural, social, political, and economic communities. With this purpose in mind, this study proposes the creation and validation of theories and measures on positive psychological constructs that can be integrated into a tool that aims at what might be called a desirable and credible global psychology. Several comparative studies that present some perspectives and measurements from various countries on optimism, generosity, and forgiveness, developed in the US, Israel, and Mexico, are included here. Different samples from university students and the open population residing in the metropolitan area of the city of Monterrey, Nuevo León, Mexico, were used. Confirmatory factor analysis was conducted to calculate the construct validity of the original instruments for each culture, the convergent validity of the premises was assessed, and a new measure for each construct was obtained, resulting from combining the original instruments and those applied to local Mexican residents, achieving adequate goodness of fit and reliability in the final version measuring optimism, generosity, and forgiveness. It is concluded that there are great advantages to combining theories and measurements of the same positive psychological construct, from various cultures, thus supporting the creation of an appropriate global positive psychology.

Chapter 3 - Qualified, trained and experienced skilled migrants from non-Western countries are becoming increasingly important drivers of economic growth in Western host countries as they help fill skill shortages in the labour market. Host countries expect skilled migrants to integrate into the socio-economic fabric of society and become contributing members. However, there are many challenges inherent in migration which can affect migrant's well-being, including language barriers, adapting to local customs, socialising with the majority population, transferring credentials, and finding suitable employment. Integrating into the host society can be more complex and challenging when there is cultural distance between migrants' sending and receiving societies. Acculturation describes a process that changes migrants' attitudes, values, customs, beliefs and behaviours in accordance with the host culture. Migrants' acculturation to a host society occurs in a number of different domains, including host country language, identity and behaviour. The current study examined the relationship between language, identity and behavioural acculturation and well-being among 306 Indian and Sri Lankan skilled migrants residing in Australia. Participants completed the Language, Identity and Behavioural Acculturation Scale (Birman and Trickett 2001) and the Personal Well-being Index (Cummins 2006) and provided demographic information. Controlling for gender, age at migration, years since migration, education, expectation to return to country of origin, and pre-migration socioeconomic status, only identity acculturation significantly predicted well-being.

Chapter 4 - Health status and well-being are individual complex dimensions where wide ranges of elements interact. With the present contribution, the authors aim to question how urban and individual objective and subjective elements will affect health status and well-being, investigating in particular the possible relationship between cultural and leisure elements and individual health conditions. The evaluation is based on research undertaken in 2010 on a statistically representative sample of Italy's Milan population. The study is aiming to assess the determinants of psychological well-being and perceived health status through a vast assembly of variables covering socio-demographic and health-related data that are widely recognized as relevant determinants in the literature. In addition fifteen cultural and community activities have been scrutinized in order to weight the incidence of these elements in relation to the general evaluation framework. The results show that the multidimensional construct of subjective well-being is extremely complex and results from a dynamic interplay of several physical, social and environmental descriptors. Furthermore, individual health status perception will be affected significantly by leisure and cultural activities.

Chapter 5 - Emotional Intelligence (EI) is associated with better performance at work, greater well-being, physical health, and higher quality of interpersonal relationships... Given the importance of EI in human life, the study had three main objectives: (1) to analyze sex differences in EI; (2) to explore the concomitant relations between EI and various behavioral, emotional, cognitive, and physical factors (positive and negative social behaviors, behavioral problems, empathy, happiness, cognitive strategies to resolve social situations, ability to analyze feelings, personality traits, state-trait anger, anger expression, and psychosomatic symptoms); and (3) to identify predictors of high EI. This study was conducted with a sample of 148 Spanish adolescents aged between 13 and 16 (45.3% boys and 54.7% girls). The study uses a descriptive, comparative, and correlational cross-sectional methodology. In order to assess the variables, the authors administered 10 assessment instruments with psychometric guarantees of reliability and validity. The results of the analysis of variance only revealed sex differences in interpersonal emotional intelligence, with significantly higher scores in females. In the rest of the variables (intrapersonal intelligence, stress management, adaptability, and general mood), and in the Emotional Intelligence Quotient (EIQ; global score that includes all the EI variables), the scores were similar in both sexes. Pearson correlation coefficients suggest that boys and girls with high EIQ were significantly more likely to display many positive social behaviors (social conformity, social sensitivity, help-collaboration, and self-assurance-firmness), many feelings of happiness, personality traits such as conscientiousness, openness, extroversion, agreeableness, and emotional stability, few social anxiety behaviors, and few psychosomatic symptoms. In addition, boys with high EIQ showed many prosocial-leadership behaviors, high empathy, high anger control-out and anger control-in, few aggressive and antisocial behaviors, few anxiety problems, and a low level of state-anger. Girls with high EIQ had high social adaptation/adjustment, a low level of trait-anger, and low anger expression-in. The results of the regression analyses revealed seven predictors of EIQ that explain 63.7% of the variance: high happiness, high agreeableness, low emotional instability, many help-collaboration behaviors, few psychosomatic symptoms, high anger control-out, and few anxiety problems. The results suggest the importance of implementing programs to promote the development of EI during childhood and adolescence, and the study identifies relevant variables to design these programs.

Chapter 6 - As the number of Chinese immigrants grows exponentially, our public school system has subsequently faced massive influxes of Chinese immigrant students. While adjusting to living in a vastly different sociocultural milieu, these immigrant students are also simultaneously adapting to a different educational system and learning a new language. All of these new academic, sociocultural, and linguistic demands can incur stress and other negative consequences that intrude on Chinese immigrant students' psychological well-being. This phenomenon, in turn, portends particular challenges to the teachers and educators working with them. It is, thus, imperative that we understand Chinese immigrant students' post-immigration experience to better address their psychological needs. This study investigated particularly three first-generation Chinese immigrant adolescents' meaning making of the factors contributing to their shaping and reshaping of their ethnic identity vis-à-vis their cultural adaptation as a means to understand their psychological well-being. To this end, the author conducted individual interviews with these adolescents. The results revealed that the three Chinese immigrant adolescents' meaning making of their formation and reformation of their ethnic identity was influenced by four major factors: (1) ethnic background; (2) cultural valuation of filial piety; (3) friendship network; and (4) English proficiency. These contributing factors are interpreted from both the cultural and contextual perspectives. Educational implications and directions for future research are also discussed.

Chapter 7 - Adolescence is a physical, sexual, cognitive, emotional and social development period. Adolescents may experience difficulties about meeting their psychological needs, adapting themselves to changing life conditions. Psychological counseling and guidance services not only focus on identifying and treating psychological disorders, but also they should focus on the positive developmental aspects of mental health. By doing so, they may contribute youths to attain better understanding about their strong aspects and sources they have, to develop effective strategies against life difficulties, to set realistic targets about future, and eventually to obtain psychological well-being (PWB). Adolescents' positive characteristics may be improved with school-based applications long before problem emerges and before adolescents' psychological well-being is not ruined, their live skills may be strengthened, and their positive coping skills and self-esteem may be increased. In this chapter the authors propose to introduce the concept of PWB, to explain variables related to PWB, to discuss the importance of PWB in the field of psychological counseling and guidance.

Chapter 8 - Social sciences have shown recurrent interest in the associations between marriage and its psychological outcomes. Marriage may provide numerous psychological benefits by offering meaning and purpose, facilitating interactions between spouses, sharing financial resources, and generating emotional and social support. Although previous research has demonstrated clear links between marital quality and well-being, the role of specific marital relations and communication styles in psychological well-being remains not fully discovered. The quality of marital interactions and the ways in which partners communicate with each other appear to be linked to their well-being.

The aim of this chapter is to examine the predictive role of marital relations and communication styles in psychological well-being within a model proposed by Ryff (1989, 2014). One hundred and five couples (105 women and 105 men) participated in this study. Their ages ranged from 23 to 62 years ($M = 41.83$; $SD = 11.16$). The group was a representative sample of Polish couples in terms of social status and age. They completed three measures: The Matched Marriage Questionnaire, The Marital Communication Questionnaire, and The Psychological Well-being Scale. Findings showed that couples tended to experience numerous psychological benefits through marital interactions and communication skills. Yet, their overall psychological well-being depend on the quality of marital relations and communication styles. The marital relations which were based on intimacy, self-realization, and similarity were positively associated with psychological well-being dimensions, while the marital relations characterized by disappointment were negatively linked to psychological well-being. The relative contribution of marital relations and communication styles to psychological well-being was different for wives and husbands. The results lead to the conclusion that a better understanding of marital relations and communication styles is likely to improve partners' well-being.

Chapter 9 - *Background*. Populations are aging and an increasing number of people are suffering from disease and disability as part of the aging process. Pain is common in older adults, and affects both their physical and psychological functioning. However, the majority of older adults who experience pain do not seek the advice of health care professionals.

Uncontrollable pain can lead to a spiral of inactivity and reduce the quality of life of older adults in the community. A self-managed health program may help to break through this spiral, thus reducing uncontrollable chronic pain among frail older adults and enabling them to live happier lives.

Method. Two community elderly centers agreed to host the Healthy Living Program (HLP). Fifty community dwelling older people from those two centers were invited to join the six-week HLP. The program covered the following topics: healthy eating habits, pain management, and information on drugs related to pain and chronic illness. The targeted participants were recruited from the community elderly centers by convenience sampling. In the study, psychological well-being among older adults was measured pre- and post- test using a subjective happiness scale. In addition, information on the participants' knowledge of healthy eating habits, fall prevention, and drugs was collected.

Results. A slight increase was seen in the participants' scores on the happiness scale after the HLP, but the change was not statistically significant. Their pain scores decreased, and their pain interference scores showed a statistically significant decrease ($p < 0.05$). Finally, a significant improvement was noted in the participants' intake of protein, vegetables, and fruit and in their knowledge of drug management.

Conclusion. A health self-management program should be offered to elderly people, and nurses should encourage them to engage in it to enrich their knowledge of how to take care of themselves, increase their happiness, and enhance their quality of life. Older adults with good habits will then be able to enjoy longer and healthier lives in the community.

In: Psychological Well-Being
Editor: Rafael Bowers

ISBN: 978-1-63484-354-6
© 2016 Nova Science Publishers, Inc.

Chapter 1

THE PSYCHOLOGY OF HOMELAND TOURISM: TRAVEL MOTIVES, TOURIST EXPERIENCES AND FEELINGS

*Man-U Io**

Institute for Tourism Studies,
Macao SAR, China

ABSTRACT

Literature review suggests that homeland tourism benefits immigrants' psychological well-being. However, immigrants' homeland visit behavior in relation to their psychological well-being is still unclear due to lack of empirical research. This study attempts to study immigrants' psychological well-being by investigating their motivation, preference of tourist activities, and emotional experiences during their visit to homeland. This study takes place in Macao and targets the Chinese immigrants from Asian regions. The statistical results reveal three major dimensions of travel motives, namely, attractiveness of the place, connect to the past, and socialize with people. These travel motives have significant effect on respondents' preference of tourist activities and emotional experiences, revealing immigrants' behavior during their homeland visit and how homeland visit contributes to immigrants' positive feelings and improvement in psychological well-being.

The value of homeland tourism should be taken into account for the management of immigrants' travel satisfaction and psychological well-being. The managerial implications for destination managers and are discussed.

Keywords: Chinese immigrants, homeland tourism, travel motives, tourist activities, emotional experiences

---

* E-mail: yan@ift.edu.mo.

INTRODUCTION

Previous studies suggested that homeland visit benefits immigrants' psychological well-being in many ways, such as consolidating family social capital by visiting friends and relatives in homeland and gaining emotional support from homeland people (Hung, Xiao, and Yang, 2013). Moreover, seeking personal identity and understanding ancestor's cultural and historical background are important motives for immigrants to visit their homeland (Maruyama and Stronza, 2010; Pearce, 2012). In recent years, homeland tourism was studied in relation to roots tourism, diasporas, and migration (Garrido, 2011; Maruyama and Stronza, 2010), as well as visiting friends and relatives (VFR) (Feng and Page, 2000; Shani and Uriely, 2011; Uriely, 2010). However, homeland visit is still an understudied form of tourism nowadays (Pearce, 2012).

Homeland is the place where immigrants grew up and formed a strong part of their biographical identity (Pearce, 2012; Picard, Reffuveille, Eustache, and Piolino, 2009). By visiting homeland, immigrants not only consolidate their connection to their homeland community and affirm their cultural identity, but also recollect their past memories and experiences vividly and in turn gaining a deep emotional bond with their homeland (Hung et al., 2013; Maruyama and Stronza, 2010; Maruyama, weber, and stronza, 2010). Immigrants' familiarity with their homeland is likely to lead them to behave differently from general sightseeing tourists or holiday makers and result in different emotional experiences and psychological well-being. However, it is not much known about immigrants' homeland visit with respect to their psychological well-being, nor is immigrants' travel behavior regarding travel motives, preference of tourist activities, and emotional experiences during homeland visit. Therefore, the investigation into immigrants' travel motives, preference of tourist activities, and emotional experiences will help to improve our understanding of how immigrants develop their travel experiences with their homeland which benefits their psychological well-being.

This research study takes place in Macao where the Chinese immigrants from mainland China make up over half of the population. While the local born residents are accounted for 40% of the population, the Chinese immigrants from Mainland China have carried 41% of the population (Statistics and Census). These immigrants also visit their homeland in mainland China regularly. In 2012, over 430,000 outbound Macao residents traveled abroad. Of the total outbound Macao residents, 49.6% used the services of travel agencies to travel to Mainland China independently and 74.2% traveled in a package tour arranged by travel agencies to Mainland China (Statistics and Census Bureau, 2012). The statistics suggested that Mainland China is the major destination for outbound Macao residents including the immigrants from Mainland China.

LITERATURE REVIEW

Immigrants' Travel Behavior

The interrelationship between tourism and immigrants was discussed widely, and the major argument suggested that many forms of migration generate tourism flows due to the geographical extension of friendship networks (Feng and Page, 2000; Lehto, Morrison, and O'Leary, 2001). Therefore, visiting friend and relatives becomes a popular travel motive for contemporary tourists, and VFR becomes a popular tourist market segment (Seaton and Palmer, 1997; Shani, 2011). VFR tourists were usually studied with respect to their expenditure, destination choice, visit duration, and demographic characteristics (Seaton and Palmer, 1997). The economic benefit of VFR tourism to a destination is also popular for research over a decade (Backer, 2012; Lehto et al., 2001). In recent years, the discussion of VFR tourism was extended to VFR tourists' experience at the destination and their interaction with the host friends and relatives (Shani and Uriely, 2011; Uriely, 2010).

Similar to VFR tourism, family reunion travel involves visiting friends and relatives in either immigrants' homeland or foreign countries. The major travel motives of family reunion tourists were identified as: enhancing family communication and interconnections, improving family adaptability, improving the stability of family relationships (Yun and Lehto, 2009). These findings revealed the similarity between VFR and family reunion tourists that seeing and talking to friends and relatives was the most important travel motive. Moreover, geographic closeness determined the destination choice of family reunion tourists, and reunion size affected their activities choices (Yun and Lehto, 2009). Family reunion tourists' choice of tourist activities were correlated with their travel motivations (Kluin and Lehto, 2012). These previous studies provide the present research with some clues for investigating why immigrants visit their homeland and what to do during their homeland tour.

Another similar form of tourism is ethnic tourism which highlights the relationship between immigrants and tourism (Yang, Wall, and Smith, 2008). Ethnic tourism could be defined in two ways that one refers to visiting an ancestral land as a tourist for visiting friends and relatives who are still living there (Feng and Page, 2000; King, 1994; Ostrowski, 1991); another one refers to visiting a foreign destination for seeking exotic cultural experiences by the interaction with ethnic groups and the consumption of ethnic products (Yang, 2010). The ethnic tourism for seeking exotic experience is more popular and widely discussed in tourism literature, whereas another type of ethnic tourism in which immigrants visit their ancestral home received little attention from tourism researchers (King, 1994).

Given the review of previous studies, VFR tourism may take place in either immigrants' homeland or foreign countries, and visiting friends and relatives is the dominant travel motive. However, for immigrants who visited their homeland, no empirical findings suggest that visiting friends and relatives is the only important travel motive. While on the contrary, some previous studies about immigrants visiting their homeland suggested that seeking personal identity and reconnection to ancestral home were the important reasons for homeland visit (Maruyama and Stronza, 2010). The same authors argued that for the descendants of Chinese immigrants living in US, visiting ancestral homeland was an effective way to understand the cultural background and ethnical identity of their ancestors and themselves. Also, for immigrants, homeland visit was a way "to gain a sense of solidarity with people who still live there and to feel a sense of empowerment to have succeeded in a country of settlement" (Maruyama and Stronza, 2010, p.23). In this sense, for immigrants, visiting homeland may not only for visiting friends and relatives, but also for connecting to and learning about their past.

Moreover, it was found that immigrants tended to narrate and construct their diasporic community by visiting their homeland and engaging in the experiences with their homeland (Powers, 2011). The same author also argued that the influence of homeland tourism on immigrants' beliefs, values and behavior could be much. Therefore, visiting friends and relatives may be a tactic for immigrants to consolidate the connection with the old community of homeland and stay in line with their cultural identity. Similarly, a recent study also argued that the Chinese immigrants, particularly, those Chinese immigrants who experienced a lower degree of acculturation in Hong Kong visited their homeland in Mainland China for consolidating their family social capital, as their homeland culture may still paly a dominant role in their identity and adaptation, and the homeland tour may help them to confirm their personal and social identities and to gain a sense of security (Hung et al., 2013).

For some immigrants and their descendants who were born and have grown up in a country of exile, seeking their ethnical identity seems to be the major reason for visiting their ancestral homeland, even though they had no friends or relatives living there and had some cultural and language barriers (Garrido, 2011). The importance of seeking personal identity for immigrants and their descendants thus was evident. The need of seeking personal identity was discussed with respect to immigrants' acculturation level in the new society (Abu-Rayya, 2009; Hung et al., 2013) and their personal and social identities in the country of exile (Maruyama et al., 2010). Given all these previous studies, homeland tourists' needs should be different from that of VFR tourists, and thus homeland tourism should not be seen as VFR tourism.

Homeland Tourism Experience

Tourism experience is always considered important for contemporary tourists in all forms of tourism. Tourism scholars discussed tourism experience widely in different forms of tourism and suggested that a quality tour should provide tourists with memorable tourism experience (Huang, Hsu, and Chan, 2010; Morgan; Reisinger and Steiner, 2006). For example, in heritage tourism it was advocated to provide tourists with a sense of authenticity of a historical site or ethnical artifact in order to improve tourists' experience and satisfaction with the tour (Wang, 1999; Yeoman, Brass, and McMahon-Beattie, 2007).

As a place where individuals spent their part or entire childhood and formed a strong part of their biographical identity, homeland provides immigrants with many cues for recollecting their past memories (Pearce2012). Recollection of past memories and experiences is an important component of memorable tourism experience and is critical to one's personal identity development (Kim, 2010; Tung and Ritchie, 2011a). It was found that memorable travel memories was much related to their past experiences in terms of family milestone and major events, relationship development, nostalgic reenactment, and freedom pursuits (Tung and Ritchie, 2011b). In homeland, through a high degree of interaction with their family, relatives, and old friends, immigrants may effectively relive their past life experiences and generate a memorable tourism experience. Meanwhile, Kim (2010) found that the experiential factors of involvement, hedonic activity, and local culture in a destination positively affected tourists' recollection of autobiographical memory vividly and resulted in a memorable travel experience.

For homeland tourists, it is easy to get involved with the place and people deeply as homeland is a familiar place. Moreover, homeland tourists' preference of activities is expected to reveal how they recollect their past memories vividly and what emotional experiences they gain during their homeland visit.

In generating a memorable tourism experience, emotion plays an important role. It was found in some psychological studies that positive emotion associated with past memories or events is more memorable and lasting in one's mind (Rasmussen and Berntsen, 2009; Rubin and Berntsen, 2003). Happiness gained from tourism is always associated with positive emotion gained during the tour (Filep and Deery, 2010). Moreover, positive emotional experiences are related to satisfaction with the destination (Hosany and Gilber, 2010). Therefore, the more positive homeland tourists feel during homeland visit, the more satisfied they are with their homeland visit and the more memorable their tourism experience will be, and the satisfied tourism experience benefits their psychological well-being.

Besides, it was found that tourists who experienced some emotional thoughts had a higher level of satisfaction with their tourism experience at the visited site (McIntosh and Prentice, 1999). Tourists could experience some emotional thoughts by linking the visited site to their cultural identity and comparing their past and present lives (Dijk and Weiler, 2009; Poria, Biran, and Reichel, 2009). Pearce (2012) argued that visiting homeland and familiar places could enrich tourists' emotional experience as the memory recollection leads them to review their past and present. The comparison between their past and present lives enables tourists to find new meanings of life and better plan their future life. The assessment of tourists' emotional thought and experience includes tourists' feelings of the visited place, perceived meaningfulness of the place, desire of return to the same place, and recollection of personal past memories (Dijk and Weiler, 2009; McIntosh and Prentice, 1999; Poria, Reichel, and Biran, 2006). These previous studies provide some guidelines for assessing homeland tourists' feelings and emotional thoughts.

METHODOLOGY

A quantitative survey method was applied to this study. The survey was conducted in Macao with self-administered methods. The target population was the Chinese immigrants from Mainland China and Hong Kong, who are currently living in Macao. Total eight institutes which served as the popular places for the immigrant community were selected as the venues for this survey. The eight institutes consist of four adult vocational schools and four community service centers in Macao. In each institute, all qualified target respondents were invited to participate in the survey through the contact person of the institute. Only the volunteers of the target population were recruited. The questionnaire was designed in Chinese. Total 500 completed survey questionnaires were collected and respondents consisted of half female and half male.

The survey questionnaire consists of four sections: demographic information, travel motivation, tourist activities, and feelings about homeland visit. the scales for measuring travel motivation, activities and feelings were adopted from previous studies related to homeland tourism (Hung et al., 2013; Io, 2014a; Io, 2014b; Io, 2014c; Maruyama et al., 2010). There were total 33 items measured, including travel motives (11 items), tourist activities (9 items), and emotional experiences (13 items). A pilot test was conducted and a minor revision on wordings was undertaken. The 33 items were measured by a five-point Likert scale, ranging from definitely disagree (1) to strongly agree (5). Regarding data analysis, exploratory factor analysis and reliability test were conducted. The structural equation model by Amos 19 was constructed to test the relationship between travel motives, tourist activities, and emotional experiences. The statistical findings are presented as follows.

RESULTS

Of 500 respondents, 77.2% had visited their homeland within the past 12 months. Moreover, 61.4% of the respondents stayed in their homeland during last visit from one to five days, and 36.2% of the respondents stayed in their homeland six days and above. The statistical results suggest that the Chinese immigrants in Macao generally visited their homeland oftentimes. Regarding respondents' travel motive, tourist activities, and emotional experiences, the results are presented and discussed in the following text.

Travel Motivation of Homeland Tourists

Exploratory factor analysis was conducted for assessing respondents' travel motivation, tourist activities, and feelings. For travel motives, the principal component extraction with Varimax rotation technique was used to reduce the eleven items of travel motives into fewer managerial factors. As shown in Table 1, the Varimax rotation extracted three factors, and the accumulated variance was 67.3%. The factor loadings of all eleven items are higher than .50, suggesting that all items have well defined the three factors. The three factors were labeled: "connect to the past" (four items, α = .82), "attractiveness of the place" (four items, α = .84), "socialize with people" (three items, α = .72). The alphas values of all three factors are over the .70 recommended threshold, suggesting that the three factors have very good internal consistency. The mean values of three factors suggest that "socialize with people" (M = 3.81) was the strongest travel motive for respondents to visit their homeland, followed by "attractiveness of the place" (M = 3.35) and "connect to the past" (M = 3.19).

In the factor of "socialize with people", the item of visiting friends and relatives (M = 4.3) had a very high mean value and thus became very important.

This result is consistent with the findings in the study of Feng and Page (2000) that the Chinese immigrants tended to visit their homeland for meeting friends and relatives. However, it is noted that the mean values of all three factors of travel motivation were over 3 (the mid-point), suggesting that respondents visited their homeland for various important reasons, and VFR is only one of the various travel motives in this present study.

Regarding homeland tourists' preference of tourist activities, as shown in Table 2, two factors were extracted from nine items by using principal component extraction with Varimax rotation: 1. "sightseeing" (five items, α = .87) and 2. "relive the past" (four items, α = .78). The accumulated variance is 65%, and the factor loadings of all items are higher than .60, suggesting that all items have well defined the two factors. The alphas values of factor one and two are 0.87 and 0.78 respectively, meaning that the two factors are highly reliable.

The factors of activities revealed that respondents enjoyed reliving their past and touring around the place like a sightseeing tourist. Meanwhile, the mean value of "relive the past" (M = 3.61) is higher than that of "sightseeing" (M = 3.04), suggesting that respondents participated in the activities of reliving their past more than sightseeing.

Table 1. Rotated factor matrix for travel motivation

	Factor loadings			Mean	Std. Deviation
	1	2	3		
Factor 1. Connect to the past Alpha = .82				**3.20**	
I want to share my past experiences with my loved ones	.776			3.29	1.38
To affirm my place identity/who I am	.775			2.99	1.45
I want to know the present development of my homeland	.720			3.27	1.35
To relive my past life	.630			3.23	1.46
Factor 2. Attractiveness of the place. Alpha = .84				**3.35**	
I like the local culture		.820		3.38	1.34
I like the scenes and sights		.736		3.42	1.37
I like shopping there		.730		2.92	1.38
I like the local cuisine		.684		3.69	1.25
Factor 3. Socialize with people. Alpha = .72				**3.81**	
Visit friends and relatives			.812	4.30	1.23
I want to spend free time with my family/friends there			.725	3.68	1.32
I want to have my vacation in a familiar place.			.540	3.44	1.39
% of Variance	**25.11**	**24.97**	**17.22**		

Similar to the above analysis of travel motives and tourist activities, by using principal component extraction with Varimax rotation, two factors were extracted from 13 items of respondents' feelings. As shown in Table 3, the two factors were labeled: 1. "feel about the past" (nine items, $\alpha = .91$, M = 3.51) and 2. "feel about the present" (four items, $\alpha = .78$, M = 4.08). Factor loadings for all items are over .05, suggesting that the items have well defined the two factors.

The accumulated variance is 60.12%, and the alphas values of factor one and two are 0.907 and 0.779 respectively, suggesting that the two factors are highly reliable. The mean values of feelings suggest that respondents felt very positive about reliving their past life during their homeland visit and about their present and future lives.

Table 2. Rotated factor matrix for tourist activities

	Factor loadings		Mean	Std. Deviation
	1	2		
Factor 1. Sightseeing. Cronbach's Alpha = .87			3.04	
Tried new games	.852		2.89	1.364
Tried new food/restaurants	.838		3.08	1.333
Visited new sites	.786		3.06	1.320
Visited historical sites	.783		3.14	1.454
Shopping	.611		3.04	1.404
Factor 2. Relive the past. Cronbach's Alpha = .78			3.61	
Meeting old friends/relatives		.833	4.11	1.233
Visited the places i visited before		.705	3.38	1.324
participated in the activities that I did before		.670	3.07	1.370
Ate the local food I ate before		.658	3.87	1.305
% of Variance	39.00	26.00		

The correlation statistics in table 4 proved the significant interrelationship among travel motives, tourist activities, and emotional experiences. As shown in Table 5, the model fit statistics indicates that the model (IFI = .99, GFI = .99, AGFI = .98, and RMSEA = .03) fit the data very well, and the statistical results of multivariate tests presented in the model indicated the significant effects of travel motives on tourist activities and emotional experiences, as well as the significant effects of tourist activities on emotional experiences. The activity factor, "relive the past" (dependent variables), was associated with the three travel motives (independent variables), "socialize with people" (β = .43), "attractiveness of the place" (β = .23) and "connect to the past" (β = .11), but "socialize with people" had no significant effect on the "sightseeing" activities.

Meanwhile, the "sightseeing" activities were significantly influenced by the "relive the past" activities (β = .37), "attractiveness of the place" motives (β = .29), and "connect to the past" motives (β = .14). The results suggest that respondents' preference of tourist activities were determined by their travel motives. Regarding respondents' emotional experiences, the statistical results revealed that their travel motives and activities had significant effects on their feelings.

Respondents' good feelings about recollecting their past memories and experiences were associated with two factors of travel motivation, "connect to the past" (β = .24) and "socialize with people" (β = .15), and two tourist activity factors, "sightseeing" (β = .19) and "relive the past" (β = .41).

Moreover, the better respondent felt good about reliving their past, the more positive they felt about their present and future lives, as the regression weight of "feel about the past" (β = .60) on "feel about the present" was much higher than other factors.

Table 3. Rotated factor matrix for emotional experience

	Factor loadings		Mean	Std. Deviation
	1	2		
Factor 1.Feel about the past. Cronbach's Alpha = .91			3.51	
Felt my values and beliefs have changed over time	.823		3.07	1.354
Felt good to share my past life with my loved ones	.770		3.53	1.342
Felt good to take the activities that I did before	.754		3.39	1.384
Felt I know myself better	.741		3.19	1.333
Felt good to relive my past life	.725		3.58	1.279
Felt good to visit the places I visited before	.678		3.78	1.259
Felt my visit was meaningful	.629		3.65	1.233
Felt good to try the food I ate before	.616		3.94	1.205
Felt good to visit my homeland again	.540		3.49	1.386
Factor 2. Feel about the present Cronbach's Alpha = .78			4.08	
Felt my present life is better than before		.849	4.10	1.076
Felt positive about my future life		.818	4.01	1.097
Felt the place has changed over time		.631	3.93	1.212
Felt good to know the present lives of old friends/relatives		.590	4.28	1.171
% of Variance	36.60	23.52		

Table 4. Correlations: Motivation, activities, and emotional experiences

	1	2	3	4	5	6	7	M	SD
Motivation									
1. Connect to the past	-	.68**	.59**	.53**	.52**	.65**	.38**	3.19	1.14
2. Attractiveness of the place		-	.59**	.59**	.56**	.59**	.36**	3.35	1.10
3. Socialize with people			-	.45**	.63**	.64**	.50**	3.81	1.05
Activities									
4. Sightseeing				-	.61**	.63**	.36**	3.04	1.12
5. Relive the past					-	.75**	.56**	3.61	1.02
Emotional experiences									
6. Feel about the past						-	.66**	3.51	.99
7. Feel about the present							-	4.08	.88

Note. **P < .01.

Table 5. Standardized Regression Weights and Model Fit Statistics

			β
Relive the past	<---	Attractiveness	.229***
Relive the past	<---	Connect to past	.114*
Relive the past	<---	Socialization	.430***
Sightseeing	<---	Connect to past	.135**
Sightseeing	<---	Attractiveness	.291***
Sightseeing	<---	Relive the past	.374***
Feel about past	<---	Relive the past	.410***
Feel about past	<---	Connect to past	.241***
Feel about past	<---	Socialization	.154***
Feel about past	<---	Sightseeing	.185***
Feel about present	<---	Relive the past	.159**
Feel about present	<---	Socialization	.133**
Feel about present	<---	Feel about past	.601***
Feel about present	<---	Sightseeing	-.119**
Feel about present	<---	Connect to past	-.111*

Model fit Statistics

X^2	df	IFI	AGFI	GFI	RMSEA
4.43	3	.99	.98	.99	.03

Note. * $p < .05$, ** $< .01$, *** $<.001$.

This result suggests that respondents had experienced some emotional thoughts by comparing their past and present lives during their homeland visit. Also the positive feelings reflected respondents' satisfaction with their homeland visit experience.

DISCUSSION AND CONCLUSION

Homeland visit is good for immigrants' psychological well-being (Hung et al., 2013; McCabe and Johnson, 2013; Pearce, 2012). However, it is ambiguous about how immigrants' behavior during their homeland visit influences their psychological well-being due to lack of empirical studies in the tourist behavior of immigrants during their homeland visit. This study has comprehensively explored the behavioral characteristics of immigrants during their homeland visit by revealing their travel motives, preferences of tourist activities, and emotional experiences.

The results of this study suggested that immigrants' travel motives for homeland visit reflect their needs for seeking their cultural identity, consolidating their connection with their homeland people, and reliving their positive past life. These travel motives are the immigrants' psychological needs which can only be fulfilled by visiting their homeland and meeting their homeland people. In addition to previous studies regarding Chinese immigrants' motives for visiting their homeland (e.g., Hung et al., 2013; Io, 2014c), this study tries to examine the influences of these travel motives on immigrants' preference of tourist activities and emotional experiences during their homeland visit. With the purposes of fulfilling immigrants' psychological needs by homeland visit, immigrants' preference of tourist experiences and activities is expected to corresponding to immigrants' travel motives. In fact, the findings of this study revealed a significant relationship between travel motives, tourist activities, and emotional experiences. Immigrants' feelings are the results of their preference of tourist activities which are corresponding to their travel motives and psychological needs for homeland visit.

The structural model in this study not only reveals the significant relationship between travel motives, tourist activities, and emotional experiences, but also the development of positive feelings and emotional experiences which benefit immigrants' psychological well-being. The multidimensional constructs of travel motives, tourist activities, and emotional experiences bring an insight into the understanding of immigrants' behavioral characteristics during their homeland visit with respect to their psychological well-being. The findings add values to the existing body of knowledge in immigrants' psychological well-being and homeland tourism. The behavioral characteristics of immigrants during their homeland visit are discussed in the following text.

Travel Motivation

Literature review suggested some travel motives for immigrants who visit their homeland, for example, visiting friends and relatives (Feng and Page, 2000; Kluin and Lehto, 2012), and seeking personal identity (Hung et al., 2013; Maruyama and Stronza, 2010). The results of this study revealed that the Chinese immigrants visited their homeland for many reasons which were categorized into three dimensions: "attractiveness of the place", "connect to the past", and "socialize with people". Immigrants visit their homeland because they are attracted by the attractiveness of their homeland. Homeland is the place where immigrants grew up since born. Immigrants are familiar with the historical attractions, landscapes, food, and culture of their homeland. The "attractiveness of homeland" reflects immigrants' psychological needs of connecting to their original cultural identity and reliving their past life in homeland (Fivush, Habermas, Waters, and Zaman, 2011; Ingram, Mickes, and Wixted, 2012; Pearce, 2012). Homeland visit not only bring immigrants relaxation, but also a chance to visit the place where contains much of their past autobiographical memories. They can escape from everyday routine and socialize with family members and relatives (Kim and Prideaux, 2003).

The motive of "connect to the past" further reflects immigrants' psychological needs for visiting their homeland. After their migration to a new place, the connection between immigrants' present and past lives gradually fades away as the longer time immigrants live in the new place, the higher level of accumulation and social capital they gain and the less connection to their homeland and past life (Abu-Rayya, 2009; Hung et al., 2013). For some immigrants, especially those who have a lower level of accumulation to the new society and place, their homeland culture still plays a dominant role in their self-concept and behavior (Hung et al., 2013). To consolidate and stay in line with their cultural identity, connecting to their past by visiting their homeland becomes important.

This motivation factor indicates the desire of Chinese immigrants for affirming their original cultural identity, reliving their past, exploring the changes of their homeland, and sharing their past stories with their loved ones. If these desires are satisfied during their homeland visit, immigrants' psychological well-being will be improved.

The last motivation factor identified in this study is "socialize with people". With the highest mean score among three factors (M = 3.81), respondents were much driven by this motive to visit their homeland. Consistent with a previous study by Hung et al. (2013), the results of this study also indicate that by socializing with relatives, friends, and old neighbors in homeland, immigrants gain several psychological benefits, such as, emotional supports, consolidating the relationship with homeland community, and staying in line with their original cultural identity. These emotional benefits from homeland visit are important for immigrants' psychological well-being. For example, Social support from the communities of the place of exile and homeland could influence immigrants' acculturation strategies and preference of homeland cultural practices (Tartakovsky, 2012). Particularly, emotional social support from friends or oversea networks is helpful for improving immigrants' psychological well-being (Williams, 2006; Wu, Chib, Plassmanc, and Guob, 2010). Talking to family members and relatives is evidenced for its contribution to lower immigrants' depressive symptoms (Gerst, Al-Ghatrifa, Beard, Samper-Ternent, and Markides, 2010). For those immigrants who have moved to a new place for few years, the cultural gap between the new place and their homeland could cause some emotional conflicts and depression (Abu-Rayya, 2009; Hiott, Grzywacz, Arcury, and Quandt, 2006; Lee, Moon). Therefore, homeland visit contributes to improving immigrants' psychological well-being by satisfying their psychological needs aforementioned.

Tourist Activities

Driven by the identified motives, immigrants participated in two types of tourist activities: "sightseeing" and "relive the past" during their homeland visit. The model in Figure 1 indicated the significant effect of three factors of travel motivation on the tourist activities. These results are consistent with some previous studies that tourists' preferences of activities was related to their travel motives (Kim and Lehto, 2013; Kluin and Lehto, 2012). Among three factors of motivation, only "socialize with people" had no effect on "sightseeing" activities, suggesting immigrants' preference of "sightseeing" activities is not driven by their travel motive of "socializing with people" but by other two travel motivation factors.

The significant relationship between immigrants' travel motives and preference of tourist activities during their homeland visit indicates how immigrants select tourist activities based on their travel motives. To understand how homeland visit benefits immigrants' psychological well-being, it is not enough to only investigate their travel motives and preference of tourist activities, but also their emotional experiences revolved around their homeland visit. All three factors of travel motivation influenced the "relive the past" activities, and the motives of "attractiveness of the place" and "connect to the past" influenced the "sightseeing" activities.

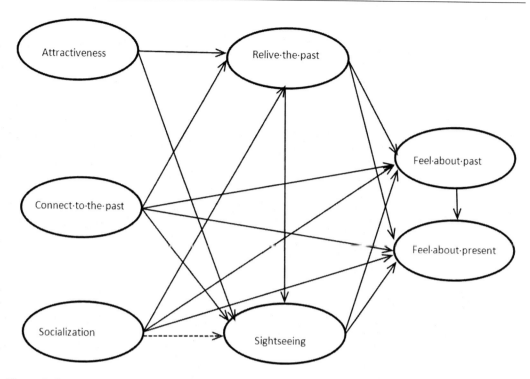

Figure 1. Structural Model of Homeland Tourist Behavior.

The results indicate that immigrants' preference of "relive the past" activities corresponded to their travel motives. Particularly, meeting friends and relatives in homeland was regarded as the most popular activity in the present study (M = 4.1), satisfying the needs of connecting to the past and socializing with family and relatives. Immigrants' participation in "sightseeing" activities helped to satisfy immigrants' needs of connecting to their past by comparing the current development and the past situation of homeland. By trying new games, new restaurants, and visiting new sites, immigrants learnt about the development and new tourist resources of their homeland. Moreover, the new experience with the new tourist resources at homeland helped to refresh and enhance immigrants' emotional bond with their homeland and in turn improve their travel experience and psychological well-being (Kim, 2010).

However, the mean value of "relive the past" activities (M = 3.61) was much higher than "sightseeing" activities (M = 3.04), suggesting that immigrants preferred the tourist activities related to "relive the past" experience much more than "sightseeing" activities. Interestingly, it was also showed that the "relive the past" activities had a significant effect on the "sightseeing" activities, suggesting that the more the Chinese immigrants participated in the "relive the past" activities, the more they participated in the "sightseeing" activities. In other words, their participation in the activities related to their past life could encourage immigrants to explore and try the new tourist activities in their homeland.

Emotional Experiences

Respondents' feelings were categorized into "feel about the past" (M = 3.51) and "feel about the present" (M = 4.08) by factor analysis. The high mean values of these two categories of feelings suggest that the Chinese immigrants generally had a very positive emotional experience with their homeland visit. By reliving their past, the Chinese immigrants had a better understanding of themselves in terms of personal identity and changes in values and appreciated their homeland visit, and in turn they had positive emotional experiences about reliving their past. Particularly, the Chinese immigrants felt very positive about their present and future lives. The significant effect of "feel about the past" on "feel about the present" indicated that the more positive the Chinese immigrants felt about their experience of reliving the past, the more positive they felt about their present and future lives. This outcome is probably because of that the Chinese immigrants had experienced some emotional thoughts about their past and present lives. The emotional thoughts led them to compare their present life with their past life and realize how good their present life is and how successfully they have settled in the new place. The good feelings about learning the current situation of their homeland (M = 3.93) and friends and relatives (M = 4.28) suggest that the Chinese immigrants have improved the connection with their homeland and people by updating their information, as well as satisfied their desire of socializing with the homeland community.

The model in Figure 1 shows that the "sightseeing" and "relive the past" activities significantly influenced the Chinese immigrants' emotional experiences, suggesting that the more the Chinese immigrants participated in these activities, the more positive they felt about their past and in turn the more positive they felt about their present. Moreover, two factors of motivation: "connect to the past" and "socialize with people" had a direct and significant effect on homeland tourists' feelings, suggesting that the Chinese immigrants' emotional experiences well responded to their travel motives too in addition to their tourist activities. The significant interrelationship among travel motives, activities, and emotional experiences has revealed the behavioral characteristics of immigrants in their homeland visit as well as the development of positive emotional experiences/feelings which benefit immigrants' psychological well-being.

The positive emotional experiences are likely to enhance the Chinese immigrants' positive memory about their homeland visit, as positive emotion associated with the past events is helpful for the recollection of the past memories and experiences vividly (Rasmussen and Berntsen, 2009; Talarico, Berntsen, and Rubin, 2009). Moreover, the recollection of past memories and socialization with the local people could help to produce a memorable tourism experience (Kim, 2010; Tung and Ritchie, 2011a) and benefit the Chinese immigrants' self-continuity development and social bonding behavior, as one's past memories and experiences affect his/her present and future behavior (Haslam, Jetten, Haslam, Pugliese, and Tonks, 2011). Also, by reliving their past life, the Chinese immigrants had a better understanding about themselves and their future, as one's past life experience directed his/her present and future development (Bluck, Alea, Habermas, and Rubin, 2005).

All in all, the present study reveals the Chinese immigrants' travel motives, preference of tourist activities and emotional experiences, particularly the emotional benefits gained from their homeland visit. To understand how immigrants improve their psychological well-being during their homeland visit, this study reveals immigrants' travel behavior by analyzing their travel motivation, preference of tourist activities, and emotional experiences. The statistical results indicated the significant relationship between travel motives, preference of tourist activities, and emotional experiences, and reflected how immigrants gain emotional benefits from their homeland visit and in turn improved their psychological well-being. According to Hung et al (2013), immigrants enjoy visiting their homeland because they gain a lot emotional benefits, such as emotional support from homeland people, emotional bond with their homeland and cultural identity. This study supports the notion that immigrants gain a lot of emotional benefits from their homeland visit and thus improve their psychological well-being. Homeland visit not only provides the Chinese immigrants with a vacation, but also positive emotional experiences and a memorable tourism experience resulted from a high degree of connection to their homeland community, participation in new and old tourist activities, and recollection of their past memories and experiences with their homeland.

Implications and Limitations

It is revealed that the reasons for visiting homeland are not limited to VFR in the present study. The analysis of "sightseeing" activities and the "attractiveness of the place" motives suggests that the Chinese immigrants enjoyed having a vacation and using the tourist resources of their homeland. Though they were familiar with their homeland, they still enjoyed seeing around and trying the new tourist resources there. This finding implies that remote and exotic destinations are not the only choice for sightseeing or pleasure tourists. Instead, familiar destinations may also attract the Chinese immigrants who cannot visit their homeland oftentimes. In familiar destinations, the familiar culture, food, landscapes, and heritage sites not only provide tourists with rich tourist resources for vacation, but also remind them of their past memories and experiences with their homeland.

Homeland tourists also partially behaved like VFR tourists who aim at socializing with friends and relatives. For homeland tourists, a homeland tour could enable them consolidate their family values and the connection with friends and relatives. Moreover, by socializing with familiar people like old friends and neighbors, homeland tourists could regain the emotional social support from their homeland community. During immigrants' homeland visit, the time for visiting friends and relatives and the chance for socializing with local people are important. For travel agencies, it is recommended to design family-oriented tours to satisfy the tourists who want to spend time with their loved ones at their homeland or familiar places.

It is noted by this study that recollecting one's past memories and experiences is one of the major characteristics of homeland tourism. Through the connection to homeland and socializing with familiar people, the Chinese immigrants not only recollected their past memories and experiences, but also experienced some emotional thoughts about their past, present, and future, resulting in positive emotional experiences which benefit psychological well-being.

However, homeland is not the only place where the Chinese immigrants can experience reliving their past life. Visiting familiar destinations may also help immigrants to recollect or relive their past experiences, as some places where are similar to immigrants' homeland or familiar to immigrants can provide them with many cues to recollect their past memories and experiences. As proved by some researchers that one's old-new memories is supported by high degrees of familiarity, familiar places should enable tourists to recollect and enhance their past memories (Ingram et al., 2012).

For travel agencies, it is recommended to design tours in some destinations where are familiar to tourists, aiming at providing them with a sense of reliving the past. For example, many places in Canton province of Mainland China share many common characteristics in terms of food and culture. For the Chinese immigrants who came from Canton province, a visit to any city of Canton province may remind them of their homeland and past life.

A major limitation of this present study should be noted. The sample respondents are Chinese immigrants from different provinces and regions of Mainland China and Hong Kong. They shared some generic Chinese culture with the local residents of Macao, and the geographical distance between their homeland and Macao is relatively short comparing to the immigrants came from other countries.

Consequently, respondents may not feel that they were living in a remote and exotic place and may not have a strong desire for returning home to search their cultural identity and relive their past life.

Therefore, the future research in homeland tourism should extend to the international immigrants who moved from remote countries, as the results may be very different from that of the present study. The present study may serve as guidelines for further research in this area to improve the understanding of homeland tourist behavior in terms of their expenditure behavior and needs for travel services.

REFERENCES

Abu-Rayya, H. M. 2009. Acculturation and its determinants among adult immigrants in France *International Journal of Psychology*, 44(3): 195-203.

Backer, E. 2012. VFR travel: It is underestimated. *Tourism Management,* 33: 74-79.

Bluck, S., Alea, N., Habermas, T., and Rubin, D. C. 2005. A Tale of Three Functions: The Self-reported Uses of Autobiographical Memory. *Social Cognition*, 23(1): 91-117.

Dijk, P. V., and Weiler, B. 2009. An Assessment of the Outcomes of a Chinese-Language Interpretive Tour Experience at a Heritage Tourism Attraction. *Tourism Analysis,* 14: 49-63.

Feng, K., and Page, S. J. 2000. An Exploratory Study of the Tourism, Migration–Immigration Nexus: Travel Experiences of Chinese Residents in New Zealand. *Current Issues In Tourism*, 3(2): 246-281.

Filep, S., and Deery, M. 2010. Towards a Picture of Tourists' Happiness. *Tourism Analysis,* 15: 399-410.

Fivush, R., Habermas, T., Waters, T. E. A., and Zaman, W. 2011. The Making of Autobiographical Memory: Intersections of Culture, Narratives and Identity. *International Journal of Psychology,* 46(5): 321-345.

Garrido, M. 2011. Home is Another Country: Ethnic Identification in Philippine Homeland Tours. *Qualitative Sociology,* 34: 177-199.

Gerst, K., Al-Ghatrifa, M., Beard, H. A., Samper-Ternent, R., and Markides, K. S. 2010. High depressive symptomatology among older community-dwelling Mexican Americans: The impact of immigration. *Aging and Mental Health,* 14(3): 347-354.

Haslam, C., Jetten, J., Haslam, S. A., Pugliese, C., and Tonks, J. 2011. 'I remember therefore I am, and I am therefore I remember': Exploring the contributions of episodic and semantic self-knowledge to strength of identity. *British Journal of Psychology*, 102(184-203).

Hiott, A., Grzywacz, J. G., Arcury, T. A., and Quandt, S. A. 2006. Gender Differences in Anxiety and Depression Among Immigrant Latinos. *Families, Systems, and Health*, 24(2): 137-146.

Hosany, S., and Gilber, D. 2010. Measuring Tourists' Emotional experiences toward Hedonic Holiday Destinations. *Journal of Travel Research*, 49(4): 513-526.

Huang, S., Hsu, C. H. C., and Chan, A. 2010. Tour Guide Performance and Tourist Satisfaction: A Study of the Package Tourism in Shanghai. *Journal of Hospitality and Tourism Research*, 34(1): 3-33.

Hung, k., Xiao, H., and Yang, X. 2013. Why immigrants travel to their home places: Social capital and acculturation perspective. *Tourism Management*, 36: 304-313.

Ingram, K. M., Mickes, L., and Wixted, J. T. 2012. Recollection Can Be Weak and Familiarity Can Be Strong. *Journal of Experimental Psychology, Learning, Memory and Cognition*, 38(2): 325-339.

Io, M.-U. 2014a. Exploring the Chinese Immigrants' Preference of Tourist Activities During Their Homeland Visit and Use of Past Memories. *Asia Pacific Journal of Tourism Research*, In-press.

Io, M.-U. 2014b. Exploring the impact of past memories on tourist experiences of homeland visit: The case of the Chinese immigrants in Macao. *Journal of Vacation Marketing*.

Io, M.-U. 2014c. Exploring the motivation of Chinese immigrants for homeland tourism. *Current Issues in Tourism*.

Kim, J. H. 2010. Determining the Factors Affecting the Memorable Nature of Travel Experiences. *Journal of Travel and Tourism Marketing*, 27: 780-796.

Kim, S., and Lehto, X. Y. 2013. Travel by families with children possessing disabilities: Motives and activities. *Tourism Management*, 37: 13-24.

Kim, S. S., and Prideaux, B. 2003. Marketing implications arising from a comparative study of international pleasure tourist motivation and other travel-related characteristics of visitors to Korea. *Tourism Management*, 26: 347 - 357.

King, B. 1994. What is Ethnic Tourism? An Australian Perspective. *Tourism Management*, 15(3): 173-176.

Kluin, J. Y., and Lehto, X. Y. 2012. Measuring Family Reunion Travel Motivations. *Annals of Tourism Research*, 39(2): 820 - 841.

Lee, H. Y., Moon, A., and Knight, B. G. 2004. Depression Among Elderly Korean Immigrants: Exploring Socio-Cultural Factors. *Journal of Ethnic and Cultural Diversity in Social Work*, 13(4): 1 - 26.

Lehto, X. Y., Morrison, A. M., and O'Leary, J. 2001. Does the Visiting Friends and Relatives' Typology Make a Difference? A Study of the International VFR Market to the United States. *Journal of Travel Research*, 40(November): 201-212.

Maruyama, N., and Stronza, A. 2010. Roots Tourism of Chinese Americans. *Ethnology*, 49(1): 23-44.

Maruyama, N., weber, I., and stronza, A. 2010. Negotiating Identity: Experiences of "Visiting Home" among Chinese Americans. *Tourism, Culture and Communication*, 10: 1 - 14.

McCabe, S., and Johnson, S. 2013. The Happiness Factor in Tourism: Subjective Well-being and Social Tourism. *Annals of Tourism Research*, 41: 42-65.

McIntosh, A. J., and Prentice, R. C. 1999. Affirming Authenticity: Consuming Cultural Heritage. *Annals of Tourism Research,* 26(3): 589-612.

Morgan, M., and Xu, F. 2009. Student Travel Experiences: Memories and Dreams. *Journal of Hospitality Marketing and Management*, 18: 216 - 236.

Ostrowski, S. 1991. Ethnic Tourism - Focus on Poland. *Tourism Management,* 12(2): 125-130.

Pearce, P. L. 2012. The Experience of Visiting Home and Familiar Places. *Annals of Tourism Research,* 39(2): 1024-1047.

Picard, L., Reffuveille, I., Eustache, F., and Piolino, P. 2009. Development of Autonoetic Autobiographical Memory in School-age Children: Genuine Age Effect or Development of Basic Cognitive Abilities? *Consciousness and Cognition*, 18(4): 864-876.

Poria, Y., Biran, A., and Reichel, A. 2009. Visitors' Preferences for Interpretation at Heritage Sites. *Journal of Travel Research,* 48(1): 92-105.

Poria, Y., Reichel, A., and Biran, A. 2006. Heritage Site Management Motivations and Expectations. *Annals of Tourism Research,* 33(1): 162-178.

Powers, J. L. 2011. Reimaging the Imagined Community: Homeland Tourism and the Role of Place. *American Behavioral Scientist,* 55(10): 1362 - 1378.

Rasmussen, A. S., and Berntsen, D. 2009. Emotional Valence and the Funtions of Autobiographical Memories: Positive and Negative Memories Serve Different functions. *Memory and Cognition,* 37(4): 477-492.

Reisinger, Y., and Steiner, C. 2006. Reconceptualising Interpretation: The Role of Tour Guides in Authentic Tourism. *Current Issues In Tourism,* 9(6): 481-498.

Rubin, D. C., and Berntsen, D. 2003. Life scripts help to maintain autobiographical memories of highly positive, but not highly negative, events. *Memory and Cognition,* 31(1): 1-14.

Seaton, A. V., and Palmer, C. 1997. Understanding VFR tourism behaviour: The first five years of the United Kingdom tourism survey. *Tourism Management,* 18(6): 345-355.

Shani, A. 2011. The VFR Experience: 'Home' Away from Home? Current Issues In Tourism: 1-15.

Shani, A., and Uriely, N. 2011. VFR Tourism The Host Experience. *Annals of Tourism Research,* 39(1): 421-440.

Statistics and Census Bureau. 2011. Population Census, Vol. 2012.

Statistics and Census Bureau. 2012. Tourism ststiatics, Vol. 2013.

Talarico, J. M., Berntsen, D., and Rubin, D. C. 2009. Positive emotions enhance recall of peripheral details. *Cognition and Emotion,* 23(2): 380-398.

Tartakovsky, E. 2012. Factors affecting immigrants' acculturation intentions: A theoretical model and its assessment among adolescent immigrants from Russia and Ukraine in Israel. *International Journal of Intercultural Relations,* 36(83-99).

Tung, V. W. S., and Ritchie, J. R. B. 2011a. Exploring the Essence of Memorable Tourism Experiences. *Annals of Tourism Research*, 38(4): 1367-1386.

Tung, V. W. S., and Ritchie, J. R. B. 2011b. Investigating the Memorable Experiences of the Senior Travel Market: An Examination of the Reminiscence Bump. *Journal of Travel and Tourism Marketing,* 28: 331-343.

Uriely, N. 2010. "Home" and "Away" in VFR Tourism. *Annals of Tourism Research*, 37(3): 854-857.

Wang, N. 1999. Rethinking Authenticity in Tourism Experience. *Annals of Tourism Research,* 26(2): 349-370.

Williams, L. 2006. Social Networks of Refugees in the United Kingdom: Tradition, Tactics and New Community Spaces. *Journal of Ethnic and Migration Studies,* 32(5): 865-879.

Wu, B., Chib, I., Plassmanc, B. L., and Guob, M. 2010. Depressive symptoms and health problems among Chinese immigrant elders in the US and Chinese elders in China. *Aging and Mental Health,* 14(6): 695-704.

Yang, L. 2010. Ethnic Tourism and Cultural Representation. *Annals of Tourism Research,* 38(2): 561-585.

Yang, L., Wall, G., and Smith, S. L. J. 2008. Ethnic tourism development: Chinese Government Perspectives. *Annals of Tourism Research,* 35(3): 751-771.

Yeoman, I., Brass, D., and McMahon-Beattie, U. 2007. Current Issue in Tourism: The Authentic Tourist. *Tourism Management,* 28: 1128-1138.

Yun, J., and Lehto, X. Y. 2009. Motives and Patterns of Family Reunion Travel. *Journal of Quality Assurance in Hospitality and Tourism,* 10: 279-300.

In: Psychological Well-Being
Editor: Rafael Bowers

ISBN: 978-1-63484-354-6
© 2016 Nova Science Publishers, Inc.

Chapter 2

TOWARD A GLOBAL CONCEPTUALIZATION AND MEASUREMENT IN POSITIVE PSYCHOLOGY

Cirilo H. García Cadena[1,2,], Arnoldo Téllez López[1],*
German Ramírez Aguillón[1], Erika Ramírez Hernández[1]
and Ezra J. Pérez Cota[2]

[1]Autonomous University of Nuevo Leon, San Nicolás de los Garza, N.L., Mexico
[2]Regiomontana University, Monterrey, N.L., Mexico

ABSTRACT

In this chapter, the reiterated need for creating psychological knowledge and measurement instruments that are universal in character is postulated. This effort would inevitably be based on the simultaneous and/or continuous study of different cultural, social, political, and economic communities. With this purpose in mind, this study proposes the creation and validation of theories and measures on positive psychological constructs that can be integrated into a tool that aims at what might be called a desirable and credible global psychology. Several comparative studies that present some perspectives and measurements from various countries on optimism, generosity, and forgiveness, developed in the US, Israel, and Mexico, are included here. Different samples from university students and the open population residing in the metropolitan area of the city of Monterrey, Nuevo León, Mexico, were used. Confirmatory factor analysis was conducted to calculate the construct validity of the original instruments for each culture, the convergent validity of the premises was assessed, and a new measure for each construct was obtained, resulting from combining the original instruments and those applied to local Mexican residents, achieving adequate goodness of fit and reliability in the final version measuring optimism, generosity, and forgiveness. It is concluded that there are great advantages to combining theories and measurements of the same positive psychological construct, from various cultures, thus supporting the creation of an appropriate global positive psychology.

---

[*] Corresponding author: Dr. Carlos Canseco 110, Mitras-Centro, CP. 64460, Monterrey, N.L., School of Psychology, Autonomous University of Nuevo Leon; Email: ciriloenator@gmail.com.

Keywords: global positive psychology, theories, measures, construct validation

INTRODUCTION

The creation of plausible explanations for the phenomena that we experience and that surround us has been a task not only important for satisfying intrinsic human curiosity but also of the highest relevance for transforming our world into a more livable place, without dangers that may lurk and put our lives at risk. This task has been accomplished, in an increasingly efficient manner, by taking advantage of technological products developed by the classical natural disciplines, such as physics, chemistry, and biology. Given that human beings are subject to universal natural laws, little has been questioned regarding the successful nomothetic approach of these disciplines. However, in the case of the human or social sciences and, particularly, in the case of psychology, the situation has been relatively different. General psychology and transcultural psychology continue working under a paradigm that strives to find universals of human nature (Kim, Yang, & Hwang, 2006). Indigenous or vernacular psychology (Díaz-Loving, 2009), however, insists that there is no contradiction with a nomothetic approximation; nonetheless, it favors the discovery and understanding of the historical, psychological, social, and cultural phenomena of the inhabitants of our countries and local social groups.

Problem Statement

Pike (1966) has already made the distinction between the etic and the emic spheres. These approaches analyze a system from the outside or from the inside, respectively. Here, the basic question is whether the knowledge derived from both perspectives is reconcilable, complementary, or contradictory. When theorizing in psychology, there is an unavoidable bias due to the psycho-cultural training of the researcher at hand. As has already be noted by Alarcón (2002), Ardila (1972), Díaz-Guerrero (1971), Díaz-Loving (1999, 2006), García, Carrascoza, and Díaz (2013), Harré (1999), Moscovici (1972), and others, theories say more about the researcher than about their research subjects and, most likely considerably less, about the human race. Therefore, even when seeking general principles that are applicable to humanity, psychological study must begin from what is inherently own. Kantor's recommendation (1978) deserves to be noted: researchers need intimate contact with the phenomena under study to understand and operationalize their theoretical efforts in an intelligible manner. For example, if one theorizes and measures optimism in individuals from a developed country, one would have to question, rather than uncritically accept, that the knowledge generated can automatically be applied to inhabitants of underdeveloped countries. Based on the previous discussion, it is possible to ask the following question:

Research Question

Is it best to theorize and measure psychological constructs from an etic or from an emic perspective, or is it more efficient to use a combination of both?

Next, 5 studies that briefly describe some theories on optimism, generosity, and forgiveness are presented, in addition to the respective operational attempts performed to measure them. It has been hypothesized that by merging various instruments into one, including the conceptual principles that encouraged their original creation in different cultures, progress can be made regarding the creation of a genuine global psychology that decreases the insidious and unacceptable ethnocentric attitude currently prevailing in the field.

STUDY 1

According to current mainstream American psychology, optimism, as defined by one of the 2 most important approaches on the subject, is a personality trait that involves the widespread expectation that the future will bring good things for oneself: " ...widespread sense of confidence" (Carver & Scheier, 2002 p.232). This type of optimism reveals a trust in one's own resources to do well in the future; that is, it refers to a personal optimism. This theory has been operationalized through the Life Orientation Test-Revised (LOT-R) created by Scheier, Carver, and Bridges (1994). The Spanish version, adapted by Otero, Luengo, Romero, Gómez, and Castro (1998), is the most commonly used in Latin America.

Recently, García, Díaz, Téllez, López, Martínez, Sánchez, and García (2013) have defined optimism as an interactive style of personality (Ribes, 2009) that results from the complex but positive historical and current relationship of the individual with his or her physical environment, with others, and with him/herself. This approach avoids the ahistorical implications derived from the US perspective briefly outlined in the previous paragraphs. It considers optimism as a positive way of seeing the world in which we live (including ourselves as unavoidable members) that emerges and develops through the multiple interactions of the individual that are beneficial for him/herself. Perhaps the amount of beneficial interactions has not always been important, but the individual sees it as favorable. Through this effective adaptation, the individual progresses in life, despite the obvious negative or conflicting vicissitudes of day-to-day life or even those major crises that arise from it. The Scale of Optimism, which is used in the 5 studies described in this chapter, represents the operationalization of such a conceptualization. Overall, optimists think, feel, and act regarding themselves, others, and the surroundings in a favorable or positive manner. They perceive themselves, others, and their surrounding world as something good. One is good, and so are others and the world itself. Optimists believe that they have done well in life and that life has been worth living. Additionally, optimistic individuals qualify life as beautiful. In the phenomenon of optimism, both experiences of the past and the experiences of the present are intrinsically interwoven.

METHOD

Participants

The study was conducted on a convenience sample of 597 residents of the metropolitan area of the city of Monterrey in Nuevo Leon, Mexico. A total of 53.60% were women (320) and 46.40% men (277) between 15 and 70 years of age, with an average of 29.67 years of age and a standard deviation of 12.87 years.

Instruments

A sociodemographic questionnaire, the 6-item Life Orientation Test-Revised (LOT-R) (Scheier, Carver, & Bridges, 1994), with alphas ranging from .78 to .83 (Carver & Scheier, 2002) (see Appendix A), and the 8-item Scale of Optimism created by the authors of this chapter, with an alpha of .847 (see Appendix B), were used.

Procedure

Five doctoral students in psychology were responsible for locating a sample of 597 participants and applying the instruments.

Data Analysis

To identify construct validity, a confirmatory factor analysis was conducted with the estimation method scale-free least squares, given that the distributions in both the American and the Mexican scales were not normal, according to the results of the Kolgomorov-Smirnov test. Faced with this abnormality, the correlations between the scores on the scales were calculated through the Spearman correlation coefficient. To calculate internal consistency, the Cronbach's alpha coefficient was used. Finally, the SPSS (version 21) and AMOS (version 21) statistical programs were used.

RESULTS

Tables 1 and 2 show the most important results of Study 1. Table 1 contains the indicators of the goodness of fit for 3 measuring models: the American test, the Mexican test, and the product of the combination of both scales, in this case called Mixed. It also contains the coefficients of internal consistency of the 3 instruments.

Table 1. Confirmatory factor analysis and reliability for the LOT-R Optimism, García, and Mixed scales (LOT-R+ GARCIA) for 597 participants

Goodness of Fit							
SCALE	n^7	CMIN[1]	RMR[2]	GFI[3]	AGFI[4]	NFI[5]	α^a
Lot-R 6 Items	597	13.698	.032	.994	.986	.974	.618
Garcia et al. 8 Items	597	54.405	.029	.990	.982	.982	.847
Mixed 8 Items	597	47.049	.028	.991	.984	.985	.850

n^7 = sample size; CMIN[1] = minimum value of the discrepancy; RMR[2] = root mean square residual; GFI[3] = goodness of fit index; AGFI[4] = adjusted goodness of fit index; NFI[5] = normed fit index; α^a = Cronbach's alpha

Table 2. Spearman correlations among the LOT-R Optimism, GARCÍA, and Mixed scales (LOT-R + García) for 597 participants

SCALE	LOT-R	GARCÍA ET AL.	MIXED
LOT-R	1.000	.568	.651
GARCÍA ET AL.	.568	1.000	.937
MIXED	.651	.937	1.000

Table 2 presents the correlations among the 3 scales used in Study 1.

STUDY 2: METHOD

Participants

This study was conducted on a non-probabilistic sample of 350 relatives of patients with cancer, mostly residents of the metropolitan area of the city of Monterrey in Nuevo León, Mexico. A total of 71.40% were women (250) and 28.60% were men (100) between 15 and 79 years of age, with an average of 39.87 years of age and a standard deviation of 14.87 years.

Instruments

A sociodemographic questionnaire, the Life Orientation Test-Revised (LOT-R) (Scheier, Carver, & Bridges, 1994) with 10 items, of which 6 were filler items, and with alphas ranging from .78 to .83 (Carver & Scheier, 2002), and the 8-item Scale of Optimism created by the authors of this chapter, with an alpha of .847, were used.

Procedure

Students in the tenth semester of the psychology program applied the instrument to families of cancer patients in hospitals. They were trained by a professor with experience in the psychological treatment of these types of patients and their families.

Data Analysis

To identify construct validity, a confirmatory factor analysis was conducted with the estimation method scale-free least squares, given that the distributions in both the American and the Mexican scales were not normal, according to the results of the Kolgomorov-Smirnov test. Similarly, the correlations between the scores on the scales were calculated through the Spearman correlation coefficient. To calculate internal consistency, Cronbach's alpha coefficient was used. Finally, the SPSS (version 21) and AMOS (version 21) statistical programs were used.

RESULTS

Tables 3 and 4 present the most important results of Study 2. Table 3 contains the indicators of the goodness of fit of 3 measuring models: the American test, the Mexican test, and the product of the combination of both scales, in this case called Mixed. It also contains the coefficients of internal consistency of the 3 instruments.

STUDIES 3 AND 4

The concept of generosity has been the object of attention since antiquity (Sommerfeld, 2009). However, it is true that this concept is a type of ugly duckling, defined indirectly and confused with other constructs such as altruism, helping others, love, or pro-social conduct, in general. It is important for different authors to define and operationalize the psychological constructs in their own cultures so that they can be eventually compared and, in this case, combined to obtain a version that is appropriate for a more inclusive segment of humanity than that in which they were originally and independently constructed. In this manner, the serious problem of ethnocentrism can be avoided or at least mitigated.

In the case of generosity, conceptualizations and operationalizations belonging to authors from Israel (Sommerfeld, 2009), the US (Smith & Hill, 2009), and Mexico are examined. These are compared, and a confirmatory factor analysis in each version is performed. Several of them are compared to know whether the resulting version adds value regarding each individual approach.

Table 3. Confirmatory factor analysis and reliability for the LOT-R Optimism, García, and Mixed scales (LOT-R+ GARCIA) for 350 participants

Goodness of Fit							
SCALE	*n*	CMIN	RMR	GFI	AGFI	NFI	A
LOT-R 6 ITEMS	350	28.932	.098	.976	.944	.806	.361
GARCÍA 8 ITEMS	350	56.478	.038	.980	.964	.961	.819
MIXED 8 ITEMS	350	36.645	.033	.987	.977	.975	.820

Table 4. Spearman correlations among the LOT-R Optimism, GARCÍA, and Mixed scales (LOT-R+ García) for 350 participants

SCALE	LOT-R	GARCÍA	MIXED
LOT-R	1.000	.456	.507
GARCÍA	.456	1.000	.959
MIXED	.507	.959	1.000

Generosity from Sommerfeld's Perspective (2009)

In general, it is agreed that generosity is a psychological disposition that involves the investment of time, effort, material resources, and even money to meet several needs of others, without expecting anything in return. However, Sommerfeld also emphasizes that it is necessary to study the subjective experience of generosity because there is a very personal satisfaction and certain complacency or self-gratification in the conduct of giving to others without expecting any reward, in addition to certain negative components, such as guilt and an emotional cost.

The measure offered by this author (Questionnaire on the experience of generosity) has 4 factors: 1) Emotional Cost and Burden (13 items, α = .88); 2) Pro-Social Orientation (10 items, α = .89); 3) Narcissistic Gratification (4 items, α = .72); and 4) Self-accusation and Guilt (7 items, α = .68). Only factor 2, Pro-Social Orientation, was used for this study (see Appendix C).

Interpersonal Generosity according to Smith and Hill (2009)

According to Smith and Hill (2009), with regard to the relationship between individuals, generosity can only exist in social terms, in which the individual who gives not only gives material resources, such as money, but also gives personal resources, such as time and energy. They also accept that to a point, this construct overlaps with altruism, pro-social guidance, and love.

They specify that generosity does not necessarily mean expecting nothing in return because sometimes the individual who gives rightly expects some degree of reciprocity. Finally, they note that it is a multidimensional construct that includes care, compassion, detachment, value, self-expansion, and verbal expression. The scale of interpersonal generosity by Smith and Hill (2009) consists of 10 items with an alpha of .89 (see Appendix D).

Generosity according to the Authors of this Chapter

From this perspective, generosity is considered a psychological disposition to share what one has with others in a desire to achieve greater equity among people. Much of this ideology is based on the Old Testament and the New Testament. For example, in accordance with the former, the individual who gives is a righteous person, and according to Paul, giving and sharing involve the search for equality (Second Epistle to the Corinthians 8:14-15 and the Old Testament/Psalms 37:11).

It is stated here that one must serve others (Mark 10:45) and that one needs to address the needs of others, as Jesus Christ himself states (Matthew 25:34-40). It is emphasized that it is better to give than to receive (Acts 20:35), that individuals should give up their own interests, subordinating them to those of others (Philippians 2:4), and that it is better to serve than to be served (Matthew 20:28).

Based on the above approaches and also according to the moral ideology that prevails in the northeast of Mexico, the authors of this chapter have developed the Scale of Generosity (see Appendix E).

STUDY 3: METHOD

Participants

The study was conducted on a convenience sample of 170 students at a public university in the northeast of Mexico. There were 87 (51.20%) women studying psychology and 83 (48.80%) male students majoring in sports management between 16 and 27 years of age, with an average of 19.19 years of age and a standard deviation of 1.81 year

Instruments

A sociodemographic questionnaire and the Experience of Generosity Questionnaire Scale (Sommerfeld, 2009, the Pro-Social factor only) were used, in addition to the Scale of Generosity created by the authors of this chapter.

Procedure

A doctoral student in psychology applied the sociodemographic questionnaire and the scales on generosity to students in sports management and psychology in their own classrooms.

Data Analysis

To assess construct validity, a confirmatory factor analysis was conducted with the estimation method scale-free least squares, given that the distributions in both the American and the Mexican scales were not normal, according to the results of the Kolgomorov-Smirnov test. Similarly, the correlations between the scores on the scales were calculated through the Spearman correlation coefficient.

To calculate internal consistency, the Cronbach's alpha coefficient was used. Finally, the SPSS (version 21) and AMOS (version 21) software programs were used.

RESULTS

Table 5. Confirmatory factor analysis and reliability of the Generosity Experience Questionnaire, Generosity, and Mixed scales for 170 participants

Goodness of Fit								
SCALE	*n*	CMIN	RMR	GFI	AGFI	NFI	A
EXPERIENCE OF GENEROSITY 9 ITEMS	170	24.90	.011	.98	.97	.95	.759
GENEROSITY 10 ITEMS	170	58.73	.053	.95	.92	.82	.675
MIXED 12 ITEMS	170	54.06	.019	.97	.96	.93	.759

Table 6. Spearman correlations among the Generosity Experience Questionnaire, Generosity, and Mixed scales for 170 participants

SCALE	EXPERIENCE OF GENEROSITY	GENEROSITY	MIXED
EXPERIENCE OF GENEROSITY	1.000	.355	.885
GENEROSITY	.355	1.000	.587
MIXED	.885	.587	1.000

Tables 5 and 6 present the most relevant results of Study 3. Table 5 contains the indicators of the goodness of fit of 3 measuring models: the American test, the Mexican test, and the product of the combination of both scales, in this case called Mixed. It also contains the coefficients of internal consistency of the 3 tests.

STUDY 4: METHOD

Participants

The study was conducted on a sample of 200 students at a public university in the northeast of Mexico. There were 100 (50.00%) females and 100 (50.00%) male students in the following programs: mechanical and electrical engineering, architecture, philosophy and literature, sports management, nursing, mathematics, criminology, biology, communications, civil engineering, public accounting, and nutrition. Ages ranged between 16 and 28 years, with an average of 20.19 years of age and a standard deviation of 2.11 years.

Instruments

A sociodemographic questionnaire and the Interpersonal Generosity scale (Smith & Hill, 2009) were used, in addition to the Scale of Generosity created by the authors of this chapter.

Procedure

A doctoral student in psychology applied the demographic questionnaire and the scales on generosity to the students belonging to the 12 aforementioned programs.

Data Analysis

To assess construct validity, a confirmatory factor analysis was conducted with the estimation method scale-free least squares, given that the distributions in both the American and the Mexican scales were not normal, according to the results of the Kolgomorov-Smirnov test. Taking this information into account, the correlations were calculated between the qualifications of the scales using the Spearman correlation coefficient. To calculate internal consistency, the Cronbach's alpha coefficient was used. Finally, the SPSS (version 21) and AMOS (version 21) statistical programs were used.

RESULTS

Tables 7 and 8 present the most relevant results of Study 4. Table 7 contains the indicators of the goodness of fit of 3 measuring models: the American test, the Mexican test, and the product of the combination of both scales, in this case called Mixed. It also contains the coefficients of internal consistency of the 3 tests.

Table 7. Confirmatory factor analysis and reliability of the Interpersonal Generosity, Generosity, and mixed scales for 200 participants

Goodness of Fit							
SCALE	*n*	CMIN	RMR	GFI	AGFI	NFI	A
INTERPERSONAL GENEROSITY 8 ITEMS	200	25.69	.043	.98	.96	.93	.71
GENEROSITY 8 ITEMS	200	30.85	.05	.97	.95	.86	.63
MIXED 11 ITEMS	200	61.64	.049	.97	.95	.92	.78

Table 8. Spearman correlations among the Interpersonal Generosity, Generosity, and Mixed scales for 200 participants

SCALE	INTERPERSONAL GENEROSITY	GENEROSITY	MIXED
INTERPERSONAL GENEROSITY	1.000	.531	.864
GENEROSITY	.531	1.000	.769
MIXED	.864	.769	1.000

STUDY 5

Conceptualization and Measurement of Thompson, Snyder, Hoffman, Michael, Rasmussen, Billings, Heinze, Neufeld, Shorey, Roberts, & Roberts (2005) on forgiveness

From this perspective, the definition of forgiveness does not require that those who feel offended empathize or reconcile with the offender. It is required that the individual changes his or her feelings, emotions, and behavior, specifically by setting aside anger and resentment. According to these authors, forgiveness is:

"...the framing of a perceived transgression such that one's responses to the transgressor, transgression, and sequelae of the transgression are transformed from negative to neutral or positive" (2005, p. 318).

These authors also include forgiving others and oneself, in addition to forgiving situations in the definition, a feature that other authors have ignored. This forgiveness scale covers 18 items, 6 of which refer to forgiving others (see Appendix F). This last sub-scale was the subject of the study reported here.

Conceptualization of Forgiveness by the Authors of this Chapter

What does "forgiving" mean? The action of forgiving arises from a dominant ideology of human relations that was governed by talion law, i.e., an eye for an eye, a tooth for a tooth, as an alternative to peace in a sociocultural climate where compensation or retaliation used to be legally and socially accepted. That is, the new maxim of forgiveness turns the blind eye and does not seek to cause the same or worse harm to those who hurt us. According to this conceptualization, unlike the definition of forgiveness offered by Thompson, Snyder, Hoffman et al. (2005) and in agreement with the authors of this study, when one forgives, any attempt, desire, or initiative to restore something lost in the process of forgiveness is abandoned (prestige, money, dignity, etc.). However, both the authors of this chapter and Thompson, Snyder, Hoffman et al. (2005) understand that the subject who was offended undergoes a process of change that allows him or her to perceive the offender and the world differently and in a more complex manner after the offense. Additionally, the conceptualization of forgiveness and the operationalization performed by the authors of this chapter are greatly based on the texts of the Old Testament and mainly the New Testament (Mark 11:25; Matthew 6:21 PM; Luke 6:37; Matthew 6:14; Ephesians 4:32; Colossians 3:12; Matthew 6:9-13). Appendix G shows the Scale of Forgiveness created by the authors of this chapter.

METHOD

Participants

This study was conducted on a convenience sample of 212 students from a public university, 110 (51.90%) men and 102 (42.10%) women between 17 and 50 years of age, with an average of 20.81 years of age and a standard deviation of 4.66 years. There were 184 undergraduate students and 28 graduate students, attending both public and private universities, but the majority were enrolled at public universities.

Instruments

We used a demographic questionnaire and the Heartland Forgiveness Scale (HFS) by Thompson, Snyder, Hoffman et al. (2005), in addition to the Scale of Forgiveness created by the authors of this chapter.

Procedure

A doctoral student and a master's student in psychology were responsible for implementing the sociodemographic questionnaire and the forgiveness scales to the participants.

Data Analysis

To assess construct validity, a confirmatory factor analysis was conducted with the estimation method scale-free least squares, given that the distributions in both the American and the Mexican scales were not normal, according to the results of the Kolgomorov-Smirnov test. Taking this information into account, the correlations were calculated between the qualifications of the scales using the Spearman correlation coefficient. To calculate internal consistency, the Cronbach's alpha coefficient was used. Finally, the SPSS (version 21) and AMOS (version 21) statistical programs were used.

RESULTS

Tables 9 and 10 present the most relevant results of Study 5. Table 9 contains the indicators of the goodness of fit for 3 measuring models: the American test, the Mexican test, and the product of the combination of both scales, in this case called Mixed. It also contains the coefficients of internal consistency for the 3 tests.

Table 9. Confirmatory factor analysis and reliability of the Heartland Forgiveness (HFS), Forgiveness, and Mixed scales for 212 participants

Goodness of Fit							
Scale	*n*	CMIN	RMR	GFI	AGFI	NFI	A
Heartland forgiveness 4 Items	212	.005	.002	1.00	1.00	1.00	.527
Forgiveness 10 Items	212	55.48	.076	.97	.96	.95	.818
Mixed 12 Items	212	72.81	.072	.97	.96	.94	.829

Table 10. Spearman correlations among the Heartland Forgiveness, Forgiveness, and Mixed scales in 212 participants

Scale	The heartland Forgiveness	Forgiveness	Mixed
The heartland forgiveness	1.000	.540	.669
Forgiveness	.540	1.000	.973
Mixed	.669	.973	1.000

GENERAL DISCUSSION

Theorizations and measurements in psychology are mainly performed in developed countries, and these models are then exported to other countries. This phenomenon occurs under the tacit or explicit assumption that results are universal and apply to any culture (Ardila, 2004; Berry, Poortinga, Segall, & Dasen, 2002; Castro Solano, 2014; García, Carrascoza, & Diaz, 2013; Vera-Villarroel, López-López, Lillo, & Silva, 2011). This assumption does not hold with the evidence gathered over the years. For example, in the case of optimism, as measured by the LOT-R test, it has been reported that in cultures other than the US, such as China (Ji, Zhang, Usborne, & Guan, 2004), Peru (Oliden Balarezo, 2014), Germany (Rauch, Schweizer, & Moosbrugger, 2006; Rauch, Schweizer, & Moosbrugger, 2007; Rauch, Schweizer, & Moosbrugger, 2008), and Chile (Vera-Villarroel, Córdova-Rubio, & Celis-Atenas, 2009), the North American scale achieves very good construct and discriminant validity but has poor to deficient reliability. According to the results reported here, this phenomenon also occurs in Mexico. The Mexican scale for optimism shows good psychometric properties in construct validity, convergent validity, and reliability.

Additionally, the scale obtained by combining the 2 versions of optimism, the American scale and the Mexican scale, which was called Mixed, proved to be valid and reliable with a component of 75.00% in the case of the Mexican scale (6 items out of 8) and 33.33% for the North American scale (2 items out of 6). Therefore, most likely, relatively different theories and measurements can be created on the same constructs in different nations due to their economic, political, social, and cultural-specific conditions. Consequently, it is essential to foster theories and measurement models that are adapted to the psychological phenomena in our own samples.

The studies described here find partial evidence in favor of promoting the construction and validation of instruments at the local level. Evidence also shows that efficient instruments result from the merging of local instruments with international instruments. It is noteworthy that with regard to optimism, the Mexican and the American tests were complementary because the latter was missing aspects concerning the past and the present, concentrating only on the future, whereas the former precisely omitted the orientation toward the future. Additionally, the Mexican scales for optimism and forgiveness turned out to be more effective than the American scales; however, regarding generosity, the opposite was true. This finding suggests that it is not possible to automatically conclude that a version used to measure positive psychological constructs is better merely because it is local. Therefore, empirical evidence would support the idea that local and international conceptualizations may be compatible. In brief: The data from this study would suggest that first, to reach a universal conceptualization, one should start from the local level. Second, it is possible, and necessary, to combine theories and instruments from various countries with our own theories and measures. Finally, the multinational theorization and operationalization of psychological phenomena would create a genuinely global psychology, avoiding the insidious ethnocentrism that currently prevails.

There are still some issues pending before achieving similar theories and measures that would map out the same positive psychological constructs that are imported. For example, the strategy recommended here should also be used in several regions of the same country because there is a clear difference between social groups within a nation. This phenomenon mostly occurs in underdeveloped countries, where there are different levels of quality of life according to the place where one dwells.

Additionally, it remains to be seen whether what has occurred here occurs in other countries: whether combining a local version with one or several foreign versions, in a foreign country, has results similar to those reported in this chapter.

To conclude, apparently, the research reported here is relatively similar to that of Hui and Triandis (1985), which is known as the "combined etic-emic approach", and had already been employed by Osgood (1967) to create a semantic differential and by Triandis (1972) to advance his concept of subjective culture. This approach is outlined in detail in its stages by Davidson, Jaccard, Triandis, Morales, and Díaz-Guerrero (1976). Nonetheless, it is not exactly the same because it lacks the last step used here, which entailed the integration of 2 or more emic measures from several countries to achieve an etic measure.

APPENDIX A.

Life Orientation Test-Revised (LOT-R) (Scheier, Carver & Bridges, 1994)

1-In uncertain times, I usually expect the best
4-Yes, 3-Maybe yes, 2-Maybe no, 1-No
2-It's easy for me to relax (filler item)
4-Yes, 3-Maybe yes, 2-Maybe no, 1-No
3-If something can go wrong for me, it will
1-Yes, 2-Maybe yes, 3-Maybe no, 4-No
4-I'm always optimistic about my future
4-Yes, 3-Maybe yes, 2-Maybe no, 1-No
5-I enjoy my friends a lot (filler item)
4-Yes, 3-Maybe yes, 2-Maybe no, 1-No
6-It's important for me to keep busy (filler item)
4-Yes, 3-Maybe yes, 2-Maybe no, 1-No
7-I hardly ever expect things to go my way
1-Yes, 2-Maybe yes, 3-Maybe no, 4-No
8-I don't get upset too easily (filler item)
4-Yes, 3-Maybe yes, 2-Maybe no, 1-No
9-I rarely count on good things to happen to me
1-Yes, 2-Maybe yes, 3-Maybe no, 4-No
10-Overall, I expect more good things to happen to me than bad
4-Yes, 3-Maybe yes, 2-Maybe no, 1-No

APPENDIX B.

Scale of Optimism (authors of this chapter)
1-Life is ugly
1-Yes, 2-Maybe yes, 3-Maybe no, 4-No
2-Life is beautiful
4-Yes, 3-Maybe yes, 2-Maybe no, 1-No
3- Life is good
4-Yes, 3-Maybe yes, 2-Maybe no, 1-No
4-I have done well in life
4-Yes, 3-Maybe yes, 2-Maybe no, 1-No
5-I have done poorly in life
1-Yes, 2-Maybe yes, 3-Maybe no, 4-No
6- Human beings are good
4-Yes, 3-Maybe yes, 2-Maybe no, 1-No
7-Human beings are evil
1-Yes, 2-Maybe yes, 3-Maybe no, 4-No
8-Men are born evil
1-Yes, 2-Maybe yes, 3-Maybe no, 4-No

APPENDIX C.

Experience of Generosity Questionnaire, Factor 2, Pro-Social Orientation (Sommerfeld, 2009)

1-I felt I wanted to help
4-Yes, 3-Maybe yes, 2-Maybe no, 1-No
2-I felt good about assisting someone in trouble
4-Yes, 3-Maybe yes, 2-Maybe no, 1-No
3-I hoped that what I was doing would make the other person feel better
4-Yes, 3-Maybe yes, 2-Maybe no, 1-No
4-I felt that I had good intentions for the other person
4-Yes, 3-Maybe yes, 2-Maybe no, 1-No
5-I wanted to give the other person a good feeling
4-Yes, 3-Maybe yes, 2-Maybe no, 1-No
6-I was satisfied that my help assisted the other person
4-Yes, 3-Maybe yes, 2-Maybe no, 1-No
7-I felt good about being able to give to the other person
4-Yes, 3-Maybe yes, 2-Maybe no, 1-No
8-I cared about the other person
4-Yes, 3-Maybe yes, 2-Maybe no, 1-No
9-I was happy that I succeeded in helping
4-Yes, 3-Maybe yes, 2-Maybe no, 1-No
10-I was happy to rescue the other person from a distressing situation
4-Yes, 3-Maybe yes, 2-Maybe no, 1-No

APPENDIX D.

Interpersonal Generosity Scale (Smith & Hill, 2009)

1-When one of my loved ones needs my attention, I really try to slow down and give them the time and help they need
4-Yes, 3-Maybe yes, 2-Maybe no, 1-No
2-I am known by family and friends as someone who makes time to pay attention to others' problems
4-Yes, 3-Maybe yes, 2-Maybe no, 1-No
3-I'm the kind of person who is willing to go the "extra mile" to help take care of my friends, relatives, and acquaintances
4-Yes, 3-Maybe yes, 2-Maybe no, 1-No
4-When friends or family members experience something upsetting or discouraging, I make a special point of being kind to them
4-Yes, 3-Maybe yes, 2-Maybe no, 1-No
5-When it comes to my personal relationships with others, I am a very generous person
4-Yes, 3-Maybe yes, 2-Maybe no, 1-No

6-It makes me very happy to give to other people in ways that meet their needs
4-Yes, 3-Maybe yes, 2-Maybe no, 1-No
7-It is just as important to me that other people around me are happy and thriving as it is that I am happy and thriving
4-Yes, 3-Maybe yes, 2-Maybe no, 1-No
8-My decisions are often based on concern for the welfare of others
4-Yes, 3-Maybe yes, 2-Maybe no, 1-No
9-I am usually willing to risk my own feelings being hurt in the process if I stand a chance of helping someone else in need
4-Yes, 3-Maybe yes, 2-Maybe no, 1-No
10-I make it a point to let my friends and family know how much I love and appreciate them
4-Yes, 3-Maybe yes, 2-Maybe no, 1-No

APPENDIX E.

Scale of Generosity (authors of this chapter)
1-What is one's becomes enhanced when it is shared with others
4-Yes, 3-Maybe yes, 2-Maybe no, 1-No
2-Nobody owns anything
4-Yes, 3-Maybe yes, 2-Maybe no, 1-No
3-I have to thank others for much of what I own
4-Yes, 3-Maybe yes, 2-Maybe no, 1-No
4- Everything I own is on loan
4-Yes, 3-Maybe yes, 2-Maybe no, 1-No
5-Serving is better than being served
4-Yes, 3-Maybe yes, 2-Maybe no, 1-No
6-Decent people share what they own
4-Yes, 3-Maybe yes, 2-Maybe no, 1-No
7-It is better to give than to receive
4-Yes, 3-Maybe yes, 2-Maybe no, 1-No
8-The poor deserve help from those of us who have more
4-Yes, 3-Maybe yes, 2-Maybe no, 1-No
9-One has to share what one owns
4-Yes, 3-Maybe yes, 2-Maybe no, 1-No
10-One gets what one has thanks to the help of others
4-Yes, 3-Maybe yes, 2-Maybe no, 1-No
11-Everything belongs to everyone
4-Yes, 3-Maybe yes, 2-Maybe no, 1-No
12-It is good to give when you have something someone else needs
4-Yes, 3-Maybe yes, 2-Maybe no, 1-No
13-Complimenting is giving part of your best
4-Yes, 3-Maybe yes, 2-Maybe no, 1-No

APPENDIX F.

Heartland Forgiveness Scale (Thompson, Snyder, Hoffman et al., 2005)

1-I continue to punish a person who has done something that I think is wrong.
1-Yes, 2-Maybe yes, 3-Maybe no, 4-No
2-With time, I am understanding of others for the mistakes they've made.
4-Yes, 3-Maybe yes, 2-Maybe no, 1-No
3-I continue to be hard on others who have hurt me.
1-Yes, 2-Maybe yes, 3-Maybe no, 4-No
4-Although others have hurt me in the past, I have eventually been able to see them as good people
4-Yes, 3-Maybe yes, 2-Maybe no, 1-No
5-If others mistreat me, I continue to think badly of them.
1-Yes, 2-Maybe yes, 3-Maybe no, 4-No
6-When someone disappoints me, I can eventually move past it.
4-Yes, 3-Maybe yes, 2-Maybe no, 1-No

APPENDIX G.

Scale of Forgiveness (authors of this chapter)

1-If someone does me wrong, I'll wrong them in return
1-Yes, 2-Maybe yes, 3-Maybe no, 4-No
2-If someone owes me, that person will pay for it
1-Yes, 2-Maybe yes, 3-Maybe no, 4-No
3-When people criticize me, I also criticize them
1-Yes, 2-Maybe yes, 3-Maybe no, 4-No
4-It is unlikely that I would hurt someone who hurt me
4-Yes, 3-Maybe yes, 2-Maybe no, 1-No
5-If someone owed money to me, I could forget the debt
4-Yes, 3-Maybe yes, 2-Maybe no, 1-No
6-I only help those who help me
1-Yes, 2-Maybe yes, 3-Maybe no, 4-No
7-If someone speaks ill of me, I speak ill of that person
1-Yes, 2-Maybe yes, 3-Maybe no, 4-No
8-It is unlikely that I would wish well for those who wish me bad
1-Yes, 2-Maybe yes, 3-Maybe no, 4-No
9-I wish that those who wish me bad do well
4-Yes, 3-Maybe yes, 2-Maybe no, 1-No
10-I Speak well of those who speak ill of me
4-Yes, 3-Maybe yes, 2-Maybe no, 1-No
11-I only speak well of those who speak well of me
1-Yes, 2-Maybe yes, 3-Maybe no, 4-No

12-I only wish evil to those who do me wrong
1-Yes, 2-Maybe yes, 3-Maybe no, 4-No
13- I only wish well to those who do me well
1-Yes, 2-Maybe yes, 3-Maybe no, 4-No
14-I wish well to those who do me wrong
4-Yes, 3-Maybe yes, 2-Maybe no, 1-No
15-If someone owes me money, he or she must pay it back
1-Yes, 2-Maybe yes, 3-Maybe no, 4-No
16-If someone insults me, I forgive that person
4-Yes, 3-Maybe yes, 2-Maybe no, 1-No
17-If someone owes me money, I forgive the debt
4-Yes, 3-Maybe yes, 2-Maybe no, 1-No

REFERENCES

Acts 20, 35 (1990)* *La Santa Biblia. Antiguo y Nuevo Testamento. Versión Reina Valera 1960* [The Holy Bible. Old and New Testaments. Reina Valera Version 1960]. Nashville: Broadman & Holman Publishers.

Alarcon, R. (2002). *Estudios sobre psicología latinoamericana* [*Latin American Studies on psychology*]. Lima: Universidad Ricardo Palma.

Ardila, R. (1972). *La psicología contemporánea. Panorama internacional* [*Contemporary Psychology. International Scene.*]. Buenos Aires: Paidós.

Ardila, R. (2004). *La Ciencia y los Científicos. A Psychological Perspective* [*Science and scientists. A Psychological Perspective*]. Medellín: Universidad de Antioquia.

Berry, J. W., Poortinga, Y. H., Segall, M. H. & Dasen, P. R. (2002). *Cross-Cultural Psychology: Research and Applications (2nd ed.).* New York: Cambridge University Press.

Carver, C. S. & Scheier, M. F. (2002). Optimism. In C. R. Snyder & S. López (Eds.), *Handbook of Positive Psychology*, pp. 231-243. Oxford, UK: Oxford University Press.

Castro Solano, A. (2014). *Positive Psychology in Latin America*. New York: Springer.

Colosssians 3, 12-13 (1990). *La Santa Biblia. Antiguo y Nuevo Testamento. Versión Reina Valera 1960* [The Holy Bible. Old and New Testaments. Reina Valera Version 1960]. Nashville: Broadman & Holman Publishers.

Davidson, A. R., Jaccard, J. J., Triandis, H. C., Morales, M. L. & Diaz-Guerrero, R. (1976). Cross-cultural model testing: Toward a solution of the etic-emic dilemma. *International Journal of Psychology, 11*, 1-13.

Díaz-Guerrero, R. (1971). La enseñanza de la investigación en psicología en Iberoamérica: un paradigma [The teaching of research in psychology in Latin America: a paradigm]. *Revista Latinoamericana de Psicología, 3*(1), 5-36.

Díaz-Loving, R. (2006). An historic-psycho-socio-cultural look at the self in Mexico. In U. Kim, K.-S. Yang, & K.-K. Hwang (Eds.), *Indigenous and Cultural Psychology: Understanding People in Context*, pp. 315-325. New York: Springer Science+Business Media, Inc.

Díaz-Loving, R. (1999). The indigenization of psychology: birth of a new science or rekindling of an old one? *Applied Psychology: An International Review, 48*(4), 433-449.

Ephesians 4, 32 (1990). *La Santa Biblia. Antiguo y Nuevo Testamento. Versión Reina Valera 1960* [The Holy Bible. Old and New Testaments. Reina Valera Version 1960]. Nashville: Broadman & Holman Publishers.

García, C. H., Díaz, H. L., Téllez, A., López, F., Martínez, J., Sánchez, L. & García, E. (2013). Construct and convergent validity of the OIS-García (Optimist Interactive Style) scales in a Mexican population. *Psychology Research, 3*(9), 518-528.

García, C. H., Carrascoza, C. A. & Díaz, H. L. (2013). Psychological theory and research in Mexico: Critical reflections. *International Journal of Psychology Research, 8*(2), 85-93.

Harré, R. (1999). The rediscovery of the human mind: The discursive approach. *Asian Journal of Social Psychology, 2*, 43-62.

Hui, C. H. & Triandis, H. (1985). Measurement in cross-cultural psychology: A review and comparison of strategies. *Journal of Cross-Cultural Psychology, 16*(2), 131-152.

Huntington, S. (1972). Society and theory in social psychology. In J. Israel & H. Tajfel (Eds.), *The Context of Social Psychology: A Critical Assessment.* London: Academic Press.

Ji, L., Zhang, Z., Usborne, E. & Guan, Y. (2004). Optimism across cultures: In response to the severe acute respiratory syndrome outbreak. *Asian Journal of Social Psychology, 7*(1), 25-34.

Kim, U., Yang, K. S. & Hwang, K. K. (2006). *Indigenous and Cultural Psychology: Understanding People in Context.* New York: Springer Science+Business Media, Inc.

Luke 6, 37-38 (1990). *La Santa Biblia. Antiguo y Nuevo Testamento. Versión Reina Valera 1960* [The Holy Bible. Old and New Testaments. Reina Valera Version 1960]. Nashville: Broadman & Holman Publishers.

Mark 10, 45 (1990). *La Santa Biblia. Antiguo y Nuevo Testamento. Versión Reina Valera 1960* [The Holy Bible. Old and New Testaments. Reina Valera Version 1960]. Nashville: Broadman & Holman Publishers.

Mark 11, 25-26 (1990). *La Santa Biblia. Antiguo y Nuevo Testamento. Versión Reina Valera 1960* [The Holy Bible. Old and New Testaments. Reina Valera Version 1960]. Nashville: Broadman & Holman Publishers.

Matthew 6, 9-14 (1990). *La Santa Biblia. Antiguo y Nuevo Testamento. Versión Reina Valera 1960* [The Holy Bible. Old and New Testaments. Reina Valera Version 1960]. Nashville: Broadman & Holman Publishers.

Matthew 6, 21 PM (1990). *La Santa Biblia. Antiguo y Nuevo Testamento. Versión Reina Valera 1960* [The Holy Bible. Old and New Testaments. Reina Valera Version 1960]. Nashville: Broadman & Holman Publishers.

Matthew 20, 28 (1990). *La Santa Biblia. Antiguo y Nuevo Testamento. Versión Reina Valera 1960* [The Holy Bible. Old and New Testaments. Reina Valera Version 1960]. Nashville: Broadman & Holman Publishers.

Matthew 25, 34-40 (1990). *La Santa Biblia. Antiguo y Nuevo Testamento. Versión Reina Valera 1960* [The Holy Bible. Old and New Testaments. Reina Valera Version 1960]. Nashville: Broadman & Holman Publishers.

Oliden Balarezo, S. N. (2014). Propiedades psicométricas del test de orientación vital revisado (LOT-R) en un grupo de universitarios de Lima Metropolitana [Psychometric properties of the Life Orientation Test – Revised (LOT-R) in a group of university students in Metropolitan Lima]. Unpublished thesis. Lima: Pontificia Universidad Catolica de Peru.

Osgood, C. E. (1967). Cross-cultural comparability in attitude measurement via multilingual semantic differentials. In M. Fishbein (Ed.), *Readings in Attitude Theory and Measurement*. New York: John Wiley.

Otero, J. M., Luengo, A., Romero, E., Gómez, J. A. & Castro, C. (1998). Psicología de la personalidad. Manual de prácticas [Psychology of the personality. Manual of practice]. Barcelona: Ariel Practicum.

Philippians 2, 4-8 (1990). *La Santa Biblia. Antiguo y Nuevo Testamento. Versión Reina Valera 1960* [The Holy Bible. Old and New Testaments. Reina Valera Version 1960]. Nashville: Broadman & Holman Publishers.

Pike, K. L. (1966). Etic and emic standpoints for the description of behavior. In A. G. Smith (Ed.), *Communication and Culture: Readings in the Codes of Human Interaction*, pp. 152-163. New York: Holt, Rinehart & Winston.

Psalms 37, 11 (1990). *La Santa Biblia. Antiguo y Nuevo Testamento. Versión Reina Valera 1960* [The Holy Bible. Old and New Testaments. Reina Valera Version 1960]. Nashville: Broadman & Holman Publishers.

Rauch, W., Schweizer, K. & Moosbrugger, H. (2006, July). *Methodological Approaches to the Problem of Dimensionality of Optimism Questionnaires*. EAM-SMABS Conference in Budapest, Hungary.

Rauch, W. A., Schweizer, K. & Moosbrugger, H. (2007). Method effects due to social desirability as a parsimonious explanation of the deviation from unidimensionality in LOT-R scores. *Personality and Individual Differences, 42*, 1597-1607.

Rauch, W. A., Schweizer, K. & Moosbrugger, H. (2008). An IRT Analysis of the Personal Optimism Scale. *European Journal of Psychological Assessment, 24*(1), 49-56. DOI 10.1027/1015-5759.24.1.49.

Ribes, E. (2009). La personalidad como organización de los estilos interactivos [Personality as the organization of interaction styles]. *Revista Mexicana de Psicología, 26*, 145-161.

Scheier, M. F., Carver, C. S. & Bridges, M. W. (1994). Distinguishing optimism from neuroticism (and trait anxiety, self-mastery, and self-esteem): A reevaluation of the Life Orientation Test. *Journal of Personality and Social Psychology, 67*, 1063-1078.

Second Epistle of Paul to the Corinthians 8, 14-15 (1990). *La Santa Biblia. Antiguo y Nuevo Testamento. Versión Reina Valera 1960* [The Holy Bible. Old and New Testaments. Reina Valera Version 1960]. Nashville: Broadman & Holman Publishers.

Smith, C. & Hill, J. P. (2009). Toward the measurement of interpersonal generosity (IG): An IG Scale conceptualized, tested, and validated. Unpublished monograph. Available at: http://generosityresearch.nd.edu/assets.

Sommerfeld, E. (2010). The subjective experience of generosity. In M. Mikulincer & P. R. Shaver (Eds.), *Prosocial Motives, Emotions, and Behavior: The Better Angels of our Nature*, pp. 303-323. Washington, DC: American Psychological Association.

Thompson, L. Y., Snyder, C. R., Hoffman, L., Michael, S. T., Rasmussen, H. N., Billings, L. S., Heinze, L., Neufeld, J. E., Shorey, H. S., Roberts, J. C. & Roberts, D. E. (2005). Dispositional forgiveness of self, others, and situations. *Journal of Personality, 73*(2), 313-359.

Triandis, H. C. (1972). *The Analysis of Subjective Culture*. New York: John Wiley.

Vera-Villarroel, P., Córdova-Rubio, N. & Celis-Atenas, K. (2009). Evaluación del optimismo: un análisis preliminar del *Life Orientation Test* versión revisada (LOT-R) en población chilena [Evaluation of optimism: a preliminary analysis of the *Life Orientation Test* revised version (LOT-R) in Chilean population]. *Universitas Psychologica, 8*(1), 61-68.

Vera-Villarroel, P., López-López, W., Lillo, S. & Silva, L. M. (2011). La producción científica en psicología latinoamericana: Un análisis de la investigación por países [Scientific production in Latin American psychology: an analysis of research in different countries]. *Revista Latinoamericana de Psicología, 43*(1), 95-104.

In: Psychological Well-Being
Editor: Rafael Bowers

ISBN: 978-1-63484-354-6
© 2016 Nova Science Publishers, Inc.

Chapter 3

THE RELATIONSHIP BETWEEN LANGUAGE, IDENTITY AND BEHAVIOURAL ACCULTURATION AND WELL-BEING AMONG NON-WESTERN SKILLED MIGRANTS IN A WESTERN HOST SOCIETY

Asanka Gunasekara, Sharon Grant
and Diana Rajendran
Swinburne University of Technology, Australia

ABSTRACT

Qualified, trained and experienced skilled migrants from non-Western countries are becoming increasingly important drivers of economic growth in Western host countries as they help fill skill shortages in the labour market. Host countries expect skilled migrants to integrate into the socio-economic fabric of society and become contributing members. However, there are many challenges inherent in migration which can affect migrant's well-being, including language barriers, adapting to local customs, socialising with the majority population, transferring credentials, and finding suitable employment. Integrating into the host society can be more complex and challenging when there is cultural distance between migrants' sending and receiving societies. Acculturation describes a process that changes migrants' attitudes, values, customs, beliefs and behaviours in accordance with the host culture. Migrants' acculturation to a host society occurs in a number of different domains, including host country language, identity and behaviour. The current study examined the relationship between language, identity and behavioural acculturation and well-being among 306 Indian and Sri Lankan skilled migrants residing in Australia. Participants completed the Language, Identity and Behavioural Acculturation Scale (Birman and Trickett 2001) and the Personal Well-being Index (Cummins 2006) and provided demographic information. Controlling for gender, age at migration, years since migration, education, expectation to return to country of origin, and pre-migration socioeconomic status, only identity acculturation significantly predicted well-being.

SKILLED MIGRATION IN THE AUSTRALIAN CONTEXT

The world today is increasingly characterised by the mobility of migrants from non-Western to Western countries (Au et al. 1998; Coleman, Casali and Wampold 2001; Chiswick and Miller, 2005; Fong and Ooka 2006; George and Chaze, 2009; Reitz et al. 2009; Sam 1998). Qualified, trained and experienced migrants are becoming important drivers of economic growth in host countries, where they help fill labour market demands. In the past, people migrated to escape from unpleasant circumstances such as extreme weather conditions or political unrest in their country of birth (Colic-Peisker 2011; De Haas and Fokkema 2011; Mara and Landesmann 2013; Nesdale and Mak 2000; Silbereisen 2008). Nowadays, people primarily migrate to Western countries to experience comparatively superior circumstances in the host country, such as economic and social benefits (Ho 2006; Mara and Landesmann 2013). Furthermore, due to skill shortages, an ageing population and decreasing fertility rates, developed countries in the Western world now invite skilled migrants to help facilitate economic growth (Ariss et al. 2012). Therefore, in recent years many migrant-receiving countries, including Australia, have given preference to the skilled migrant category within their migration programs (Boucher 2007; Colic-Peisker 2011; Hugo 1999; Lee 2013).

Australia is one of the world's major recipient nations of skilled migrants (Berry 2010; Islam and Fausten 2008, 66). Currently, 26% of the total labour force (12 million people) in Australia was born overseas (Australian Bureau of Statistics [ABS] 2013). Furthermore, skilled migrants now comprise the majority of new arrivals in Australia (Department of Immigration and Citizenship of Australia [DIAC 2012]; Fong and Ooka 2006; Kramar et al. 2011; Murdie and Ghosh 2010; Syed and Kramar 2010). All types of Australian organisations, from multinational companies to family businesses, employ skilled migrants from different cultural and ethnic backgrounds (Dagher and D'Netto 1997; Syed and Kramar 2010). Skilled migrants help to fill chronic skill shortages across different professions and occupations, including construction, education, engineering and health sectors (Wulff and Dharmalingam 2008; Ziguras and Fang Law 2006).

Australia, like other migrant-receiving societies, such as Canada, the U.S and the U.K, has a long history of migration, which ranges from humanitarian migration to skilled and business migration (Chow 2003; Collins 2013). Since the establishment of the Department of Migration and Citizenship Australia in 1945, over seven million people have been granted visas for permanent migration (DIAC 2010-2011). More than 43.1% of the current Australian population was born overseas or has at least one parent who was born overseas (ABS 2013). As such, Australia is considered one of the most culturally diverse nations in the world (Ho 2006; Hugo 1999; 2004). With the end of the White Australia Policy in 1973, which had lasted for over 70 years, a new migration policy of non-discrimination on the grounds of colour, race or nationality was established (Colic-Peisker 2011; Government of Western Australia 2012). Thus, individuals and families from different societies all over the world gained the opportunity to enter to Australia.

Since 1998, the skilled stream has been the primary pathway for migrants who come to Australia (DIAC 2010-2011). In the past six decades, the Australian migration plan has allocated more places to skilled migrants, expecting to fill existing skill shortages and to achieve a sustainable economic boom in the country (Bahn 2014; Boucher 2007; Colic-Peisker 2011; Collins 2013; Ho 2006; Parliament of Australia, 2013). In addition, Australia has been a major education provider for international students. In 2012-2013, 259,278 student visas were granted for students from countries around the world, including China, India, South Korea, Vietnam and Brazil (DIAC 2013). Hawthorne (2010) found that international students who completed their studies in Australia were a major source of skilled migration.

ASIAN CENTURY IN MIGRATION

The above policy changes paved the way for Asian skilled migrants to enter Australia (Colic-Peisker 2011; Hugo 1999; 2004). The current Australian skilled migration policy encourages skilled migrants from all around the world, but Asian skilled migrants have been given prominent attention in this program since the 1990s. Skilled migration has been a practical solution to Australia's skill shortage and to balance the ageing population of the country.

In 2011-2012, the Indian sub-continent provided 24% and North Asia 25% of the migrants to Australia. Possibly for this reason, Australia's migration discourse has named this period the Asian Century in migration (DIAC 2011-2012). In recent years, skilled migration from Asia has constituted the largest influx of migrants into Australian society, with South Asian migrants, such as Indian and Sri Lankan migrants, accounting for a considerable percentage of this influx (Collins 2013; Hugo 1999; 2004). Indian and Sri Lankan born skilled migrants are significant minority groups in present-day Australia. Despite this significant representation, this group is neglected in the academic literature and little is known about their experiences after migration.

Skilled migrants differ from other migrant categories in various ways. They have recognised qualification, possess work experience in a given field, and mostly work within the profession for which they have been trained (DIAC 2013; Hawthorne 2010). In addition, skilled migrants generally intend to live in the host country permanently or extend their stay for a longer period than temporary migrants (Groutsis and Arnold 2012; Roberts 2011). Studies that focus on skilled migrants are on the increase (Boucher 2007; Hawthorn 2002; 2010; Ho 2006; Islam and Fausten 2008; Massey and Parr 2012; Roberts 2011; Wulff and Dharmalingam 2008; Ziguras and Fang Law 2006). Nevertheless, there remains a lack of studies that focus on particular ethnic groups of skilled migrants and their migration outcomes.

CHALLENGES FOR SKILLED MIGRANTS

People may migrate to escape from undesirable circumstances in their country of birth or to experience a better life in the host country (Nesdale and Mak 2000). Therefore, many skilled migrants who migrate to Western countries expect better outcomes in their personal lives as well as their work lives (Amit 2010a; Choudhry 2001; George and Chaze 2009; Malinen and Johnston 2011; Sam 1998). Likewise, skilled migrants are expected to readily contribute to the host society's economy (DIAC 2013). Realistically, however, in the initial stages of migration, it can be challenging for migrants to adapt to a new culture and a new lifestyle (George and Chaze 2009; Valento 2009). For many skilled migrants, the migration process is not necessarily a smooth one. Migration is considered to be a major life event (Foroughi et al. 2001; George and Chaze 2009; Gudykunst and Kim 2003; Safdar et al. 2003; Safi 2010), and it is evident that ethnic migrants to the Western world in particular can experience 'culture shock' in the early stages of arrival (Gijsberts and Dagevos 2007; Kisselev et al. 2010; Murdie and Ghosh 2010). Thus, migration is not simply a decision to change where one lives, but a much more complex process that is associated with a number of significant changes which can affect migrants' subjective experiences, including their well-being (George and Chaze 2009; Gudykunst and Kim 2003; Foroughi et al. 2001; Safdar Lay and Struthers 2003; Safi 2010).

Despite their potential to contribute to host societies, skilled migrants are not always accepted and absorbed into the host society labour market with their existing credentials (Ho 2006; Neto and Barros 2007; Valenta 2009) and the likelihood of finding a suitable job can be low (see also Chowhan et al. 2012). For instance, Chowhan et al. (2012) found that a large proportion of new skilled migrants in Canada reported difficulty in finding a job due to non-recognition of their foreign credentials. Australian research has similarly shown that some skilled migrants fail to secure employment in their field (Chiswick et al. 2005; Hawthorne 1994, Ho 2006). In addition, Cobb-Clark (2000) and Lee (2013) identified that skilled migrants from non-English speaking countries experience more hardship than migrants from English-speaking countries in the Australian labour market. This situation may come about as a result of discounted recognition for foreign credentials (Amit 2012b; Somerville and Walsworth 2009; Syed and Murray 2009). As a consequence of these issues, skilled migrants may experience deteriorating economic outcomes such as high unemployment rates, low initial wages, displacement, low earnings or early retirement (Hawthorne 2002, 55; Qureshi et al. 2013; Somerville and Walsworth 2009). These difficulties are likely to impact on their well-being.

Hawthorne (2010) found that, regardless of ethnic background, Australian employers prefer to employ skilled migrants who studied in Australia as international students. However, Parasnis et al. (2008) found no advantage in having Australian qualifications for labour market integration among their study participants, with factors such as education level, labour market experience, marital status, country of birth and years since arrival being more influential factors. Parr and Guo (2005) found that there has been an upward mobility in the occupational structure of Asian-Australian skilled migrants in recent years. In 2013, the overall unemployment rate among Indian and Sri Lankan migrants were six percent and five percent, respectively while the national unemployment rate stood at 5.8 percent (DIAC 2013a and 2013b).

Adapting to the host society can be complex and challenging when there is social distance between migrants' sending and receiving societies (Barret and Duffy 2008; Berry 2001; Chiswick and Miller 2002). Many migrants feel vulnerable due to the new environment due to their minority status, especially in the early stages of arrival (George and Chaze 2009; Lu, Samarathunge and Härtel 2011; Safi 2010). Migrants from non-English speaking countries that have basic cultural differences from Australia and may suffer emotional distress when adjusting to their new lives (Birman and Taylor-Ritzler 2007; Coleman 1995; Coleman et al. 2001); regardless of the official resettlement support that newcomers receive from the host government and other migrant-supporting institutions, anxiety, fear, helplessness and the desire to return home are some of the common feelings that migrants experience during this journey (Au et al. 1998; Sam 1998; Valenta 2009). For instance, the following quote illustrates the experiences of a new skilled migrant to Canada (George and Chaze 2009, 274):

> 'I remember there was once last year when I was turned down from another job, I was really, really upset and I called my husband and I started crying on the phone and I told him I am going to take my life because I just feel, I was just depressed, I had never in my life considered things like that, and I told him that am just going to hang myself. What am I doing here [...] I have nothing to look forward to [...].'

Several studies have examined the well-being of migrants in different host societies (Amit 2010a; Daig et al. 2009; Mara and Landesmann 2013; Verkuyten 2008). However, these studies report mixed findings across different migrant groups (Amit 2010a; Neto and Barros 2007; Sam 1998; Verkuyten 2008). Furthermore, previous studies have primarily focused on first- and second-generation refugee or humanitarian migrant groups in other host societies such as Canada and Norway (Dalgard and Thapa 2007; George and Chaze 2009; Valento 2009). More research is needed on the well-being of skilled migrants in Australia; in particular, studies that focus on increasingly prevalent groups such as Indian and Sri Lankan skilled migrants are needed due to the limited availability of research that examines these important groups. Understanding the level of well-being among a minority skilled migrant group is important because researchers have long recognised that employees do not leave their non-work life experiences on the 'door step' but carry them into the workplace and vice versa (Ragins 2009). Furthermore, well-being may affect propensity to stay in the host society (Mara and Landesmann 2013).

ACCULTURATION AND MIGRATION OUTCOMES

Berry (1997) noted that the majority of migrants adjust as time spent in the host country increases (see also Martinovic, Tubergen and Maas 2009; Remennick 2004; Sam 1998). Furthermore, migration can expand individuals' worldviews, cultural competence and adaptability, leading to higher well-being in the long run (Mahmud and Scholmerich 2011). Some migrants establish themselves in the new destination by building new links with people, institutions and workplaces to recreate feelings of belonging and self-worth (Berry 2001; Gordon 1964; Remennick 2003; Valenta 2009; Vergunst 2008). Therefore, adapting to the beliefs, norms and practices of the new culture and building new social networks are also seen as common outcomes of migration (Dalgard and Thapa 2007).

Some scholars (Valenta 2009; Vergunst 2008) have argued that the extent to which migrants adapt to the host society forms the foundation for a successful life after migration. The adaptation of migrants in host societies has been described variously in the literature as 'acculturation' (Berry 2001; Birman and Taylor-Ritzler 2007; Gordon 1964), 'assimilation' (Gordon 1964; Nesdale and Mak 2000; Safda et al. 2003) and 'social integration' (Dalgard and Thapa 2007; Reitz et al. 2009). In the present study, the term 'acculturation' is used and is defined as *the degree of migrants' adaptation to the mainstream society in terms of host country language, identity and behaviour.*

There is consensus in the literature that acculturated migrants overcome many of the challenges inherent to migration and contribute to the socio-economic growth of the host society (Amit 2010b; Au et al. 1998; Lu et al. 2012; Sam 1998). These studies suggest that the acculturation of migrants is likely to be linked to their well-being (Dalgard and Thapa 2007; Sam, 1998; Valenta 2009). The benefits of skilled migrants' acculturation for migrant receiving societies are clear. Acculturation reflects the degree of cultural acceptance and social cohesion among migrants in a host society (Adachi 2011; Safdar et al. 2003; Yoon and Lee 2010). Despite a large representation of Indian and Sri Lankan skilled migrants in Australia, there has been little research on this segment of skilled migrants, including their experiences after migration.

THE CURRENT RESEARCH

The present research explores the acculturation of Indian and Sri Lankan skilled migrants in Australian society, in terms of host country language, identity and behavior.The relationship between acculturation and well-being in this group of migrants is also examined. Understanding the level of well-being among migrants is important for migration policy-makers, since poor well-being may result in costs rather than benefits to the host country, including high unemployment rates and dependency on social benefits, or political and social unrest due to psychological stressors. In the sections that follow, we define acculturation and provide an operational definition of well-being for the current research before examining the possible relationship between acculturation and well-being. Additional factors which might influence skilled migrants' well-being are also discussed.

Definition of Key Terms

The adaptation of migrants to host societies has evoked considerable interest in the current migration literature. Due to the complexity of the process, studies have used various terms to explain the extent to which migrants adapt to the host society. These include 'acculturation' (Berry 2001; Birman and Taylor-Ritzler 2007; Gordon 1964; Nesdale and Mak 2000; Sam and Berry 2010), 'assimilation' (Gordon 1964; Nesdale and Mak 2000; Sam and Berry 2010), and 'social integration' (Dalgard and Thapa 2007, Martinovic et al. 2009; Remennick 2003, 2004; Valento 2009; Wu et al. 2012). Due to the interchangeable usage (Garrido et al. 2012; Selvarajah 2004; Stark and Jakubek 2013) of such terms within migration literature, the following section provides a brief overview of these terminologies and discusses the similarities and differences among them in order to understand their appropriateness in the present study.

Acculturation

Acculturation is one of the most researched areas in the migration literature (Au et al. 1998; Berry, 2001; Birman and Taylor-Ritzler 2007; Coleman et al. 2001; Ea et al. 2008; Lu et al. 2011; Remennick 1999; Safdar et al. 2003; Sakamoto 2007). Acculturation is primarily described as "a process that entails contact between two cultural groups, which results in numerous cultural changes in both parties" (Arends-to´th and Van de Vijver 2003; Redfield, Linton and Herskovits 1936, as cited in Berry 2001, 616). Therefore, acculturation has been described as a bidirectional process. That is, changes occur within both the groups in contact (Berry 2001; Sayegh and Lasry 1993).

Berry et al. (2006) argued that even though contact experiences change migrants' and mainstreamers' behaviours, there is a greater impact on migrants (see also, Arends-to´th and Van de Vijver 2003). Perhaps for this reason, some authors have described acculturation mainly in relation to migrants, an approach that was also adopted in the present study. Mendoze (1989) has defined acculturation as the process of ethnic minorities integrating into mainstream society (as cited in Sanchez and Brock, 1996). Similarly, acculturation was defined by Abraido-Lanza (2004) as the process by which migrants adapt their attitudes, values, customs, beliefs and behaviours to a new culture. Berry et al. (2006) offered a similar definition, describing acculturation as "an accumulative social learning process through which ethnic minority individuals adapt to the dominant culture and the corresponding changes in their beliefs, values, and behaviours that result from their exposure to the host culture and its members" (as cited in Kumar and Nevid 2010, 275). When all of these definitions of acculturation are taken into account, the similarities in the definitions are clear: acculturation is a process that changes migrants' attitudes, values, customs, beliefs and behaviours in accordance with the host culture.

Gordon (1964) proposed two types of acculturation, 'behavioural acculturation' and 'structural acculturation' (as cited in Selverajah 2004). 'Behavioural acculturation' refers to changes in the cultural patterns of migrants in accordance with the host society, including language, interests, daily living habits, food and entertainment choices of migrants (Miller 2010). 'Structural acculturation' refers to migrants' becoming members of social clubs in the host society (Selverajah 2004). The focus of the present study is on acculutration in terms of language, identity and behaviour dimensions. This may be more closely linked with 'behavioural acculturation' introduced by Gordon, because changes among first-generation ethnic migrants (such as Indian and Sri Lankan skilled migrants in Australia) can be mainly expected in 'behavioural' realms rather than 'structural' realms.

Acculturation also involves alterations in the migrants' sense of self-identity (Garrido et al. 2012; Ryder et al. 2000; Worrell and Gardner-Kitt 2006). These alterations have been discussed using two predominant models. These are the unidimensional model and the bidimensional model (Berry 2006; Ryder et al. 2000; Sakamoto 2007). In the historical unidimensional model, acculturated individuals are placed on different identities that range from exclusively heritage culture to exclusively mainstream culture (Ryder et al. 2000, 49). For instance, according to this model, heritage and mainstream cultures are mutually exclusive and compete with each other (Sayegh and Lasry 1993). Suinn-Lew's Asian Self Identity Acculturation Scale (SL-ASIA Scale, Suinn et al. 1992), an often-used scale in acculturation studies, assumes a 'unidimensional' construct that ranges from highly traditional to bicultural competence to highly assimilated (for instance, one of the items in the scale is 'What language can you speak: Asian only; Asian and English equally; English only?').There is no option for Asian and English other than adopting both equally when in fact someone may adopt both but to differing degrees. Therefore, as a critique of this unidimensional model, the bidimensional model was proposed (Ryder et al. 2000).

The bidimensional model assumes heritage and mainstream cultures are free to vary independently and migrants are capable of having multiple cultural identities (Ryder et al.

2000). Therefore, the bidimensional model posits that individuals are able to maintain their own cultural identification and behaviours while developing mainstream cultural identification and behaviours simultaneously (Berry 2006; Sakamoto 2007; Sayegh and Lasry 1993). Thus, LaFromboise et al. (1993) claimed acculturated individuals may perceive themselves as members of an ethnic group, as well as members of mainstream society, depending on the situation (see also Remennick 2004). However, past research findings (Birman and Taylor-Ritzler 2007; Remennick 2003; Saghafi et al. 2012; Sakamoto 2007; Sam 1998) suggest that first-generation ethnic migrants are more likely to maintain their own culture while adding host country cultural dimensions. Therefore, it is sensible to assess the extent to which migrants are acculturated to the host society rather than the extent of their acculturation to the culture of their country of origin. Hence the current study focused on skilled migrants' acculturation to the host country only. Furthermore, with the introduction of the bidimensional model, earlier researchers have measured migrants' acculturation to the host culture and to their own country of origin culture as two separate variables; measuring migrants' acculturation to their new and old cultures independently has received support in the literature (Birman and Tyler 1994; Birman 2006; Birman et al. 2014; Ryder et al. 2000).

Assimilation

Assimilation represents a complete change in minorities, whereby they shift from their old culture and way of life to the new culture and way of life (Berry 1990; Eshel and Rosenthal-Sokolov, 2000; Remennick 2003, 2004; Safdar et al. 2003). In addition, assimilation is based on the expectation that migrants will abandon their own traditional values and practices in order to adapt to those of the majority culture (Berry 1990; 2006 Remennick 2003; Sakamoto 2007). Therefore, researchers believe that assimilation results in greater socio-cultural changes within migrants (Eshel and Rosenthal-Sokolov 2000; Safdar et al. 2003; Sakamoto 2007). Early studies (Gordon, 1964) on assimilation suggested that assimilating into the host culture is desirable and unavoidable for migrants over a span of a few generations. However, with the significant increase in the number of migrants from non-English speaking background in Australia, Barda (2006) argued that nowadays assimilation is far from the reality. Therefore, in a host society with policies of multiculturalism, the assimilation of first-generation migrants is debatable. For this reason, the present study has omitted this concept.

Sakamoto (2007) stated that assimilation is not completely achievable for first-generation ethnic migrants in multicultural societies, mainly because nowadays migrants are structurally permitted to maintain their own 'cultural heritage' (Barda 2006, 6; Coleman et al. 2001; Eshel and Rosenthal-Sokolov, 2000; Lu et al. 2011; Nesdale and Mak, 2000; Safi 2010). For instance, Sakamoto's study of Asian migrants in North America (2007)[1] suggested that complete assimilation of migrants is no longer valid for a number of different reasons such as the unbridgeable socio-cultural gap between migrants sending and receiving societies, host country policies of multiculturalism, and technological and communication improvements

---

[1] This study was conducted with Mainland Chinese skilled migrants to Canada. Specific demographic characteristics were a high level of education, diverse professions such as IT, engineering, management, university professors etc., employment, and between four and ten years' duration living in Canada. (These demographics were somewhat similar to the present study sample, with the exception of ethnicity).

that enable continued connections with family members in home countries (see also Amit 2010b; Li 2003; Remennick 2003; 2004; Sakamoto 2007). In addition, many other scholars (Coleman et al. 2001; Fanning, Haase and O'Boyle, 2011; Li 2003; Remennick 2003; Sakamoto 2007) agree that the basic differences between ethnic groups do not completely disappear even after a few generations.

Li (2003) stated that, under multiculturalism ideologies, the goal of migrant-receiving societies is to facilitate migrants' integration. However, in the case of countries with relatively smaller migrant groups, migrants can be forced to assimilate into the host society, mainly due to a lack of government policies such as those of multiculturalism (Dalgard and Thapa 2007). Similarly, Sayegh and Lasry (1993) pointed out that assimilation is appropriate when migrants who come from similar religious, cultural or value systems are accepted into the host society as they are more ready to accept values and beliefs of the host society. However, none of these exceptions are valid in relation to the present study participants, first generation migrants.

Assimilation is a long-term process; it might take a few generations to assimilate into a host culture (Sakamoto 2007). A common characteristic in multicultural societies is that people of different ethnic groups are structurally allowed to continue their own original cultural values, beliefs and social norms while adapting to the new way of life in the host country (Safdar et al. 2003). Therefore acculturation is more realistic than assimilation, as assimilation expects migrants to fully integrate into the host society.

Social Integration

Garrido et al. (2012) described 'social integration' as a process of acculturation that deals with multidimensional phenomena that change migrants' attitudes, values, behaviours or identity when interacting with mainstreamers. This is the same as acculturation, as defined earlier in this chapter. The extent to which migrants integrate into the host society is an individual choice and depends on their expectations, preferences, skills and opportunities in the host society (Birman et al. 2014; Coleman 1995b; Lafromboise et al. 1993). Safdar et al. (2003) took the view that every individual integrates into a new society at a different rate and level of motivation. Even though social integration is viewed as optional for migrants, Adachi (2011) argued that, from a multicultural host society's perspective, it is an urgent issue that needs to be addressed; failed integration can harm the social unity of such host societies (see also Gijsberts and Dagevos 2007).

It is evident that researchers at times refer acculturation as a bidirectional construct but at other times refer to the construct as related to migrants only (Ryder et al. 2000). Studies have empirically supported that the preferred acculturation strategy is integration (Berry 2006; 2010; Kunst and Sam 2013; Sakamoto 2007); the separation strategy also seems to be relevant to a certain extent (Lu et al. 2011; 2012; 2013). Nowadays assimilation and marginalisation strategies are far from the reality; furthermore, no studies have suggested marginalisation as the preferred strategy (Berry 2010; Kunst and Sam 2013). Moving forward, if integration is the preferred strategy, then the next question is to what extent are migrants integrated into the host society and what is the preferred 'level' of integration among different groups of migrants. Therefore, identifying the extent to which skilled migrants are acculturated to the host society is a main focus of this study.

Dimensions of Acculturation

The most common dimensions which migrants tend to change when adapting to a new country are (a) host language skills, (b) host country identity and (c) host country behaviour (Adachi 2011; Amit 2012; Au et al. 1998; Birman and Trickett 2001; Birman and Taylor-Ritzler 2007; Ersanilli and Koopmans 2010; Garrido et al. 2012; Safdar et al. 2003; Suinn et al. 1987; Vergunst 2008). However, a few studies have explored migrants' acculturation in terms of these three dimensions within the same study (Birman and Taylor-Ritzler 2007; Ho and Birman 2010). Hence, the present study explores all three dimensions.

The present study assessed skilled migrants' acculturation using the Language, Identity and Behaviour Acculturation Scale(LIB) (Birman and Trickett 2001), which consists of separate subscales for language, identity and behaviour. The LIB Scale was selected based on its reliability and the appropriateness of scale items for the present study cohort. For instance, items in the scale are easy to understand, can be related to migrants' daily lives in Australia and cover a range of different perspectives across three distinct dimensions (multidimensional) to capture migrants' acculturation in language, identity and behaviour dimensions (Birman and Trickett 2001; Birman 2006). The sections that follow describe each of these dimensions separately.

Language. Chiswick and Miller (1999) considered language to be a primary element of acculturation (see also Chiswick and Miller 2002; Kisselev et al. 2010). Migration is a challenging process in a number of ways ranging from practical (how to take a bus), to social (making new friends) to economic (finding a new job). Language barriers can lead to negative outcomes, such as difficulty finding employment, inability to establish contacts in the host society, and frustration and psychological distress (Aycan and Berry 1996; Chiswick and Miller 2002). Therefore, language is an important dimension of acculturation. Many researchers (Birman and Trickett 2001; Chung, Kim and Abreu 2004; Suinn, Ahuna and Khoo 1992) have included language acculturation in their scales or at least measured language acculturation separately in their studies (Chiswick and Miller 2001; 2002; Dalgard and Thapa 2007; Lu et al. 2012; Remennick 2003 2004; Valenta 2009).

Identity. Identity involves the individual's self-perception of their cultural character (Worrell and Gardner-Kitt 2006). The migration literature describes two dimensions of identity: ethnic identity and host country identity (Remennick 2003; Safdar et al. 2003). Ethnic identity describes one's self-concept related to sense of belonging, familiarity and attachment to one's own ethnic group (Schwartz et al. 2012; Worrell and Gardner-Kitt 2006). On the other hand, host country identity refers to the extent to which migrants feel a sense of belonging, familiarity and attachment to the host culture (Schwartz et al. 2012; Worrell and Gardner-Kitt 2006). Migrants' level of host-country identity reflects the extent to which they are integrated into a host society (Birman and Taylor-Ritzler 2007; Sakamoto 2007). Therefore, host country identity was included as a measure of acculturation within the present study (Birman and Taylor-Ritzler 2007).

Researchers (Amit 2012; Saghafi et al. 2012; Sam 1998; Schwartz et al. 2012) agree that some migrant groups prefer to retain their own ethnic identity, while other groups show a relatively weaker preference; thus levels of own- and host-country identity can vary among individuals and among groups. This study assesses the extent to which Indian and Sri Lankan skilled migrants identify with the host country (Australia), not their country of origin. The identity dimension in the LIB scale measure (a) the extent to which migrants feel positive about being an Australian and (b) the extent to which migrants consider themselves as Australian (Trickett and Birman 2005).

Behaviour. Change in behaviour, in accordance with host country norms and values, is a prominent dimension that has been used to assess the extent to which migrants are acculturated to the new society (Kim and Omizo 2010; Saghafi et al. 2012). Researchers (Birman et al. 2014; Mahmud and Schölmerich 2011; Martinovic et al. 2009) have emphasised the importance of exploring host-country behaviour such as making friends, entertainment, media, music and food consumption. Some migrants tend to completely change their behaviour, from the old cultural way to the new, whereas for others only a negligible change occurs in behaviour after migration (Kim and Omizo 2010; Saghafi et al. 2012; Worrell and Gardner-Kitt 2006).

The present study seeks to assess the extent to which skilled migrants engage in behaviours related to host society in a range of domains: media, food and entertainment consumption as well as other behavioural domains, such as visiting English-speaking doctors and socialising with Australian friends.

WELL-BEING: LIFE SATISFACTION

The Personal Well-being Index (Cummins 2006) was used to measure well-being in the current study. This index assesses life satisfaction (as an indicator of well-being) across domains such as 'standard of living', 'achievements in life', 'personal relationships', 'feeling part of community', 'health' and 'safety', amongst others. Life satisfaction has received considerable research attention as an indicator of well-being (Cummins & Nistico, 2002; Daig et al. 2009; Neto & Barros, 2007; Safi, 2010; Sam 1998) and, possibly for that reason, has been used to measure individuals' well-being in many societies (Amit, 2010a; Daig et al. 2009; Mara & Landesmann, 2013; Neto & Barros, 2007).

Life satisfaction is defined as an overall assessment of an individual's quality of life according to his or her own personal judgment or criteria (Daig 2009; Diener 1984). Respondents may be asked to evaluate their life satisfaction globally, or in specific life domains that are then aggregated to indicate overall life satisfaction. The advantage of using the latter approach is that researchers are then able to assess the contribution of each domain to overall life satisfaction (Wu and Yao 2007).

Researchers have measured individuals' life satisfaction in various life domains. The domains examined in any study will likely depend on the researcher's objectives (Rojas 2006; Wu and Yao 2007). Argyle (2001) emphasised (a) money, (b) education, (c) health, (d) employment, (e) community relationships and (f) housing as important domains when analysing one's overall life satisfaction. Similarly, Heady and Wearing (1992) concluded that domains such as (a) marriage, (b) work, (c) quality of living, (d) friendships, (e) health and (f) sex life are important to an individual's overall life satisfaction. These domains were derived after conducting a large number of Australian studies and with cross-cultural justification. Such domains are generally considered important life domains by other researchers (Cummins 2006; Rojas 2006; Wu and Yao 2007), and are thought to be important for assessing ethnic migrants' life satisfaction (Wu and Yao 2007).

Life satisfaction is comparative (Diener et al. 2003). Thus, individuals tend to compare their present state of affairs with (a) set goals, (b) past experiences, (c) future expectations, or (d) others' achievements (Clark et al. 2008; Diener et al. 2003). In the context of migration, individuals tend to compare their life satisfaction with satisfaction prior to migration, satisfaction of co-ethnics or other groups of migrants, and satisfaction of mainstreamers (Mara and Landesmann 2013). The focus of the present study is to examine life satisfaction among Indian and Sri Lankan skilled migrants. Hence the present study does not have a reference point for comparison; however, the results of this study can be compared with prevailing research findings related to life satisfaction of migrants.

Does Acculturation Influence Migrants' Well-being?

Herrero, Fuente and Gracia (2011) noted that migration changes almost every aspect of life. Migrants are separated from people and places they are accustomed to; they must find a job, build a new social life, and negotiate between their old and new cultural practices. In this sense, acculturation in the new community offers a potentially important pathway to well-being, by allowing the migrant population to gain access to resources in the wider community. In this study, we examine the effect of language, identify and behavrioural acculturation on migrants' well-being in the host society. This section explores how acculturation may influence migrants' experiences in the host society and hence their well-being.

Competence in the language of the host country has been identified as a pathway to a better life in the host society in several ways (Amit 2012; Ersanilli and Koopmans 2010; Lu et al. 2011; Martinovic et al. 2009; Remennick 2003; 2004). Migrants who are more proficient in the host country language show better economic and labour market integration (Amit 2010a; Borjas 1990; Mahmud and Schölmerich 2011; Massey and Parr 2012). Massey and Parr (2012) stated that migrants to Australia with high English-language proficiency are less discriminated against in the labour market than their less proficient counterparts. Mahmud and Schölmerich (2011) revealed similar findings in relation to temporary migrants from 24 different countries in Germany. A study of socio-cultural integration and naturalisation of migrants in the Netherlands, France and Germany (Ersanilli and Koopmans 2010) found that insufficient host-country language proficiency impacted the economic and social independence of migrants. Amit's (2010a) study on factors that influence migrants' life satisfaction revealed that highly skilled Western migrants in Israel who were more proficient in the host society language were more satisfied with their lives, largely because they perceived themselves as being able to utilise their skills and contribute to Israeli society.

Remennick's (2004) study of first-generation former Soviet migrants in Israel and found that host-country language competency (a) positively impacted communication within occupational and public realms and (b) improved migrants' cultural and media consumption (e.g., newspapers, magazines, TV channels, shows and concerts of host country artists; see also Chiswick and Miller 2001; Chiswick et al. 2003; Choi and Thomas 2009; Li 2007). Martinovic et al. (2009) found that migrants who had more exposure to the official language (Dutch) at the time of their arrival had greater opportunities to interact with mainstreamers. Valenta (2009), in a study of the acculturation of first-generation of migrants in Norway, also highlighted the importance of host-language proficiency in building relationships. Findings revealed that even though migrants interacted with mainstreamers at a personal level, this interaction could be difficult when there were language barriers. For instance, the following quote illustrates the perspective of a migrant from Iraq in Norway:

> We socialise with each other. We have invited them to dinner from time to time. They are nice, but on the whole, the situations are somehow tense and forced, [...] I do not know why ... No; [ ] maybe we cannot relax due to language problems... Maybe all of us are afraid to do something wrong, to insult each other. You never know what they think. (Valenta 2009, 187)

Communication is important for social mobility as it enhances the ability to include locals in one's social networks (Remennick 2004). Migrants who experience language barriers may develop a sense of isolation in the host society (Valenta 2009). This is likely to have a negative effect on their well-being.

Asukura (2008) found that Japanese Brazilian visiting migrants with good host-language skills secured jobs in better work environments and in more reputable organisations, and in turn had access to a wider social community. It is also suggested that migrants with better host-language skills are more often included in informal organisational social groups (Asukura 2008). Furthermore, they seem to gradually include co-workers from other ethnic groups including the majority group in their personal networks (Mor Barak 2000; Syed and Kramar 2010). Syed and Kramar (2010) suggested that this feeling of social inclusion assists migrant employees in enhancing their level of belonging in the new destination. These findings are relevant to the present study, which focuses specifically on skilled migrant employees and their well-being.

Migrants from countries that have strong English-language influence (e.g., North Europe, South Asian regions that had British influence in the past, the Philippines) are more efficient at language acquisition in Australia, and some mother tongues are more linguistically close to English, thus providing an advantage in language acquisition (Chiswick and Miller 1999). Indian and Sri Lankan migrants come from regions that have British influence (Bernhardt 2011). Bernhardt (p. 90) suggested that 'today English is spoken by more people in India than in any other country'. Therefore English is not a complete foreign language to skilled migrants from Sri Lanka and India. Furthermore, the minimum English language proficiency requirement to be eligible as an Australian skilled migrant applicant is a score of six out of eight in each of the four components (speaking, reading, writing, listening) in the International English Language Testing System (IELTS) (DIAC 2013). Therefore, little variability is expected in first-generation skilled migrants' level of English language proficiency. The foregoing leads to the assumption that language acculturation may not be a strong predictor of well-being in this sample for the following reasons: English is not a completely foreign language to Indian and Sri Lankan skilled migrants and skilled migrants are expected to already have high English language proficiency. In addition, skilled migrants tend to increase language acculturation the longer they stay in the host society (Borjas 1990; Chiswick and Miller 2002; Reitz et al. 2009).

Finadings regarding the relationship between migrants' host-country identity and well-being have been mixed (Birman et al. 2014; Dalgard and Thapa 2007; Sam 1998; Verkuyten 2008). Some studies have suggested that migrants who demonstrate less host-country identification experience more discrimination and social exclusion, leading to lower well-being (Asakura et al. 2008; Eshel and Rosenthal-Sokolov 2000; Gijsberts and Dagevos 2007; Safi 2010; Verkuyten 2008). In particular, this experience may be more relevant to ethnic migrant groups living in Western societies, who suffer from higher ethnic discrimination (LaFromboise et al. 1993; Malinen and Johnston 2011; Nesdale and Mak 2000; Verkuyten 2008). For instance, Paterson and Hakim-Larson (2012) found that Canadian identity was important for well-being among Arab youth migrants. Sam (1998) found that the association between host-country identity and well-being was positive for a Turkish adolescent group in Norway, but for Pakistanis and Vietnamese adolescent groups, ethnic identity was more important than host-country identity. Based on the study findings, Sam argued that Turks in Norway may identify themselves as Europeans, and thus host-country identity is important for their life satisfaction, whereas Pakistanis and Vietnamese – who are Asians – may perceive themselves more as belonging to an ethnic group; thus making ethnic identity more important.

In light of Sam's (1998) argument, one could infer that a positive relationship may not exist between host-country identity and well-being among Indian and Sri Lankan first-generation migrants. However, a recent study by Birman et al. (2014) found that ethnic identity and host-country identity contributed to well-being of migrants differently. According to Birman et al. (2014), host-country identity positively influences well-being via occupational success and (reduced) discrimination, whereas ethnic identity positively influences well-being via co-ethnic social support (Birman et al. 2014). Birman et al. further argued that for migrants who are working in owned businesses that are supported by co-ethnics, ethnic identity might be important. Host-country identity may be more influential for a skilled migrant group that can be employed in occupations other than owned businesses. Nesdale and Mak's study (2000) shows that Australians more readily accept migrants who are willing to live according to Australian values.

While behavioural changes occur faster than other types of changes (Kim et al., 1999), some ethnic migrants remain locked into their traditional ways of life and mix only with members of their own ethnic groups (Borjas 1994; Dalgard and Thapa 2007; Lu et al. 2012, 2013; Nesdale and Mak 2000; Valenta 2009; Zhou 1997). Valento's (2009) study of acculturation among first-generation Croatian, Bosnian and Iraqi migrants in Norway found that a majority of participants perceived having Norwegian friends and acquaintances as central to achieving a sense of belonging in the host society. Other researchers have also stated that building social ties with the dominant group in the host society helps migrants to enhance their sense of belonging (Martinovic et al. 2009; Verkuyten 2008).

Skilled migrants bring relevant knowledge and skills needed to participate in the labour market to the host society, which is likely to increase wider participation in the host society over a period of time (Amit 2010b; Borjas 1994). However, research findings suggest that generation (first generation and second generation, for example) also influences host-country behaviour acquisition; for instance, the second generation is faster to behaviourally acculturate in comparison with the first generation (Birman 2006; Birman and Taylor-Ritzler 2007; Schwartz et al. 2012).

Based on the above discussion, it is reasonable to argue that skilled migrants who are acculturated (language, identity and behaviour dimensions) are more likely to report higher well-being for a range of reasons. For example, language acculturation is important for navigating the workplace and the broader environment, identity acculturation for participation and acceptance by mainstreamers, and behavioural acculturation for a sense of belonging, However, there are several other factors which may influence how migrants experience host societies, and hence their well-being, including age at migration, years since migration, level of education, pre-migration socio-economic status (SES), and expectation to return to the country of birth (see e.g., Amit 2010a; Daig et al. 2009; Mara and Landesmann 2013; Morrison Tay and Diener 2011; Neto and Barros 2007). These factors were included as possible covariates in the current study and are hereafter referred to collectively as 'socio-demographic factors'. To the best of the authors' knowledge, the current study is the first to simultaneously examine the influence of all of these variables on migrants' life satisfaction within a single study and among Indian and Sri Lankan skilled migrants in Australia. Hence a secondary aim of the current research was to identify the relative importance of various socio-demographic factors to life satisfaction among skilled migrants representing a particular ethnic group in the Australian context.

Although studies have also shown that host country, migration purpose, employment status, and ethnicity can predict migration outcomes these variables were excluded from the current study on the basis that all participants were skilled migrants working in Australia and participants in this study were limited to Indian and Sri Lankan skilled migrants. Indian and Sri Lankan people share commonalities, such as (a) non-English speaking background; (b) maintaining close ties with country of birth; (c) strong sense of belonging to the country of birth; (d) strong values towards ethno-cultural relationships; (e) high regard for religious beliefs and traditional customs; (f) maintaining multigenerational households; and (g) similar sporting interests, such as supporting cricket teams (Frank, Hofstede and Bond, 1991; Hofstede, 2001). Therefore, clear differences between Sri Lankans and Indians were not expected, as they might be if, for instance, we were studying the acculturation of Indian sub-continent migrants and European migrants, who are culturally distinct.

SOCIO-DEMOGRAPHIC FACTORS AND MIGRANTS' EXPERIENCES

Age at Migration

Age, age at migration, and years since migration are variables that overlap to a certain extent, as they all reflect migrants' level of exposure to country of birth and to the host country. In some studies (e.g., Fong and Ooka 2006; Lu et al. 2011), present age and age at migration have been included as two separate variables; in other studies, either one or the other has been included (e.g., Dalgard and Thapa 2007; Martinovic et al. 2009; Nesdale and Mak 2000). The present study focuses on age at migration and years since migration, which are expected to correlate with present age; age reflects possible generational differences in the experiences of migrants.

Several studies (Chiswick and Miller 2001; Lu et al. 2012; Martinovic et al. 2009; Remennick 2003, 1999; Sanchez and Brock 1996) indicate that migrants who arrive at a younger age possess greater capacity to adapt to the new society than those who arrive at a later age. Martinovic et al. (2009) found that non-Western migrants who arrived in the Netherlands at younger ages were less socialised into their home cultures by third parties such as parents, extended family members, educational institutions, social functions and media in the country of birth and showed greater capacity to accept the social norms of the host society compared to individuals who had migrated at later ages.

Age at migration has also been shown to influence social participation (Chiswick and Miller 2001; Martinovic et al. 2009). In addition to being less socially-oriented in the culture of their country of birth, those who arrive at a younger age are more likely to include locals in their personal networks, as they encounter more opportunities to interact with mainstreamers, for example at school (Chiswick and Miller 2001; Fong and Ooka 2006). Even though at the point of entry there is no perceptible difference between younger and older migrants socially, age at migration affects the development of inter-ethnic contacts longitudinally, with the younger migrants making inter-ethnic contacts at a faster rate than individuals who migrate at later ages (Chiswick and Miller 2001; Martinovic et al. 2009). A study of patterns of social participation of Chinese migrants in Canada (Fong and Ooka 2006), found that exposure to educational institutions and patterns of social behaviour among migrants who arrive at a younger age can positively influence their participation in social activities in the wider society. Remennick (2003) similarly found that younger Russian migrants in Israel spent more time with host country associates than older Russian migrants. The association between age at migration and the social participation of migrants has been established in several societies across different migrant groups (Bisin et al. 2008; Chiswick and Miller 2001; Fong and Ooka 2006; Jasinska-Lahti et al. 2011; Lance 2010). However, with respect to skilled migrants in Western societies, this relationship is uncertain, due to a lack of studies in this area (Lu et al. 2011; 2012). Nevertheless, based on the above findings, this variable was expected to influence the social experiences of skilled migrants and hence their well-being in the host destination.

Years since Migration

Jasinskaja-Lahti et al. (2011) suggested that the adaptation of migrants generally stabilises after a few years of migration. Thus, satisfaction in the host society may increase over time. Generally, when migrants arrive in a new country, they tend to accept the first job opportunity available to them, due to reasons such as lack of knowledge and experience of the host country labour market, the host society's lack of recognition of overseas qualifications earned in developing countries, and family strain in the new destination (Barrett and Duffy 2008; Li 2000; Nakhaie 2007; Parr and Guo 2005; Reitz 2001). This situation may be true especially where Indian and Sri Lankan skilled migrant employees are concerned, as they have migrated from a collectivist society that emphasises family commitments (Frank, Hofstede and Bond 1991; Hofstede 2001). As time passes, migrant employees accumulate work experience and knowledge of the labour market, and tend to perform better in terms of income and other objective dimensions such as housing. Some scholars have reported that migrant employees' wages converge with those of mainstream employees the longer they stay in the host country (Borjas 1994; Chiswick 1978; Chiswick and Miller 2008; Sabharwal 2011). Furthermore, the longer migrant employees stay in the host country, the more structurally bound they are to participate in social mediums in the new society. Thus, years since migration may positively influence well-being via successful economic and social integration. However, some studies show that certain migrant groups such as refugees find it difficult to narrow the gap in areas such as work and social participation, even when they have resided in the host country for a long period of time (Borjas 1994; Dalgard and Thapa 2007; Valenta 2009; Zhou 1997). Therefore, the effect of years since migration on migration outcomes varies based on the migration category.

Level of Education

The likelihood of being in higher-ranking employment increases with education level. Migrants with more formal education have a wider range of job opportunities from which to choose (Asukura 2008; Barrett and Duffy 2008; Martinovic et al. 2009; Nakhaie 2007). In contrast migrants with lower levels of skills and qualifications have poorer work conditions and restricted job opportunities, as they are often compelled to take on opportunities with little or no preference. For example, Au et al. (1998) pointed out that migrants with lower levels of education have traditionally settled in low-paid occupations and ethnic economies in Canada (see also Hou 2009). In contrast, educated migrants get more opportunities to interact with a wider community through more diverse job opportunities. In addition, studies in organisational psychology have revealed that migrants' education level influences discrimination in the workplace in multicultural societies (Asakuara et al. 2008; Syed and Kramar 2010): the higher the level of education, the lower the level of organisational discrimination (Asakuara et al. 2008; Kwok-bun and Plüss 2013). For instance, Kwok-bun and Plüss (2013) stated that highly educated migrants experience less discrimination than unskilled and less educated migrants in American society. It can be argued that the feelings of inclusion may positively influence well-being among migrants.

Highly educated migrants are likely to get exposure to mainstreamers at educational institutions and workplaces, which positively influences host-language acquisition and learning of local norms and values (Chiswick and Miller 2002; Martinovic et al. 2009). As argued by Berry et al. (1986; cited in Au et al. 1998), migrants with a higher educational background perceive acculturation as a challenge or opportunity rather than an unpleasant or stressful experience, and submerge themselves in in the host society (see also Pham and Harris 2001). This is likely to facilitate greater satisfaction in the host society.

However, the importance of education may differ based on factors such as the host society's attitude towards migrants and the quality of education in the home country (Kwok-bun and Plüss 2013; Rudiger and Spencer 2003). Notably, job markets in Western societies do not always readily accept formal qualifications earned from non-Western societies at the initial stage of migration (Chiswick et al. 2003; George and Chaze 2009; Li 2000; Reitz 2001; Nakhaie 2007; Parr and Guo 2005). For instance, the following quote from an Indian migrant in Canada reveals the experience in the job market:

> I just thought that I will be OK. I was a family counsellor in India and I did not know the scope over here right? I just thought...I will get a job because I am from social work background...but when I came here I knew...you have to have (Canadian) experience, and you have to have Canadian education. (George and Chaze 2009, 272)

Therefore, even though formal qualifications are recognised at the point of granting the migration visa, the level of recognition attributed by employers in the job market is uncertain.

Negative recognition may impact migrants' well-being in the host society via poor labour market integration, low income, job dissatisfaction etc.

The participants in the present study came from non-Western societies and may have earned their qualifications in their own countries; it is unknown whether the education level of this group is an influential determinant of their well-being in Australia. Lu et al. (2012) found that there was no significant relationship between education level and acculturation among a Chinese professional migrant sample in Australia. Massey and Parr (2012) also stated that in regional Australia highly educated skilled migrants did not have many advantages, as the benefits of a high level of education were cancelled out by a lack of networking opportunities, language difficulties and social discrimination.

Qualifications of Australian skilled migrants vary from doctoral level to diploma level (DIAC 2013). Due to the mixed nature of the findings in previous research, variations in the education level in the current sample, and limited research focusing on Australian skilled migrants, education level was thought to be appropriate for inclusion in the present study.

Pre-Migration Socio-Economic Status

Researchers suggest that pre-migration SES is an important variable when assessing migrants' success in the host country (De la Cruz, Padilla and Agustin 2000, cited in Ea et al. 2008; Li 2007; Nakhaie 2007). Recently, Riosmena and Dennis (2012) revealed that Mexican migrants with higher pre-migration SES (measured in terms of income and education) experienced smoother adaptation into American mainstream society due to greater acceptance from mainstreamers. A study of Mexican-American women (Fitzgerald 2010) found an association between pre-migration SES (again, measured by income and education) and acculturation, which was measured in terms of language proficiency and social interaction.

Bourdieu and Passerson (1977, cited in Li 2007) found that individuals with higher pre-migration SES (measured by parents' education) behaved differently to their counterparts, participating in highbrow cultural activities, such as frequent visits to theatres, movies, and museums that promote an intercultural climate. Bisin et al. (2008) suggested that migrants' pre-migration SES may lead to different attitudes towards acculturation. In their study, the speed of socio-cultural integration among Muslim participants was lower than that among non-Muslim participants due to their socio-economic characteristics, which included lower education level and higher unemployment rates prior to migration. Notably, strong religious identity and cultural attitudes were also explanatory variables for socio-cultural integration in Bisin et al.'s study. In addition, pre-migration SES influences the fluency of English language and education source of migrants (Li 2007). Li (2007) argued that individuals with wealthier family backgrounds can afford to access facilities such as internationally recognised forms of education offered in the English language in the host country, which may have a positive influence when adapting to the host society.

Further research findings have revealed that pre-migration SES may influence characteristics such as dress sense and basic norms and values of migrants (Pio 2010). For example, early migration study findings in Australia indicated that Persian migrants were disadvantaged in the acculturation process, as most of them reported lower pre-migration SES and their customs and basic values were quite different from that of other (native) Australians

(Cummins 1996; Foroughi et al. 2001). Therefore, pre-migration SES may impact migrants' acceptance of host culture practices, which may in turn influence their satisfaction with life in the host society.

The quality of support that new migrants receive from formal or informal networks may depend on their pre-migration SES. Migrants with higher pre-migration SES have access to individuals with higher standing in their community (Connor and Massey 2010; Nakhaie 2007). For instance, Nakhaie (2007) found that individuals with higher pre-migration SES had access to people with better social capital (measured in terms of associational participation, family contacts, religious participation, ethnic-based networks) and human capital (measured in terms of years of education and host country credentials). Nakhaie suggested access to such capital can help migrants to overcome labour market discrimination, act as a substitute (or add value) when migrants' credentials are not recognised in the host country labour market, and help with initial access to the job market and other resources in the host country (see also George and Chaze 2009). Furthermore, George and Chaze (2009) suggested that the informal relationships in which migrants participate impact their first job, housing, formal social networks and so forth, especially for migrants of non-English speaking backgrounds. These social resources have been shown to positively facilitate their lives in the host destination (see also Lance 2010; Li 2007; Remennick 2003).

The above studies use income, education, occupation, or combinations of these dimensions to measure pre-migration SES. In the current study, education level was considered as a separate variable from pre-migration SES. Although some variability in income is expected among the present study's participants (according to 2011 Australian census data, 10% of Indian and Sri Lankan migrants have $0 household income [no income] and 10% have income of over $104,000), income-related data were not collected, as a high percentage of missing data can be expected in a convenience sample. In the current study, pre-migration SES was operationalised as the 'town of residence before migration to Australia'. The reasons for selecting this variable to measure pre-migration SES in the present study are discussed below (see also Remennick, 2004).

It is argued that migrants who grew up in an urban city may have attitudes, values, norms, and experiences (e.g., 'highbrow' culture) that fit well with Western society, and that such migrants may therefore find it easier to grasp the host country's way of life (Bourdieu and Passerson 1977, cited in Li 2007). English is the second official language in India and Sri Lanka but families in metropolitan cities tend to use English more often in their day-to-day lives than people in rural cities (Bernhardt 2011, 90). Furthermore, programs in private schools and private higher education institutes located in urban cities are taught in English, and only individuals with higher socio-economic backgrounds can afford to access these facilities. For instance, the Sri Lankan Institute of Information Technology (SLIT), located in the capital city of Sri Lanka, offers a Bachelor's degree in Information Technology accredited by Curtin University, Australia, and an Electronic Engineering degree accredited by Sheffield Hallam University, UK (SLIT 2013). When former students of these educational institutions migrate to Western countries, they may encounter less acculturation stress and culture shock (Li 2007).

Both India and Sri Lanka are countries that experience a high level of disparity in income and other socio-economic dimensions (Bandyopadhyay 2011; Naranpanawa and Bandara 2012). For instance, India is the tenth richest country in the world, yet is home to the largest number of poor people in the world (Bandyopadhyay 2011). Therefore, a certain amount of disparity is expected in the pre-migration SES of the present study participants. Town of residence anticipates some differences in individual characteristics, such as attitudes towards host society norms and values and ability to build social capital (Bisin et al. 2008). For these reasons, town of residence before migration (i.e., highly rural to highly metropolitan) was used to operationalise participants' pre-migration SES.

Expectation to Return to Country of Birth

Both forced migrants (humanitarian) and voluntary migrants often consider returning to their country of birth to be the end of the migration journey (Marta Bivand and Oeppen 2013). Irrespective of the migrant category, reasons for increased return migration include ethnic discrimination in the host society, financial hardship, feeling excluded, homesickness, long-term unemployment, strong cultural orientation towards the country of birth and implementation of attractive return migration strategies by the migrant-sending societies e.g., economic expansion (Arguin 2010; Brenick and Silbereisen 2012; DIAC 2013; Mara and Landesmann 2013; Tsuda 2010).

Mara and Landesmann (2013) suggested that migrants make plans based on their anticipated the length of stay; migrants who plan to stay permanently attempt to find jobs that are compatible with their education and skills,   and to settle in terms of family needs such as housing. Lack of investment in pursuing a life in the host society, the desire to one day return 'home' may reduce satisfaction with life in the host society. By the same token, low satisfaction might have implications for expectation to return to country of birth. Recently, researchers have found that leaving the host country is an option that educated migrants may consider more often than refugee migrants (Mara and Landesmann 2013; Marta Bivand and Oeppen 2013). Marta Bivand and Oeppen (2013, 274), referring to refugee migrants, stated that 'in the case of forced migration, the inability to return safely is part of the defining characteristic.'

Studies related to non-Western skilled migrants returning home are limited (Labrianidis and Lyberaki 2004). Some studies (Arguin 2010; Brenick and Silbereisen 2012; Silbereisen; 2008; Tsuda 2010) have been conducted targeting diaspora migrants. These previous studies have looked at return migration policies, post-return experiences (Tsuda 2010), or reasons for leaving the host society (Arguin 2010; Brenick and Silbereisen 2012). This study examines the relationship between expectation to return to country of birth and well-being (life satisfaction). This is an appropriate variable to take into account in the present study context for two reasons. Firstly, first-generation skilled migrants' extended families live in their country of birth (Amit 2010b; Mara and Landesmann 2013; Sakamoto 2007; Sanderson 2009); migrants who seek to reunite with their families tend to leave host societies (see also De Haas and Fokkema 2011). Secondly, Sri Lankan citizens are allowed to maintain dual citizenship (Colombo Page 2013; The High Commission of the Democratic Socialist Republic of Sri Lanka Canberra, Australia 2013), while Indians who have Australian citizenship can also obtain an 'Overseas Citizen of India Certificate', which provides the option to live in India for the long term (Australian High Commission India 2013). Indian and Sri Lankan citizens who are also Australian citizens have the option to go back to and settle in their country of birth. Current statistics from the Australian government state that 25% of Sri Lankan migrants intend to leave Australia on a permanent basis. In 2011, 12, 243 permanent migrants left Australia, of whom 37% were professionals (e.g., accountants and managers; DIAC 2013); 39% of Indian permanent migrants intend to leave Australia, and in 2011-12, a total of 1007 left the country permanently (DIAC 2013). Thus the expectation to return to country of birth is a feasible option for the participants in the present study, which may affect life satisfaction in this study context.

To summarise, the following gaps in the literature on skilled migrants have been identified and provide the basis for the current study.

1. Lack of research on skilled migrants in Australia, especially Indian and Sri Lankan skilled migrants.
2. Limited studies on acculturation and well-being among skilled migrants.
3. A lack of studies that consider the influence of a broad range of socio-demographic factors well-being among migrants.

Thus, the aim of the research was to examine the relationship between language, identity and behavioural acculturation and well-being (operationalized by life satisfaction) among Indian and Sri Lankan skilled migrants working in Australia, while controlling for variation in socio-demographic factors that may influence migrants' well-being. Understanding the factors that contribute to well-being among skilled migrants could inform intervention strategies to improve the migration outcomes for these ethnic skilled migrants in Australia.

METHOD

Participants

Only Indian or Sri Lankan first-generation[2] skilled migrants in Australia were eligible to participate in the study. As shown in Table 1, the total sample consisted of 306 participants, 61% of whom were male and 39% of whom were female. There was a higher proportion of Sri Lankan than Indian respondents. The majority of participants were Australian citizens. The average age at migration was 30.33 years (SD = 6.72).

Approximately 90% were married with or without children, although a third of participants had arrived in Australia as singles. Most had been living in Australia for less than 10 years. Participants were predominantly highly educated, with almost 80% having a Bachelor degree or higher. Most had obtained their highest qualification in their country of birth.

---

[2] First-generation migrants are defined as migrants who were born outside of the host country (Smith, 2003).

Table 1. Summary of Demographic Background of the Sample

Demographic Variable	Category	Frequency	Valid percentage
Gender	Male	187	61.0%
	Female	119	39.0%
	No response	1	
Country of birth	Sri Lanka	212	69.3%
	India	94	30.7%
Visa Category	Australian Citizen	183	59.8%
	Permanent Resident	119	38.9%
	Bridging Visa	4	1.3%
Present marital status	Single	35	11.7%
	Married	79	26.3%
	Married with Children	186	62.0%
	No response/Other	3	
Migration status	Single	101	33.0%
	With parents	9	2.9%
	With spouse	84	27.5%
	With spouse and children	112	36.6%
Years since migration	Less than 5 years	99	32.4%
	5 – 10 years	127	41.5%
	11 – 15 years	40	13.1%
	16 – 20 years	18	5.9%
	More than 20 years	22	7.2%
Education level	Secondary or equivalent	3	1.0%
	Certificate level	6	2.0%
	Diploma level	23	7.5%
	Bachelor's degree/equivalent, professional	225	63.5%
	Postgraduate level	49	16.0%
Highest qualification attained in country	Country of birth	172	57.0%
	Australia	130	43.0%
	No response	4	
Town of residence before migration	1 Highly metropolitan	127	41.5
	2	73	23.8
	3	58	19
	4	33	10.8
	5	9	2.9
	6	3	1
	7 Very rural	3	1
Current occupation (coded)	Clerical and administrative	72	23.5%
	Community and personal services	15	4.9%
	Labourer	2	0.7%
	Machine operator/driver	8	2.6%
	Manager	35	11.4%
	Professional	150	49.0%
	Sales	14	4.6%
	Technician/trade worker	10	3.3%

All participants were actively involved in the labour market at the time of the survey; just under half had professional jobs, while approximately a third had administrative and clerical or managerial jobs. Community or personal services, sales, and technical and trade jobs showed fairly low representation.

MEASURES

Demographic Information. Personal demographic information, as detailed in the table above, was gathered using a combination of close-ended questions (choosing from multiple response options) and open-ended, short answer questions. Expectation to return to country of birth was assessed by asking the participants to rate their expectation to return to country of origin in a 11 point Likert scale, which ranged from 0 (most unlikely) to 10 (highly likely).

Language, Identity and Behavioural Acculturation Scale (Birman and Trickett 2001). This scale was used to assess host country acculturation, in this instance the Acculturation of Indian and Sri Lankan skilled migrants to Australia. Scale items are divided into three subscales that assess language, identity and behaviour acculturation respectively. With the permission of the scale author, a seven-point Likert scale response format, that ranged from 1 (low - not at all) to 7 (high - very much) was used rather than a 1 to 4 response scale format, as in the original version of the instrument. The response format was changed to allow for more variability in the range of responses. Therefore, possible scores for each subscale ranged from 1 to 7 (responses were averaged across subscale items to obtain a total score for each subscale). According to the scale author (Dina Birman, e-mail message to author, April 5, 2012), an average score of 6 and above in the seven-point Likert scale represents very high acculturation; an average score below 3 represents low acculturation; and scores between 3.5 and 6 indicate average acculturation.

The original Language subscale consists of 9 items that ask participants to rate their ability to speak and understand English as a measure of language integration in the host society, specifically 'How would you rate your ability to speak English - (1) at work, (2) with friends, (3) on the phone, (4) with strangers and (5) overall?' and 'How well do you understand English – (6) on TV or at the movies, (7) in newspapers or in magazines, (8) in songs, and (9) overall?'. However, in the present study, the subscale was modified to consist of three parallel items that measured overall ability to speak and understand English language in different situations: 'How would you rate your ability to speak English (1) now and (2) in social situations now?' and (3) 'How would you rate your ability to understand English now?' Determining overall ability to speak and understand English was thought to be more appropriate than measuring ability to speak and understand English in specific situations. This format also avoided repetition in the scale. Subscale reliability (Cronbach's alpha) for this study was .80.

The Identity subscale consists of 7 items. These were replicated from the original subscale with only the names of the countries altered to reflect the present study context. This subscale measures the extent to which participants consider themselves as 'Australian' (e.g., 'I think of myself being Australian') and assesses to what extent they feel positive about being 'Australian' (e.g., 'I feel good about being Australian'). Subscale reliability (Cronbach's alpha) for this study was .96.

The Behaviour subscale consists of 11 items that assess to what extent migrants engage in behaviours related to host society culture (e.g., language use, media consumption, grocery habits, food consumption). One new item was added for the purpose of the current study: 'How much do you attend Australian sporting events?'. This item was added on the basis that sporting events are an important aspect of Australian culture. Other sample items in the scale are 'How much do you read Australian books, newspapers or magazines?', 'How much do you eat Australian food?'. Subscale reliability (Cronbach's alpha) for this study was .82.

Personal Well-being Index (Cummins 2006). The Personal Well-being Index consists of 9 items, of which one item represents global life satisfaction, i.e., 'How satisfied are you with your life as a whole?'. The remaining items correspond to eight domains that represent the first-level of deconstruction of 'life as a whole satisfaction'. The domains are (a) standard of living, (b) health condition, (c) achievement in life, (d) relationships, (e) feeling of safety, (f) feeling part of the community, (g) future security, and (h) spirituality or religion. The response format for the Personal Well-being Index is an 11-point Likert scale that ranges from 0 (low - completely dissatisfied) to 10 (high - completely satisfied) with a mid-point of neutral (neither dissatisfied nor satisfied). The total life satisfaction value derived in the present study was the mean of the eight domains (PWI manual, 2006). For the purpose of creating results that can be simply compared with other PWI data sets, we converted all data to a standard form, which made it look as though responses had been rated on a 0 – 100 point scale i.e., 'percentage of scale maximum' scores (see Cummin 2006). Cummins noted that this simple linear conversion does not alter the statistical properties of the data. Scale reliability (Cronbach's alpha) for this study was .82.

Procedure

Data collection commenced after receiving ethical clearance from the University's Human Research Ethics Committee. Data were collected using a self-report, cross-sectional survey. A mixed mode data collection technique was employed, which included mail and on-line surveys. Potential survey participants were approached through promoting the study and providing a link to the survey on the websites of organisations and Indian and Sri Lankan community groups in Australia e.g., Buddhist Society, Victoria, University of Colombo, Alumni Society in Melbourne. Hard copies of the survey were distributed at shopping malls, Indian and Sri Lankan grocery shops, Indian and Sri Lankan temples, and to Indian and Sri Lankan parents at schools. Survey completion took approximately 20 minutes and completed surveys were at a time and location convenient to the participant. Participation in the survey was anonymous and voluntary, and consent was implied by return of a completed questionnaire.

RESULTS

Descriptives for the continuous scales are shown in Table 2.

Table 2. Descriptives for Acculturation and Life Satisfaction

Variable	Mean	Standard Deviation
Expectation to return to COB (0-10)	4.92	3.25
Language acculturation (1-7)	5.47	1.01
Identity acculturation (1-7)	4.08	1.66
Behaviour acculturation (1-7)	4.63	1.44
Life satisfaction (0-10)	77.29	15.90

Note. Descriptives for socio-demographic factors which are possible covariates in examining the relationship between acculturation and life satisfaction are shown in Table 1 above.

With regard to acculturation, participants were most integrated in language, followed by behaviour and then identity respectively. Only 2% of participants scored below 3.5 (low acculturation) for the language dimension and 35% scored over six (high acculturation) for this dimension. For the identity dimension, 35% participants recorded a low acculturation score, and 15% recorded a high acculturation score. For the behaviour dimension, 16% of participants recorded a low acculturation score and 13% recorded a high acculturation score.

The average PWI score in the Australian Unity Well-being Index for 2012 was 75.40 and the average PWI score for the present sample group was 77.27 points, which is a difference of only 1.87. The normative range for Australia is 73.4 to 76.4 points (Cummins 2006). Hence it can be suggested that the sample were fairly satisfied with their lives in Australia on average.

Pearson's product moment correlation analysis was conducted to examine bivariate relationships among the socio-demographic factors, language, identity and behaviour acculturation, and life satisfaction (see Table 3).

Table 3. Correlation Matrix for Study Variables

	1	2	3	4	5	6	7	8		10
1 Language	1									
2 Identity	.38	1								
3 Behaviour	.53	.45	1							
4 Gender	-.14	-.00	-.00	1						
5 Age at migration	-.02	-.10	-.18	.10	1					
6 Years since migration	.36	.35	.28	.01	-.18	1				
7 Level of Education	.05	-.02	.16	-.04	-.00	-.05	1			
8 Expectation to return to COB	-.23	-.44	-.23	-.06	-.01	.25	-.07	1		
9 Pre-migration SES	.30	.03	.14	-.09	-.02	.19	.03	-.03	1	
10 Life Satisfaction	.33	.35	.30	-.08	-.05	.26	.10	-.26		.14

Note. $N = 306$. $R > |.14|$ are significant at $p < .05$; $r > |.16|$ are significant at $p < .01$. COB: Country of Birth, SES: Socio-Economic Status.

The correlation results indicated that language, identity and behaviour acculturation were positively correlated with life satisfaction, suggesting the more acculturated the migrants are, the more satisfied they are with their lives. As expected, number of years since migration was positively correlated with life satisfaction. Pre-migration SES was also positively correlated with life satisfaction indicating migrants who lived more metropolitan areas before migrating were more satisfied with their lives in Australia. As expected, a high expectancy of returning to one's country of birth was negatively correlated with life satisfaction. Age at migration and education level were not correlated with life satisfaction.

In the next step, language, identity and behaviour acculturation, years since migration, expectation to return to country of birth and pre-migration SES were entered into a regression equation predicting life satisfaction. Results (Table 4) showed that the overall model was significant, $R = .44$, $F (6, 304) = 12.05$, $p < .001$. However, only language and identity acculturation contributed uniquely to the prediction of life satisfaction.

Table 4. Regression results for direct relationship between socio-demographic variables, acculturation and life satisfaction

No	Variable	Beta	Sig
1	Language	**0.13**	.042
2	Identity	**0.19**	.005
3	Behaviour	0.08	.192
4	Years since migration	0.10	.138
5	Expectation to return to COB	-0.11	.050
6	Pre-migration SES	0.07	.208

$R = .44$, $R^2 = .20$, Adjusted $R^2 = .18$.

DISCUSSION

The current research aimed to examine the relationship between acculturation and well-being (life satisfaction) among Indian and Sri Lankan skilled migrants in Australia, after controlling for various socio-demographic factors which may influence migrant well-being. Currently, India and Sri Lanka are first and fourth largest skilled migrant-sending countries to Australia; thus migrants from these countries represent a large minority group in present-day Australia. However, there is a dearth of literature that focuses on this migrant group and their level of acculturation and life satisfaction is not known. Thus the findings of the present study contribute new knowledge in relation to Indian and Sri Lankan skilled migrants' subjective outcomes in Australia. It is important that the findings of the present study be interpreted in the context of demographic characteristics of the sample (for instance, educated skilled migrants mainly employed in professional jobs, with high English language proficiency and an average age of 38 years, who had been living in Australia for an average of eight years).

Literature on migrants' adaptation to host societies has identified acculturation as a positive indicator of migrants' contribution to economic growth in the host society (Drever and Hoffmeister 2008; Hawthorne 2002; Wulff and Dharmalingam 2008), and as a factor that minimises social issues which can arise through differences and inequalities among migrants from different parts of the world (Hughes 2002; Kwok-bun and Plüss 2013). Therefore, exploring the level of acculturation among the current study participants was also a focus for the current study.

Although a predominant motive for individuals to migrate to developed countries is to improve life satisfaction (Mara and Landesmann 2013; Sam 1998; Verkuyten 2008), some research findings suggest that life satisfaction is relatively low among ethnic minorities in Western countries (e.g., Amit 2010; Berry 1998; Dalgard and Thapa 2007; Reitz et al. 2009; Safi 2010; Sabharwal 2011; Verkuyten 2008). However, skilled migrants may experience better outcomes than other migrant groups given their education, skills and experience. In the present study, acculturation (assessed in terms of host country language, identity and behaviour) and the following six demographic factors were included as possible predictors of skilled migrants' life satisfaction: (a) age at migration, (b) education level, (c) expectation to return to country of origin, (d) gender, (e) pre-migration SES, and (f) years since migration.

Acculturation

The Language, Identity and Behaviour Acculturation Scale (Birman and Trickett 2001) was employed to measure acculturation. Notably, past research has used the LIB scale in humanitarian migrant-related studies (Birman and Taylor-Ritzler 2007; Birman 2006; 2011; Ho and Birman 2010; Trickett and Birman 2005); hence the current study also tested the validity of the LIB scale for a skilled migrant sample.

The LIB Scale (Birman and Tricket 2001) was originally developed to measure refugee migrants' adaptation to host societies in terms of language, identity and behaviour. Going beyond the refugee migrant category, this study used the LIB scale to assess skilled migrants' acculturation in these three dimensions, adding new scope to existing literature on the validity of the scale. The factor structure of the scale was generally confirmed and all three dimensions showed meaningful associations with outcomes. Although average scores were relatively consistent across the acculturation dimensions, the language dimension recorded the highest average score, followed by behaviour and identity, respectively. The finding that participants were more acculturated in the language dimension than in the identity and behaviour dimensions, is consistent with previous findings related to different groups of migrants, such as refugee migrants (Birman and Taylor-Ritzler 2007; Birman 2006; Ho and Birman 2010). These findings show that, even though skilled migrants bring unique skills and work experiences when compared to refugee migrants, this does not necessarily mean that they will integrate more consistently across all acculturation dimensions.

Findings for acculturation suggested that the majority of Indian and Sri Lankan skilled migrants were moderately acculturated across the language, identity and behaviour dimensions. Therefore, the frequently documented (Berry et al. 2006; Birman 2006; George and Chaze 2009; Sakamoto 2007; Valento 2009) low level of acculturation among first-generation ethnic migrants in Western societies was not observed in this study.

In a multicultural society like Australia, where migrants have access to clothing, food, entertainment and spiritual options from their own cultures on a daily basis, migrants have the option of being bi-cultural (Adachi 2011; Au et al. 1998; George and Chaze 2009). As a result, migrants in the current study may not have fully acculturated to Australian society, thus explaining their moderate level of acculturation. Furthermore, given that India is the first and Sri Lanka is the fourth largest skilled migrant-sending society to Australia, the large representation of those groups may limit such migrants from fully acculturating to Australian society (Martinovic et al. 2009) on the basis that they can maintain close ties with co-ethnics.

Although acculturation was not high in the current study, it was higher than might be expected based on findings in past studies, which have generally reported low acculturation among migrants (Adachi 2011; Birman and Taylor-Ritzler 2007; Ho and Birman 2010; Martinovic et al. 2009; Stark and Jakubek 2013). However, past studies have focused on migrant categories other than *skilled* migrants. The current study findings suggest that *skilled* migrants may be more capable of acculturating to Western societies than other migrant categories such as humanitarian migrants, perhaps due to their education, skills and occupational characteristics.

As noted above, acculturation in the language dimension was higher than acculturation in the identity and behaviour dimensions in the present study context. One of the key selection criteria for skilled migration is a high level of English language proficiency. Furthermore, English is the second official language in India and Sri Lanka, is prominently used within higher educational institutions, and is the official language of the majority of workplaces in these two countries (Bandyopadhyay 2011; Kumar and Nevid 2010). Therefore, it is not surprising to see higher scores for language acculturation among the present study participants.

With regard to identity acculturation, past research findings (Collins 2013; Sam 1998; Trickett and Birman 2005) suggest that first-generation ethnic migrants prefer to maintain their own ethnic identity. In line with these findings, the present study participants reported lower scores for identity acculturation compared to host country language and behaviour acculturation, on average. The results may also reflect the age of the present sample (Worrell and Gardner-Kitt 2006): ethnic identity is mainly developed in adolescence and the average age at migration among the present study participants was 30 years, with an average current age of 38 years. In line with Worrell and Gardner-Kitt (2006), it can be argued that the study participants had already established their ethnic identity when they left their birth country as adults (see also Ho 2012). In addition, the freedom to maintain one's own ethnic identity in multicultural societies (Ho and Birman 2010) may be another explanation for the participants reporting comparatively lower scores in the Australian identity acculturation dimension. However, the present study did not measure identity related to country of origin, so it is unclear whether participants idetnified more or less with Australia than their country of origin. This could be investigated in future studies.

Remennick (2004) identified host country language skills as a key trigger for reshaping migrants' host country identity. Consistent with this, the present study also found a moderate correlation between language and identity dimensions, suggesting that Indian and Sri Lankan skilled migrants with higher English language proficiency have a stronger Australian identity.

Well-Being

Well-being (life satisfaction) was assessed using the Personal Well-being Index (Cummins 2006), which has been used with Australian samples. According to the results, the majority of Indian and Sri Lankan skilled migrants were satisfied with their lives in Australia. Average life satisfaction scores in the sample were above the average Australian's life satisfaction score, as reported in Cummins' (2012) study. Given that the present study involved a skilled migrant sample, it is possible that education, income and occupational characteristics might have contributed to higher life satisfaction than would be found in the Australian population taken as a whole. In contrast to study findings that show culturally distinct migrants are less satisfied in host societies (Amit 2010; Choudhry 2001; Sam 1998; Sabharwal 2011; Verkuyten 2008), Indian and Sri Lankan skilled migrants in the current study were satisfied with their lives in Australia. Past research has shown that perceived discrimination could influence the life satisfaction of migrants (Verkuyten 2008). Perhaps skilled migrants are less likely to experience discrimination than other migrant groups. In addition, Australia is considered a 'migrant-friendly' country with positive multicultural policies towards migrants. As a result, ethnic skilled migrants in Australia may feel more accepted.

Past research (Amit 2010a; Martinovic et al. 2009) has found that co-ethnic group size can influence the well-being of migrants in host societies. There is a large Indian (295,362) and Sri Lankan (86,412) migrant population living in Australia (DIAC 2013), and thus these migrants may receive more support from friends and relatives compared to migrant groups with lower representation, leading to greater satisfaction with life in the host society. Another reason for relatively high life satisfaction scores among the study participants could be that *skilled* migrants choose where to live, and can return to their country of origin if unhappy with their lives in the host country. For other migrant categories, such as humanitarian migrants, rather than choosing their destination, they may be forced to migrate due to unfavourable circumstances in their country of origin (Safi 2010; Sam 1998; Verkuyten 2008). Future studies could compare life satisfaction between humanitarian and skilled migrants in Australia.

Lifestyle improvements between the migrant sending and receiving society could also account for the high level of life satisfaction among study participants (see e.g., Diener and Diener 1995; Morrison et al. 2011; Pan et al. 2008), however the present study did not assess pre-migration versus post-migration life satisfaction. Future studies in the field could compare pre- and post-migration life satisfaction of skilled migrants to determine whether positive social conditions are related to changes in life satisfaction.

Relationship between Acculturation and Well-Being

The current research predicted that language, identity, and behaviour acculturation is positively related to life satisfaction. However, language acculturation was expected to be less important for Indian and Sri Lankan skilled migrants in Australia because they come from countries where English is a predominant language and therefore may not need to adapt their language significantly. While all three dimensions showed a positive relationship with life satisfaction at bivariate level, only identity and language acculturation uniquely predicted life satisfaction. Lu et al. (2011) have suggested that the Australian population is favourably disposed towards migrants who are committed to contributing to Australia, therefore having a stronger Australian identity may positively influence life satisfaction of skilled migrants because it promotes acceptance by mainstreamers.

Past research findings (Chiswick and Miller 1999; Kisslev et al. 2010; Kogan 2010; Remennick 2003, 2004) have suggested that host country language skills influence migrants' well-being. Language as a primary means of communication should support migrants in handling practical and social challenges in the host country. For instance, connecting with mainstreamers and other ethnic groups, day-to-day activities or even finding a job should be easier for migrants with good language skills (Kisselev et al. 2010). In terms of behavioural acculturation (e.g., host country entertainment, food, media and music consumption), country–of-origin alternatives are readily available in Australia (Birman et al. 2014), thus, the relationship between behaviour integration and life satisfaction may not be as strong as expected in other contexts.

Acculturation may be a less important predictor of life satisfaction among skilled migrants in a migrant friendly country such as Australia that allows migrants to maintain their own cultural values and contacts (Barda 2006; Eshel and Rosenthal-Sokolov 2000; Lu et al. 2011; Safi 2010). Skilled migrants may not consider integrating into the society as essential for well-being in a post multicultural era when they have access to own cultural materials and events (Adachi 2011). Furthermore, given there is a large Indian and Sri Lankan population in Australia, integrating into the host society may not be desirable for migrants. Rather other general factors like career achievements, income, quality/standard of living may be relatively more important for life satisfaction (Dalgard and Thapa 2007; Mara and Landesmann 2013; Neto and Barros 2007; Sam 1998; Verkuyten 2008).

Past research has identified various socio-demographic variables which can affect migration outcomes however the factors that affect Indian and Sri Lankan skilled migrants' subjective outcomes in Australia were not known in the literature. Thus the findings of the present research contribute by addressing this gap in literature. It can be said that factors that have traditionally been considered important, such as age at migration (Dalgard and Thapa 2007; Martinovic et al. 2009; Nesdale and Mak 2000; Remennick 2003) and education (Fong and Ooka 2006; Helliwell 2003; Nauck 2001; Pham and Harris 2001; Remennick 2004; Selvarajah 2003) appear to be less important for Indian and Sri Lankan skilled migrants in Australia.

LIMITATIONS AND FUTURE RESEARCH

The findings of this study should be interpreted with due consideration of the limitations of the research design. A widely acknowledged limitation of cross-sectional survey data is its inability to capture the cause and effect relationship among variables (Schwartz et al. 2012). A longitudinal survey design would enable change in acculturation and life satisfaction to be measured over a period of time, so that change in the acculturation factors could be related to change in well-being. For instance, acculturation and life satisfaction could be measured at time intervals such as one year since arrival, five years since arrival, ten years since arrival etc.

Another limitation of the research design is the use of self-report surveys. Urlacher (2010) suggested that there is a tendency for participants to rate their language skills as higher than their actual language skill level in a self-report survey. English language skills among the present study participants were generally at the high end of the scale. Future research could use objective test scores such as IELTS or interviews in order to more accurately assess skilled migrants' language skills. The high life satisfaction scores reported in the present study may also have been reflective of social desirability response bias.

Sampling limitations in the current study included that the majority of participants were recruited from highliy metropolitan States in Australia and had been living in Australia for at least five to ten years. As such, the sample was not representative of the overall Indian and Sri Lankan skilled migrant population in Australia and, in particular, new migrants, who are likely to be less acculturated. Sampling bias in the present study may have limited the variability in socio-demographic factors, such as age at migration, years since migration, neighbourhood concentration of co-ethnic migrants, pre-migration SES and English language proficiency, which could have obscured the relationship between socio-demographic factors, acculturation and life satisfaction. Therefore, it would be appropriate to replicate the study with proportionate representation of the other States, also sampling migrants who have lived in Australia for different time periods. In addition, it is possible that individuals in the sampling frame (Indian and Sri Lankan skilled migrants) who were not acculturated and felt distressed about life in Australia did not volunteer to participate in the survey, since participation was by self-selection. Future research may also consider incorporating employment status such as employed, unemployed and underemployed to contribute to better understanding of the topics addressed in the research. For example, it is possible that skilled migrants who are unemployed or under employed may have negative subjective feelings about the host country (Kwok-bun and Plüss 2013; Safi 2010; Schmidt 2007).

The current research findings refer exclusively to first-generation skilled migrants from India and Sri Lanka. Future research could focus on comparing different skilled migrant groups within Australia (e.g., important skilled migrant groups in Australia such as the People's Republic of China, the UK and South Africa) and in other migrant-receiving societies, such as the UK, New Zealand and Canada, in order to determine the impact of ethnicity and host country on the acculturation and life satisfaction of skilled migrants.

Diener et al. (2003) suggested that life satisfaction is comparative (i.e., present life satisfaction can be compared with one's life satisfaction 'x' years ago or with others' life satisfaction). This study did not compare the life satisfaction of skilled migrants with other migrant groups. Therefore, in future studies, the life satisfaction of skilled migrants could be compared with other migrant groups in Australia, such as humanitarian migrants, or with people in their country of birth with similar demographic backgrounds. It would also be informative to compare pre- and post-migration life satisfaction to determine if migrating to a Western country is associated with increased life satisfaction among skilled migrants.

The positive life satisfaction experiences reported in the present study may enhance confidence among potential future Indian and Sri Lankan skilled migrants who are considering migration to Australia. Previous research (Choudhry 2001; George and Chaze, 2009) has shown that Asian migrants experience loneliness and isolation in Western host societies. Therefore it is important that skilled migrants have realistic expectations about migration outcomes. Nevertheless, the present study results suggest that positive subjective outcomes are achievable for Indian and Sri Lankan skilled migrants in Australia. Achieving higher life satisfaction soon after migration may not be realistic, but could be a more realistic goal with increased time spent in the country. Notably, the majority of participants in the current study had been in Australia for some time.

CONCLUSION

This study contributes to the migration literature by establishing the level of acculturation and life satisfaction among a unique ethnic group of skilled migrants in the Australian context. Findings indicated that Indian and Sri Lankan skilled migrants are moderately acculturated to Australian society, thus the traditional social separation that many first-generation migrants or humanitarian migrants experience in other Western host societies was not observed in this context. This may reflect fact that participants were skilled migrants and thus possessed the skills and abilities necessary to integrate well, unique characteristics of migrants from this region (India and Sri Lanka), or the migration experience in Australia.

The present study found that Indian and Sri Lankan skilled migrants were generally satisfied with their lives in Australia. Therefore, the low level of life satisfaction observed among some ethnic migrants in Western societies was not present among these skilled migrants. These findings suggest that 'migrant category' is likely to be an influential variable for migrants life satisfaction. The current study also found that only identity and language acculturation significantly predicted well-being. This suggests that acculturation may be a less important predictor of life satisfaction among skilled migrants in a migrant friendly country such as Australia that allows them to maintain their own cultural values.

In conclusion, the findings suggest that Indian and Sri Lankan skilled migrants in Australia are successful in achieving positive migration outcomes related to acculturation and life satisfaction that support the Australian 'common bond' concept. Future research in the field should aim to explore acculturation and life satisfaction among other skilled migrant groups in Australia in order to determine whether these positive outcomes in the Australian context can be generalised to other groups.

REFERENCES

Abraído-Lanza, Ana. 2004. "Social support and psychological adjustment among Latinas with arthritis: A test of a theoretical model," *Annals of Behavioural Medicine*, 27:162-171.

Adachi, Satoshi. 2011. "Social integration in Post-multiculturalism: an analysis of social integration policy in post-war Britain," *International Journal of Japanese Sociology*, 20:107-120.

Amit, Karin. 2010b. "Socio economic integration of second generation immigrants in Israel: examining alternative ethnic classification", *Journal of Immigrant & Refugee Studies*, 8: 50-75.

Amit, Karen. 2012. "Social integration and identity of immigrants from western countries, the FSU and Ethiopia in Israel," *Ethnic and Racial Studies*, 35:1287-1310.

Arends-to´th, Judit. and Van de Vijver, Fons. 2003. "Multiculturalism and acculturation: Views of Dutch and Turkish–Dutch," *European Journal of Social Psychology*, 33: 249-266.

Arguin, Paul M. 2010. "A definition that includes first and second generation immigrants returning to their countries of origin to visit friends and relatives still makes sense to me," *Journal of Travel Medicine*, 17:147-149.

Ariss, Akram All, Koall, Iris, Ozbilgin, Mustafa. and Suutari, Vesa. 2012. "Careers of skilled migrants: towards a theoretical & methodological expansion," *Journal of Management Development,* 31:92-101.

Asakura, T, Gee, GC, Nakayama, K. and Niwa S. 2008. "Returning to "home land": work related ethnic discrimination & the health of Japanese Brazilians in Japan," *American Journal of Public,* 98: 743-750.

Au, AYV, Garey, JG, Bermas, N, and Chan, MM.1998. "The Relationship between Acculturation and Job satisfaction among Chinese Immigrants in the New York City Restaurant Business," *Hospitality Management,* 17:11-17.

Australian Bureau of Statistics. 2010. *Forms of Employment,* cat.no. 6359.0, ABS, accessed December 31, 2012, http://www.ausstats.abs.gov.au/ausstats/subscriber.nsf/0/ED7010B1774DA4D4CA2578800019CAFB/$File/63590_november%202010.pdf.

Aycan, Z and Berry, John. 1996. "Impact of employment related experience on immigrants' psychological well-being & adaptation in Canada," *Canadian Journal of Behavioural Science,* 28:240-251.

Bahn, Susanne. 2014. "Migrant workers on temporary 457 visas working in Australia: implications for human resource management," *Asia Pacific Journal of Human Resources,* 52:77-92.

Bandyopadhyay, Sanghamitra. 2011. "Rich states, poor states: Convergence and polarisation across Indian states," *Scottish Journal of Political Economy,* 57: 414-436.

Barda, Rachel Marlene. 2006. "The migration experience of the Jews of Egypt to Australia 1948-1967: A model of acculturation," PhD diss., University of Sydney, Sydney.

Barrett, Alan, and Duffy, David. 2008. "Are Ireland's immigrants integrating into its Labor market?", *International Migration Review,* 42:597-619.

Berry, John. 1990. *Psychology of acculturation: understanding individual's moving between culture, applied cross-cultural psychology,* Sage, London.

Berry, John. 1997. "Immigration, acculturation & adaptation," *Applied Psychology: An International Review,* 46: 5-68.

Berry, John. 2001. "A psychology of immigration," *Journal of Social Issues,* 57:615-631.

Berry, John and Sam, David. 1997. *'Acculturation and adaptation'* in JW Berry, MH Segall & C Kagitcibasi (eds.), *Handbook of cross-cultural psychology, Social Behaviour and applications,* Allyn and Bacon, Boston, pp.291-326.

Birman, Dina. 2006. "Acculturation gap and family adjustment: Findings with Soviet Jewish refugees in the United States and implications for measurement," *Journal of Cross-cultural Psychology,* 37: 568-589.

Birman, Dina. 2011. "Migration and Well-being: Beyond the macro system,", *Psychosocial Intervention,* 20:339-342.

Birman, Dina and Tyler, Forrest. 1994. "Acculturation and alienation of Soviet Jewish refugees in the United States," *Genetic, Social & General Psychology Monographs,* 120:103-116.

Birman, Dina, and Trickett, EJ. 2001. "Cultural transitions in first generation Immigrants: A study of Soviet Jewish refugee adolescents and parents," *Journal of Cross-Cultural Psychology,* 32: 456-477.

Birman, Dina and Taylor-Ritzler, T. 2007. "Acculturation & psychological distress among adolescence immigrants from the former Soviet-Union: exploring the mediating effect on family relationship", *Cultural Diversity & Ethnic Minority Psychology,* 13:337-346.

Birman, Dina, Simon, Corrina, Chan Wing and Tran, Nellie. 2014. "A life domains perspective on acculturation and psychological adjustment: a study of refugees from the Former Soviet Union," *American Journal of Community Psychology*, 53:60-72.

Bisin, Alberto, Patacchini, Eleonora, Verdier, Thierry and Zenou, Yves. 2008. "Are Muslim migrants different in terms of cultural integration?" *Journal of the European Economic Association*, 6: 445-456.

Borjas, George. 1990. *Friends or strangers: The impact of immigrants in on the US economy*, Basic Books, New York.

Borjas, George. 1994. "The economies of migration," *Journal of Economic Literature*, 32:1667-1717.

Boucher, Ana. 2007. "Skill migration & gender in Australia & Canada: The case of gender-based analysis", *Australian Journal of Political Science*, 42: 383-401.

Brenick, Alaina & Silbereisen, Rainer K. 2012. "Leaving (for) home: Understanding return migration from the Diaspora', *European Psychologist*, 17: 85-92.

Chiswick, Berry. 1978. "The effects of Americanisation on the earnings of foreign born Men," *Journal of Political Economy*, 86:897-921.

Chiswick, Berry and Miller, Paul. 1999. "Immigration, language & multiculturalism in Australia," *The Australian Economic Review*, 32:369-385.

Chiswick, Berry and Miller, Paul. 2001. 'A model of destination-language acquisition: Application to male immigrants in Canada', *Demography*, vol.38, no.3, pp.391-410.

Chiswick, Berry, and Miller, Paul. 2002, "Immigrants earnings: language skills, linguistic concentrations & the business cycle," *Journal of Population Economy*, 15: 31-57.

Chiswick, Berry, Lee, YL, and Miller, Paul. 2003. "Patterns of immigrant occupational attainment in a longitudinal survey," *International Migration*, 41:47-70.

Chiswick, Berry, Lee, YL and Miller, PW 2005, 'A longitudinal analysis of immigrant occupational mobility: A test of the immigrant assimilation hypotheses', *International Migration Review*, vol.39, no.2, pp.332-353.

Chiswick, Berry and Miller, Paul. 2008. "Occupational attainment & immigrants economic progress in Australia," *The Economic Record*, 84:S45-S56.

Choi, Jong, and Thomas, Madhavappallil. 2009. "Predictive factors of acculturation attitudes & social support among Asian immigrants in the USA," *International Journal of Social Welfare*, 18:76-84.

Choudhry, UK. 2001. "Uprooting & resettlement experience of South Asian immigrant women," *Western Journal of Nursing Research*, 23:376-393.

Chow, Ben. 2003. "The challenges of immigration & integration in Australia & European union," *Opening address, National Europe Centre, paper no 1, University of Sydney*, accessed 22 February 2011, https://digitalcollections.anu.edu.au/bitstream/ 1885/41480/3/chow.pdf.

Chowhan, James, Zeytinoglu, Isic U and Cooke, Gordon B. 2012. "Are immigrants' pay and benefits satisfaction different than Canadian-born?," *Industrial Relations*, 67:3-24.

Chung, Ruth H, Kim, Bryans S and Abreu, Jose M. 2004. "Asian American multidimensional acculturation scale: development, factor analysis, reliability, & validity', *Culture Diversity Ethnic Minority Psychology*, vol.10, no.1, pp.66-80.

Clark Andrew, Frijters, Paul and Shields, Michael. 2008. "Relative income, happiness and utility: an explanation for the Easterlinparadox and other puzzles," *Journal of Economic Literature*, 46: 95-144.

Cobb-Clark, Deborah A. 2000. "Do selection criteria make a difference? Visa category & the labour market status of immigrant to Australia." *The Economic Records,* 76:15-31.

Coleman, Hardin LK. 1995. "Cultural factors and the counselling process: Implications for school counselors," *The School Counsellors,* 42:180-185.

Coleman, Hardin LK, Casali, Sherry B and Wampold, Bruce E. 2001. "Adolescent strategies for coping with cultural diversity," *Journal of Counselling & Development,* 79:356-364.

Colic-Peisker, Val. 2011. "A new era in Australian multiculturalism? from working-class "Ethnics" to a "multicultural middle-class," *International Migration Review,* 45: 562-587.

Collins, Jock. 2013. "Multiculturalism and immigrant integration in Australia," *CES,* 45:133-149.

Colombo Page. 2013, "Drafting new legislation for granting dual citizenship to expatriate Sri Lankans completed," accessed October 20 2013, http://www.colombopage.com/archive_13B/Jul20_1374339598JR.php.

Connor, Phillip and Massey, Douglas S. 2010. "Economic outcomes among Latino migrants to Spain and the United States: differences by source region and legal status." *International Migration Review,* 44:802-829.

Cummins, Robert. 1996. "The domains of life satisfaction: an attempt to order chaos," *Social Indicators Research,* 303-328.

Cummins, Robert. 2006. "Personal Wellbeing Index manual, Deakin University, Melbourne," accessed June 15 2010, http://www.deakin.edu.au/research/acqol/instruments/wellbeing_index.htm.

Cummins, Robert. 2010. "Subjective well-being, homeostatically protected mood & depression: A synthesis," *Journal of Happiness Studies,* 11:1-17.

Dagher, J and D'Netto, Brian. 1997. "Managing workforce diversity in Australia," Australia, Monash University, Faculty of Business & Economics, Working Paper, 05/97.

Daig, Isolde, Herschbach, Peter, Lehmann, Anja, Knoll, Nina & Decker, Oliver. 2009. "Gender & age differences in domain-specific life satisfaction & the impact of depressive & anxiety symptoms: a general population survey from Germany," *Quality of Life Research,* 18: 669-678.

Dalgard, Odd, and Thapa, Suraj. 2007. "Immigration, Social Integration & mental health in Norway with focus on gender differences," *Clinical Practice & Epidemiology in Mental Health,* 3:1-10.

De Bree, June, Davids, Tine and De Haas, Hein 2010, 'Post-return experiences & transnational belonging of return migrants: a Dutch-Moroccan case study', *Global Networks,* vol. 10, no.4, pp.489-509.

De Haas, Hein and Fokkema, Tineke. 2011. "The effects of integration and transnational ties on international return migration intentions," *Demographic Research,* 25:755-782.

Department of Immigration & Boarder Protection. 2014. "Annual Report 2012–13," accessed April 04 2014, http://www.immi.gov.au/about/reports/annual/2012-13/html/performance/outcome_1/economic_migration.htm.

Department of Immigration & Citizenship. 2011a, "Annual Report 2010-2011," accessed December 31 2012, http://www.immi.gov.au/about/reports/annual/2010-11/pdf/2010-11-diac-annual-report.pdf.

Department of Immigration & Citizenship. 2011b. "Trends in Migration: Australia 2010:11," accessed November 11 2012, http://www.immi.gov.au/about/reports/annual/2009-10/pdf/.

Department of Immigration & Citizenship. 2012a. "Country Profile: Republic India," accessed December 31 2012, http://www.immi.gov.au/media/statistics/country-profiles/_pdf/india.pdf.

Department of Immigration & Citizenship. 2012b, "Annual Report 2009-2010," accessed December 31 2012, http://www.immi.gov.au/about/reports/annual/2009-10/pdf/.

Department of Immigration & Citizenship. 2012c, "Country Profile: Sri Lanka," accessed December 31 2012, http://www.immi.gov.au/media/statistics/country-profiles/_pdf/sri-lanka.pdf.

Department of Immigration & Citizenship. 2013a, "Fact sheet 5-Emigration from Australia," accessed October 20 2013, http://www.immi.gov.au/media/fact-sheets/05emigration.htm.

Department of Immigration & Citizenship. 2013b, "Migrant economic outcomes & contributions," accessed August 22 2013, http://www.immi.gov.au/media/publications/research/_pdf/outcomes-contributions-apr11.pdf.

Department of Immigration & Citizenship. 2013c, "Migration program report 2012-13," accessed August 26 2013, http://www.immi.gov.au/media/statistics/pdf/report-on-migration-program-2012-13.pdf.

Department of Immigration & Citizenship. 2013d, "Professionals & other skilled migrants," accessed August 15 2014, http://www.immi.gov.au/skilled/general-skilled-migration/new-skilled.htm.

Department of Immigration & Citizenship. 2013e, "Australian Citizenship, our common bond," accessed December 16 2013, http://www.citizenship.gov.au/learn/cit_test/test_resource/_pdf/our-common-bond-2014.pdf.

Department of Immigration & Citizenship. 2014, Business migration, accessed April 22, 2014, https://www.immi.gov.au/media/fact-sheets/27business.htm.

Diener, Ed. 1984. "Subjective well-being," *Psychological Bulletin*, 95:542-575.

Diener, Ed, Oishi, Shigehiro and Lucas, Richard E. 2003, "Personality, culture, and subjective well-being', emotional and cognitive evaluations of life," *Annual Review of Psychology*, 54: 403-25.

Ea Emerson E., Griffin Mary Q., L'Eplattenier Nora and Fitzpatrick Joyce J. 2008. "Job satisfaction and acculturation among Filipinoregistered nurses," *Journal of Nursing Scholarship*, 40: 46-51.

Ersanilli, Evelyn and Koopmans, Ruud. 2010. "Rewarding integration? Regulations & the socio-cultural integration of immigrants in the Netherlands, France & Germany," *Journal of Ethnic & Migration Studies,* 36:773-791.

Eshel, Yohanan and Resenthal-Sokolov, Marianna. 2000. "Acculturation attitudes & socio-cultural adjustment of sojourner youth in Israel," *The Journal of Social Psychology,* 140: 677-691.

Fanning, Bryan, Hasse, Truts and O'Boyle, Neil. 2011. "Well-being, cultural capital, & social inclusion: Immigrants in the Republic of Ireland," *International Migration & Integration,* 12:1-12.

Fitzgerald, Nurgul. 2010. "Acculturation, socioeconomic status, and health among Hispanics," *Napa Bulletin,* 34:28-46.

Fong, Eric and Ooka, Emi. 2006. "Patterns of participation in informal social activities among Chinese immigrants in Toronto," *International Migration Review,* 40:348-374.

Foroughi, Ehsan, Misajon, RoseAnne, Cummins, Robert. 2001. '"The relationship between migration, social support & social integration on quality of life'", *Behaviour Change,* 18:156-167.

Franke, Richard H, Hosftede, Geert & Bond, Michael H. 1991. "Cultural roots of economic performance: A research note," *Strategic Management Journal,* 12:165-173.

Garrido, Angeles A. Olmos, Juan CC. García-Arjona, Noemi. and Rodrigo, P. 2012. "Immigration, school, physical activity and sports," *Kinesiology,* 4:83-93.

George, Usha and Chaze, Ferzana. 2002. "Tell me what I need to know, South Asian women, social capital and settlement," *International Migration & Integration,* 10: 265-282.

Gijsberts, Merove, and Dagevos, Jaco. 2007. "The socio-cultural integration of ethnic minorities in the Netherlands: Identifying neighbourhood effects on multiple integration outcomes," *Housing Studies,* 22:805-831.

Gordon, Milton M. 1964. *Assimilation in American life, the role of race, religion & national origins*, Oxford University press, New York.

Government of Western Australia. 2012. "The Economic & social contribution of migrants to Western Australia," accessed August 23, 2013, www.omi.wa.gov.au/resources/publications/localgovernment/Economic_Social_Contributions_MigrantsWA_Full_Report.pdf.

Groutsis, Dimitria and Arnold, PC. 2012. "Tracking the career decisions & experience of migrant elites: The case of South African trained medical professionals in the Australian labour market," *Health Sociology Review*, 21:332-342.

Gudykunst, William B and Kim, Young Y. 2003. *Communication with strangers: an approach to intercultural communication*, Mc-Graw-Hill, Bostan.

Hawthorne, Lesleyanne. 2002. "Qualifications recognition reforms for skilled migrants in Australia: applying competency based assessment to overseas qualified nurses," *International Migration,* 4:55-91.

Hawthorne, Lesleyanne. 2010. "How Valuable is "Two-Step Migration"? Labor Market Outcomes for International Student Migrants to Australia," *Asian & Pacific Migration Journal*, 19:5-36.

Hawthorne, Lesleyanne, 1994. *Labour market barriers for immigrants engineers in Australia,* Canberra, ACT.

Ho, Christina. 2006. "Migration as feminisation? Chinese women's experiences of work & family in Australia", *Journal of Ethnic & Migration Studies,* 32:497-/514.

Ho, Joyce, and Birman, Dina. 2010. "Acculturation gaps in Vietnamese immigrant families: Impact on family relationships," *International Journal of Intercultural Relations,* 34:22-33.

Hofstede, Geert. 1980. *Culture's Consequences: International Differences in Work-Related Values*, Sage, Beverly Hills, CA.

Hofstede, Geert. 2001. *Culture's consequences: comparing values, behaviours, institutions and organizations across nations*, 2nd edn, Sage, Thousand Oaks, CA.

Hou, Feng. 2009. "Immigrants working with co-ethnics: who are they & how do they fare?", *International Migration,* 47:70-100.

Islam, Asadul and Fausten, Dietrich K. 2008. "Skilled immigration & wages in Australia," *The Economic Record*, vol.84, Special Issue, PP.s66-s82.

Jasinskaja-Lahti, Inga. Horenczyk, Gabriel and Kinunen, Tamara. 2011. "Time and context in the relationship between acculturation attitudes and adaptation among Russian-speaking immigrants in Finland and Israel," *Journal of Ethnic and Migration Studies,*37:1423-1440.

Kim, Bryan S and Omizo, Michael M. 2006. "Behavioral acculturation and enculturation and psychological functioning among Asian American college students," *Cultural Diversity & Ethnic Minority Psychology,* 12:245-258.

Kisselev, Paulina, Brown, Margaret A, and Brown, Jonathan D. 2010. "Gender differences in language acculturation predict marital satisfaction: A dyadic analysis of Russian-speaking immigrant couples in the United States," *Journal of Comparative Family Studies,* 41:767-782.

Kramar, Robin, De Cieri, Helen, Noe, Raymond A, Hollenbeck, JR and Wright, PM. 2011. *Human resource management in Australia,* 4th edn, McGraw-Hill Irwin, Sydney.

Kramar, Robin and Syed, Jawad. 2012. *Human resource management in a global context: a critical approach,* Palgrave, Macmillan Basingstoke, New York.

Kumar, Asha. and Nevid, Jeffrey S. 2010. "Acculturation, enculturation, and perceptions of mental disorders in Asian Indian immigrants," *Cultural Diversity & Ethnic Minority Psychology,* 16:274-283.

Kunst, Jonas R and Sam, David L. 2013. "Expanding the margins of identity: A critique of marginalization in a globalized world," *International Perspectives in Psychology: Research, Practice, Consultation,* 2:225-241.

Kwok-bun, Chan and Plüss, Caroline. 2013. "Modeling migrant adaptation: Coping with social strain, assimilation, and non-integration," *International Sociology,* 28:48-65.

Labrianidis, Lois, and Lyberaki, Antigone. 2004. "Back & forth & in between: returning Albanian migrants from Greece & Italy," *Journal of International Migration & Integration,* 5:77-106.

Lafromboise, Teresa. Coleman, Hardin LK and Gerton, Jennifer. 1993. "Psychological impact of biculturalism: evidence & theory," *Psychological Bulletin,* 114:395-412.

Lance, Bram. 2010. "The economic returns of immigrants' bonding and bridging social capital: the case of the Netherland," *International Migration Review,* 44:202-226.

Lee, Gyung-Sook J. 2013. "English ain't English in the Australian workplace' a narrative analysis of Korean migrant women's labour market experiences," *Gender, Place & Culture,* 20:53-69.

Li, Peter. 2000. "Earning disparities between immigrants & native-born Canadians," *Canadian Review of Sociology & Anthropology,* 37:289-312.

Li, Peter. 2003. "Deconstructing Canada's discourse of immigrant integration," *Journal of International Migration & Integration,* 4:315-333.

Li, Guofang. 2007. "Home environment & second language acquisition: the importance of family capital", *British Journal of Sociology of Education',* 28:285-299.

Lu, Ying, Samaratunga, Ramani and Härtel, Charmine. 2011. "Acculturation strategies among professional Chinese immigrants in the Australian workplace," *Asia Pacific Journal of Human Resource Management,* 49:71-86.

Lu, Ying, Samaratunga, Ramani and Härtel, Charmine. 2013, "Acculturation attitudes and affective workgroup commitment: evidence from professional Chinese immigrants in the Australian workplace," *Asian Ethnicity,* 14:206-228.

Lu, Ying, Samaratunga, Ramani and Härtel, Charmine. 2012. "The relationship between acculturation strategy and job satisfaction for professional Chinese immigrants in the Australian workplace," *International Journal of Intercultural Relations,* 36:669-681

Mahmud, SH and Schölmerich, Axel. 2011. "Acculturation & life satisfaction: immigrants in Germany," *Psychology Research,* 1:278-286.

Malinen, Sanna and Johnston, Lucy. 2011. "Seek a better work life balance: Expectations & perceptions of work related practices & attitudes of recent immigrants to New Zealand," *Asia & Pacific Migration Journal,* 20:233-252.

Mara, Isilda and Landesmann, Michael. 2013. *Do I stay because I am happy or am I happy because I stay? Life satisfaction in migration, and the decision to stay permanently, return and out-migrate, Norface Migration,* Discussion Paper No. 2013-08, accessed 12 October 2013, http://www.norface-migration.org/publ_uploads/NDP_08_13.pdf.

Marta Bivand, E and Oeppen, Ceri. 2013. "Migrant balancing acts: understanding the interactions between integration and transnationalism," *Journal of Ethnic & Migration Studies,* 39:867-884.

Massey, Simon JL and Parr, Nick. 2012. "The socio-economic status of migrant populations in regional and rural Australia and its implications for future population policy", *Journal of Population Research,* 29:1-21.

Mor Barak, ME. 2000. "Diversity in the work place: Beyond affirmative action: towards a model of diversity & organisational inclusion," *Administration in Social Work,* 23:47-68.

Murdie, Robert, and Ghosh, Sutama, 2010, "Does spatial concentration always mean a lack of integration? Exploring ethnic concentration & integration in Toronto," *Journal of Ethnic & Migration Studies,* 36:293-311.

Nakhaie, Reza M. 2007. "Ethno racial origin, social capital & earnings," *International Migration & Integration,* 8:307-325.

Naranpanawa, Athula and Bandara, Jayatileke S. 2012. "Trade liberalisation and income distribution: evidence from a small open economy," *The Empirical Economics Letters,* 11:239-249.

Nesdale, Drew and Mak, Anita S. 2000. "Immigrant acculturation attitudes & host country identification," *Journal of Community & Applied Social Psychology,* 10: 483-495.

Neto, Félix and Barros, Jose. 2007. "Satisfaction with life among adolescents from Portuguese immigrant families in Switzerland," *Swiss Journal of Psychology,* 66:215-223.

Parasnis Jaai, Fausten, Dietrich and Cheo, Roland. 2008. "Do Australian qualifications help? Host country qualifications on migrants participation & unemployment," *The Economic Records,* 84:131-140.

Parliament of Australia. 2013, *Skilled migration: temporary & permanent flows to Australia,* accessed August 23, 2013, http://www.aph.gov.au/About_Parliament/Parliamentary_ Departments/Parliamentary_Library/pubs/BN/2012-2013/SkilledMigration#_Toc342559466.

Parr, Nick and Guo, Fei. 2005. "The occupational concentration and mobility of Asian immigrants in Australia," *Asian and Pacific Migration Journal,* 14:351-380.

Paterson, Ashley D and Hakim-Larson, Julie. 2012. "Arab youth in Canada: acculturation, enculturation, social support, and life satisfaction," *Journal of Multicultural Counselling and Development,* 40:206-215.

Pham, Thuy B and Harris, Richard J. 2001. "Acculturation strategies among Vietnamese-Americans," *International Journal of Intercultural Relations*, 25:279-300.

Pio, Edwina. 2010. "Weaving contentment: Ethnic minority women at work in New Zealand," *Revue Sciences de Gestion*, 43-62.

Qureshi, Kaveri, Varghese, VJ and Osella Filippo. 2013., "Indian Punjabi skilled migrants in Britain: of brain drain & under-employment", *Journal of Management Development*, 32:182-192.

Reitz, Jeffery. 2001. "Immigrant success in knowledge economy: Institutional change and immigrant experience in Canada," *Journal of Social Issues*, 57:579-613.

Reitz, Jeffery, Banerjee, Rupa, Phan, Mai and Thompson, Jordan. 2009. "Race, religion & social integration of new immigrant minorities in Canada," *International Migration Review*, 43:695-726.

Remennick, Larrisa. 1999. "Women with a Russian accent' in Israel: on the gender aspects of immigration," *The European Journal of Women's Studies*, 6:441-461.

Remennick, Larrisa. 2003. "What does integration mean? Social insertion of Russian immigrants in Israel," *Journal of International Migration & Integration*, 4:23-49.

Remennick, Larrisa. 2009. "Exploring intercultural relationships: A study of Russian immigrants married to native Israelis," *Journal of Comparative Family Studies*, 40:719-738.

Riosmena, Fernando. and Dennis, Jeff A. 2012. "Gradient importation, SES-selective acculturation, and the weaker SES-health gradients of Mexican immigrants in the US," *The Social Science Journal*, 49:325-329.

Roberts, Rosie. 2011. "Unfolding stories of skilled migrants," *Social Alternatives*, 30:35-39.

Rojas, Mariano. 2006, 'Life satisfaction and satisfaction in domains of live: is it a simple relationship?' *Journal of Happiness Studies*, vol.7, pp.467-497.

Rudiger, A and Spencer, S. 2003. "Social integration of migrants and ethnic minorities, policies to combat discrimination conference," *Conference proceedings of The European Commission and the OECD*, Brussels, 21-22 January, accessed November 21, 2011, http://www.oecd.org/els/mig/15516956.pdf.

Ryder, Andrew G, Alden, Lynn E and Paulhus, Delroy L. 2000. "Is acculturation unidimensional or bidimensional? A head-to-head comparison in the prediction, of personality, self-identity and adjustment", *Journal of Personality and Social Psychology*, 79:49-65.

Sabharwal, Meghna. 2011. "High skilled immigrants: How satisfied are foreign born scientists & engineers employed at American universities?", R*eview of Public Personal Administration*, 31:143-169.

Safdar, Saba. Lay, Clarry. and Struthers, Ward. 2003. "The process of acculturation & basic goals: testing a multidimensional individual difference acculturation model with Iranian immigrants in Canada," *Applied Psychology: An International Review*, 52:555-579.

Safi, Mirna. 2010. "Immigrants' life satisfaction in Europe: between assimilation & discrimination," *European Sociology Review*, 26:159-176.

Saghafi, Nazanin. Asamen, Joy. Rowe, Daryl. and Tehrani, Rozalin. 2012. "The Relationship of religious self-identification to cultural adaptation among Iranian immigrants & first-generation Iranians professionals," *Psychology Research & Practice*, 43:328-335.

Sakamoto, Izumi. 2007. "A critical examination of immigrant acculturation: toward an Anti-oppressive social work model with immigrant adults in a pluralistic society," *British Journal of Social Work*, 37:515-535.

Sakamoto, Izumi. Wei, Yi. and Truong, Lele. 2008. "How do organisations and social policies acculturate to immigrants? Accommodating skilled immigrants in Canada," *American Journal of Community Psychology*, 42:343-354.

Sam, David L. 1998. "Profiling life satisfaction among adolescents from immigrant families in Norway," *Journal of Ethnicity & Health*, 3:5-14.

Sanchez, Juan I. and Brock, Petra. 1996. "Outcomes of perceived discrimination among Hispanic employees: Is diversity management a luxury or a necessity?", *Academy of Management Journal*, 39:704-719.

Sayegh, Liliane. and Lasry, LJean-Claude. 1993. "Immigrants' adaptation in Canada: Assimilation, acculturation and orthogonal cultural identification," *Canadian Psychology*, 34:98-109.

Schaefer, David R. & Dillman, Ddon A. 1998, 'Development of a standard email methodology: Result

Schwartz, Seth J. Kim, Su Y. Whitbourne, Susan K. Zamboanga, Byron L. Weisskirch, Robert S. Forthun, Larry F. Vazsonyi, Alexander T. Beyers, Wim and Luyckx, Koen. 2012. "Converging identities: dimensions of acculturation & personal identity status among immigrant college students," *Cultural Diversity and Ethnic Minority Psychology*, vol.19, no.2, accessed January 02, 2012 https://www.ncbi.nlm.nih.gov/m/pubmed/23148900/?i=5&from=/23082833/related.

Selvarajah, Chris. 2004. "Equal employment opportunity: acculturation experience of immigrant medical professionals in New Zealand in the period of 1995-2000," *Equal Opportunities Journal*, 23:50-70.

Silbereisen, Rainer K. 2008. "New research on acculturation among diaspora migrants," *International Journal of Psychology*, 43:2-5.

Stark, Oded and Jakubek, Marcin. 2013. "Integration as a catalyst for assimilation," *International Review of Economics and Finance*, 28:62-70.

Suinn, Richard M, Rickard-Figueroa, Kathryn, Lew, Sandra and Vigil, Patricia. 1987. "The Suinn-Lew Asian Self-Identity Acculturation Scale: An initial report," *Educational & Psychological Measurement*, vol.47, no.2, pp.401-407, accessed August 6, 2011, http://www.antiochne.edu/multiculturalcenter/test/test_titles32/.

Suinn, Richard M, Ahuna, Carol and Khoo, Gillian. 1992. "The Suinn-Lew Asian Self-Identity Acculturation Scale: Concurrent and factorial validation," *Educational and Psychological Measurement*, 52:1041-1046.

Syed, Jawad and Kramar, Robin. 2010. "What is the Australian model for managing cultural diversity?", *Personnel Review*, 39:96-115.

Syed, Jawad and Murray P. 2009. "Combating the English language deficit: the labour market experiences of migrant women in Australia," *Human Resource Management Journal*, 19:413-432.

Trickett, Edison and Birman, Dina. 2005. "Acculturation, school context and school outcomes: Adaptation of refugee adolescents from the former Soviet Union," *Psychology in the Schools*, 42:pp.27-38.

Tsuda, Takeuki. 2012. "Ethnic return migration and the nation-state: encouraging the diaspora to return 'home,'" *Nations and Nationalism*, 16:616-636.

Valenta, Marko. 2009. "Selective networking as identity project: the social integration of first generation immigrants in Norway," *International Migration & Integration,* 10:117-195.

Verkuyten, Maykel. 1994. "Ethnic self-identification & psychological well-being among minority youth in the Netherlands," *International Journal of Adolescence & Youth,* 5:19-34.

Verkuyten, Maykel. 2008. "Life satisfaction among ethnic minorities: the role of discrimination and group identification", *Social Indicators Research,* 89:391-404.

Verkuyten, Maykel. 2010. "Assimilation ideology and situational well-being among ethnic minority members," *Journal of Experimental Social Psychology,* vol.46, pp.269-275.

Worrell, Frank C and Gardner-Kitt, Donna L. 2006. "The Relationship between racial & ethnic identity in black adolescents: The cross racial identity scale & the multi-group ethnic identity measure, identity," *An International Journal of Theory & Research,* 6:293-315.

Wu, Chia-Huei and Yao, Grace. 2007. "Examining the relationship between global and domain measures of quality of life by three factor structure models," *Social Indicators Research,* 84:189-202.

Wu, Zhen, Schimmele, Christoph M and Hou, Feng. 2012. "Self-perceived integration of immigrants and their children," *Canadian Journal of Sociology,* 37:381-408.

Wulff, Maryann and Dharmalingam, Arunachalam. 2008. "Retaining skilled migrants in regional Australia: The role of social connectedness," *International Migration & Integration,* 9:147-160.

Yoon, Eunju and Lee, Richard M. 2010. "Importance of social connectedness as a moderator in Korean immigrants' subjective well-being," *Asian American Journal of Psychology,* 1:93-105.

Zhou, Min. 1997. "Segmented assimilation: issues, controversies & recent research on the new second generation," *International Migration Review,* 31:975-1008.

Ziguras, Christopher and Fang-Law, Siew. 2006. "Recruiting international students as skilled migrants: the global 'skills race' as accessed from Australia & Malaysia," *Globalisation, Societies & Education,* 4:59-76.

In: Psychological Well-Being
Editor: Rafael Bowers

ISBN: 978-1-63484-354-6
© 2016 Nova Science Publishers, Inc.

Chapter 4

WELL-BEING, HEALTH STATUS AND CULTURE: FINDINGS FROM THE MILAN STUDY

Enzo Grossi[1,] and Giorgio Tavano Blessi[2,†]*
[1]Ce.P.Ci.T. Centro Studi sui Problemi della Città e del Territorio,
Department of Sociology and Economic Law, Bologna University,
[2]Department of Sociology and Economic Law,
Bologna University, Bologna, Italy,
Faculty of Arts, Markets, and Heritage, IULM University, Milan, Italy

ABSTRACT

Health status and well-being are individual complex dimensions where wide ranges of elements interact. With the present contribution, we aim to question how urban and individual objective and subjective elements will affect health status and well-being, investigating in particular the possible relationship between cultural and leisure elements and individual health conditions. The evaluation is based on research undertaken in 2010 on a statistically representative sample of Italy's Milan population. The study is aiming to assess the determinants of psychological well-being and perceived health status through a vast assembly of variables covering socio-demographic and health-related data that are widely recognized as relevant determinants in the literature. In addition fifteen cultural and community activities have been scrutinized in order to weight the incidence of these elements in relation to the general evaluation framework. The results show that the multidimensional construct of subjective well-being is extremely complex and results from a dynamic interplay of several physical, social and environmental descriptors. Furthermore, individual health status perception will be affected significantly by leisure and cultural activities.

* 40126, Bologna, Italy Tel: +39 051 20 9 2877, Tel. +39-02-21772808, E-mail: Enzo.Grossi@bracco.com.
† +39 051 20 9 2877, E-mail: g.tavano@iuav.it.

INTRODUCTION

Culture has been long recognized as an important component of individual and social development, and in the last twenty years a growing scientific literature has investigated the role and impact of culture in both theoretical and/or empirical research. Starting in the 1980s, the cultural dimension has been advocated within the development process both at a tangible level, e.g., urban areas and neighborhoods, or at an intangible level, such as in the case of individuals and social dimension, while policy lines and action have been directed at the possible exploitation of this resource with the aim of achieving different goals ranging from economic to environmental issues, and quite recently in relation to increased individual well-being and health conditions. In this perspective, improvements in cultural infrastructure, access to cultural activities and cultural policies targeted at capability building, just to give a few examples, seem to bring about substantial beneficial effects at the economic, environmental, social and human levels, thus qualifying as major tools for local and urban development (Tavano Blessi et al., 2012). The need to define a development strategy focusing on the accumulation of culture-related assets is ever more frequently seen as a political priority and as a direct way to generate social and economic value for spaces and individual; existing studies provide evidence that culture may have significant impact on key aspects of human life such as health and perceived well-being.

In regards to the specific relationship between culture and individual philological and physical conditions, it is quite commonly perceived that this element will be important and anyone would be willing to negate the social, psychological and health-based influence of culture, and thus the indirect impact that this resource may have on individual dimensions such as longevity or life satisfaction. However, reasoning about culture as a possible determinant of physical and psychological individual conditions, such as producing a direct outcome in terms of increasing the health and well-being dimensions, is a less uncontroversial point. This is due to the fact that, compared to other health-related factors such as, to name just a few, exposure to a polluted environment as is the case of most Western urban areas, stress endured in the work place, habits and addiction to alcohol and smoking, and genetic endowment. Yet also in comparison to socio-economic features such as level of income or quality of social relationships, culture is often intuitively judged to have a relatively minor impact on significant quantities such as life expectation or (suitably measured) well-being. At most, there may be the recognition that some of these major factors such as dietary and smoking habits can be at least in part culturally determined. Again, concern for culture is instrumental to the fact that it is revealed to act upon other, intrinsically relevant matters.

This article aims to provide a possible estimation of the contribution provided by cultural participation on individual conditions, and has two manifold objectives: firstly, to provide a possible ranking of psychological well-being determinants in the group of objective and subjective elements affecting well- being and, secondly, to define the incidence of these in modulating individual health status perception.

In order to achieve the above aims, we have employed the MMWP – Milan Municipality Well Being Project – database. The study undertaken in 2010 aimed to assess the determinants of psychological well-being among a vast assembly of variables covering socio-demographic and health-related data which are widely recognized as relevant determinants of well-being: gender, age, schooling, civil status, monthly income level, presence/absence of diseases, 15 different leisure activities, dietary patterns and BMI, in a representative sample of the general population consisting of 1,000 inhabitants. Subjective well being was measured on the Psychological General Well-Being Scale, which gives a global index of psychological well-being ranging from 0 (lowest level of well-being) to 110 (highest level of well-being). The survey was conducted with the assistance of Doxa, an Italian pollster company, through telephone interviews, according to the Computer Aided Telephone Interview system.

Thanks to the opportunity provided by supervised artificial neural networks, the evidence shows that the multidimensional construct of subjective well-being and also health status perception is extremely complex and results from a dynamic interplay of several physical, social and environmental descriptors. Furthermore, not only individual psychological well-being but also health status perception will be affected significantly by leisure and cultural activities.

1. THEORETICAL BACKGROUND

In the last 20 years, researchers have tried to investigate the possible contribution of cultural participation on individual psychological health. A literature review of the main evidence-based contributions seems to supply clear and concrete confirmation that participation in cultural activities may act toward the establishment of better individual well-being conditions. One of the first attempts made to measure the impact of art on the quality of life of individuals has been undertaken by Michalos (Michalos, 2005). Through a mailed-out questionnaire sent to a sample of 315 adults (18+) of Prince George residents (CA), it emerged that the arts have a very small impact on QOL, and could only explain from 5% to 11% of the variance in four plausible measures of the self-perceived quality of respondents' lives. In a second research drive, Kalhke (Michal and Kalhke, 2008) has tried to widen the research using a larger sample, and over 10,000 questionnaires were distributed to households forming part of five different communities of British Columbia Province (CA). A total of 1027 questionnaires were completed and returned, and evidence showed that that arts-related activities, and the satisfaction obtained from those activities, had relatively little impact on the respondents' perceived or experienced quality of life. In the same year, 2008 Nummela et al. (Nummela et al., 2008) undertook a postal survey of 2,800 residents in Southern Finland. The results of the study showed significant associations between certain cultural practices and psychological well-being, in particular music practices, in a sample of elderly (65-75) Swedes. One of the major deficiencies in the research studies described above has to do with the weak statistical significance of the outcomes, given the fact the sample under investigation was not statistically representative. The gap opened by the absence of a statistical representative sample has been closed thanks to Grossi et al. (Grossi et al., 2011a, Grossi et al., 2011b). The authors have explored the relationship between cultural access and individual psychological well-being thanks to a statistically representative sample of Italian residents in order to provide a possible estimation of the impact of cultural participation upon subjective perceptions of well-being. The results suggest that culture has a relevant role as a well-being determinant, in that a selected subset of cultural variables turns out to be among the best predictors of psychological well-being, ranking from second to third position in the element greatly affecting the individual quality of life.

The literature contains a number of studies that also seem to provide solid evidence (including clinical) concerning the role played by participation in cultural activities and physical health. Starting from the contribution of culture attendance and life expectation, a 14-year longitudinal study undertaken by Koonlaan et al. (Koonlaan et al., 2000) between the 1980s and 1990s has showed that cultural participation such as attending museums, theatres and exhibitions improves individual chances of survival in longitudinal samples. In addition, the study found an important element regarding those rarely attending various kinds of cultural events or visiting cultural institutions; these showed a higher mortality risk in comparison to those attending them more often.

In addition to the previous study, Hyppa et al. (Hyppa et al., 2006) undertook a study concerning cultural participation as a predictor of survival. The research was based on a sample of 8000 Finns, and with the data gathered it has been possible to observe a direct correlation between cultural frequency and mortality risk, with a lower risk of mortality observed among frequent attendees of cultural events. Furthermore, Väänänen et al. (Väänänen et al., 2009) managed a longitudinal study based on 12,173 employees of all grades, from blue-collar workers to management grade, of the major Finland forestry company. Researches collected data from a questionnaire submitted in terms of socio-demographic factors (including age, marital status, educational level, social contact, smoking, alcohol consumption and exercise), stress, diabetes and hypertension, investigating also individual engagement in socially-shared culture- and arts-related activities on a daily to yearly scale (every day vs. once a year). The study scheduled two additional waves, re-surveying the original cohort in 1996 and 2000. The results showed that the risk of all-cause mortality and deaths, from cardiovascular to external causes (such as suicides, accidents and violence-related deaths) was found to be reduced in those regularly engaging with culture.

These preliminary findings indicate that more research should be undertaken in order to gather more fundamental evidence and reach better understanding concerning the influence of the cultural dimension on self-reported psychological individual and health-status perception. This contribution seeks to bridge this gap, with particular focus on the relationship between cultural participation, the cultural experience undergone by individuals and the two aforementioned dimensions. Should we find that cultural habits are indeed effective predictors of psychological well-being and also a powerful instrument in relation to health status conditions, then, combining these results with the already existing evidence about the impact of culture on life expectancy, we would have a promising empirical platform to construct a model that illustrates in some depth and explains this connection, thereby providing further insights and avenues for new empirical research.

2. METHODOLOGY

We have re-analyzed the cross-sectional survey which has been conducted on a relatively large sample (n = 1000) of residents living in the municipality of Milan, with the aim of assessing how different urban well-being determinants scrutinized in the literature review will affect individual psychological well-being and also health-status perception, and in this respect how the modes and intensity of access to cultural experiences will promote these elements. The survey has been conducted with the assistance of DOXA, an Italian pollster company, through telephone interviews, according to the CATI system. A multi-step random sampling method has been adopted to draw a large representative sample from the Milanese adult population (15 + years) with a telephone home landline. The survey has collected information covering socio-demographic and health-related data that are widely recognized as relevant determinants of well-being: gender, age, schooling (no schooling, primary education, secondary education, high school, college), civil status (single, married, widow, divorced/separated), monthly income level (<1.000 Euros, 1.000-1.500 Euros, 1.500- 2.500 Euros, >2.500 Euros, no data) and the presence/absence of diseases from the following list: Hypertension, Heart Attack, Heart Disease, Diabetes, Angina, Cancer, Allergy, Arthritis, lower back pain, lung diseases, skin diseases, deafness, limited functionality of the arms or legs, blindness, psychiatric disorders and depression.

In addition, fifteen different variables related to cultural access have been added, after a scrutiny of the relevant literature pertaining to the cultural field; the totality of these variables are considered as being a proxy of individual levels of 'cultural access'. These variables are: Jazz music concerts, Classical music concerts, Opera/ballet, Theatre, Museums, Rock concerts, Disco dance, Painting exhibitions, Social activity, Watching sport, Practicing Sport, Reading of Novels, Poetry reading and Cinema and Local community development.

Each subject surveyed in the study had to go through a structured questionnaire where the frequency of access to all the activities previously listed (how many times in a year did you perform a given activity?) was researched. The intensity of access to a specific cultural activity could thus be measured on a quantitative scale through a composite sum of frequencies, expressing therefore the number of days in a year in which at least one cultural activity was present.

2.1. The Psychological General Well-being Index (PGWBI)

The level of subjective psychological well-being has been measured by means of an index that has been validated by decades of clinical practice: The Psychological General Well-Being Index (PGWBI). The PGWBI has been developed as a tool to measure self-representations of intra-personal affective or emotional states reflecting a sense of subjective well-being or distress, and thus it captures what we might call a subjective perception of well-being (Dupuy 1990).

The original PGWBI consists of 22 self-administered items, rated on a 6-point scale, which assess the psychological and general well-being of respondents in six health-related quality-of-life (HRQoL) domains: anxiety, depression, positive well-being, self-control, general health and vitality. Each item has six possible scores (from 0 to 5), referring to the last four weeks of the subject's lifetime. Each domain is defined by a minimum of 3 to a maximum of 5 items. The scores for all domains can be summarized into a global summary score, which reaches a theoretical maximum of 110 points, representing the best achievable level of well-being (Dupuy 1990), a sort of 'state of bliss.'

In this survey, we have utilized the Italian version of PGWBI, which has been already utilized in two previous waves of research on the well-being of the Italian population (Grossi et al., 2006), and we have added questions regarding cultural access, such as frequency of participation in culture-related activities, considered in the present research.

2.2. Data Analysis

The sample selected for analysis (n = 1000) is relatively large, as required by the nature of the research question. This allows enough variability to make meaningful inferences as to the predictive capacity of the single variables. Univariate analysis has been carried out with standard statistical tests (Pearson linear correlation index; unpaired t-test to compare means). A P value of < 0.05 has been accepted as being significant.

Supervised artificial neural networks have been employed to build up a predictive model able to identify participants defined as being in a distressed state (PGWBI score range of first decile from those defined to be in a state of well-being (PGWBI score range of 10th decile) starting from 46 input variables, after a pre-processing phase employing a particular evolutionary system called "TWIST" developed at Semeion Research Centre, Rome (Buscema, 2005). The TWIST system is specifically designed for sorting out the most relevant variables for the sake of prediction/classification, removing redundant and noisy information from complex data sets.

According the distribution of the PGWBI score, we divided the population in deciles. The first and tenth deciles were used as the target for the neural network and thus with a view to providing insight into our hypothesis.

3. RESULTS

Sample Description

The sample consists of 1000 of citizen selected randomly from the general population and has been carefully described in a previous publication (Grossi et al., 2013).

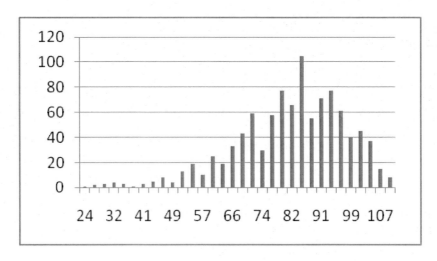

Figure 1a. PGWBI score distribution.

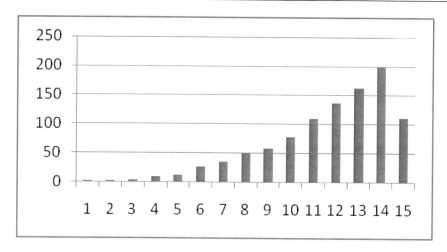

Figure 1b. HSP score distribution.

Figure 1a shows the distribution of PGWBI in the population and Figure 1b shows the distribution of the population in relation to the perceived health score. The health-status perception-HSP score is the result of the sum of three items of PGWBI standard scale and ranges from 0 to 15.

Table 1 shows the comparison of the two groups relevant to first and tenth decile of PGWBI and perceived health-status distribution. Two extremes subsets of records were selected in both cases, in relation to PGWBI distress (N = 98; PGWBI score range 0 - 60) and well-being (N = 104; PGWBI score range 99 - 110), and in relation to HSP - health status perception, poor health perception (N = 92; score range 0-7) and very good health perception (N = 112; score = 15). The variables with a statistically significant difference between the two groups are marked in yellow.

ANN Analysis

The starting point of our ANN methodology is to apply the already mentioned TWIST system (see Appendix 1) to process the full data set with a view to understanding those variables that really matter in predicting both targets, the PGWBI and health-status perception HPS. In the case of PGWBI, the process led to the selection of 17 variables, which together provide a sufficient statistic for the problem under study. The list of such variables is reported in Table 2. In the case of health-status perception, the system selected 14 out of 45 independent variables, as listed in Table 2.

Concerning the cultural dimension, the system selected 7 variables in the PGWBI example and 6 variables in the HSP example belonging to cultural participation All variables listed have been independently selected in the relevant informational base by the TWIST system.

Figures 2a and 2b show the AUC ROC curve of goodness of prediction of the target variables (PGWBI and HSP). In the case of PGWBI and HSP targets, the mean had a very good value, 0.79 and 0.85.

Table 1. Statistical significance of variables considered in the HSP (poor health/good health) and PGWBI (distress and well-being)

Feature	Poor health (n= 92) Mean	IC 95%	Good health (n = 112) Mean	IC 95%	Distress (n = 98) Mean	IC 95%	Well-being (n = 104) Mean	IC 95%
Male	**35,87%**	**9,99%**	**62,50%**	**9,11%**	**31,63%**	**9,37%**	**58,65%**	**9,62%**
Female	**64,13%**	**9,99%**	**37,50%**	**9,11%**	**68,37%**	**9,37%**	**41,35%**	**9,62%**
Age	**61,73**	**3,09**	**46,05**	**3,63**	57,01	3,19	53,88	3,60
Education level	**2,91**	**0,39**	**3,95**	**0,30**	**3,04**	**0,36**	**3,83**	**0,32**
Blue-collar	**75,00%**	**9,02%**	**53,57%**	**9,38%**	63,27%	9,71%	64,42%	9,36%
White-collar	**25,00%**	**9,02%**	**46,43%**	**9,38%**	36,73%	9,71%	35,58%	9,36%
Single	**16,30%**	**7,69%**	**37,50%**	**9,11%**	29,59%	9,20%	25,00%	8,46%
Married	54,35%	10,37%	48,21%	9,40%	47,96%	10,07%	64,42%	9,36%
Widower	**19,57%**	**8,26%**	**5,36%**	**4,24%**	13,27%	6,84%	5,77%	4,56%
Divorced	9,78%	6,19%	8,93%	5,36%	9,18%	5,82%	4,81%	4,18%
Number members family	**2,40**	**0,19**	**2,88**	**0,22**	2,60	0,21	2,83	0,23
Income don't know	38,04%	10,11%	46,43%	9,38%	38,78%	9,82%	43,27%	9,68%
Income < 1000	11,96%	6,76%	8,04%	5,11%	9,18%	5,82%	8,65%	5,49%
Income_1000_1500	18,48%	8,08%	13,39%	6,41%	23,47%	8,54%	12,50%	6,46%
Income_1500_2500	17,39%	7,89%	12,50%	6,22%	14,29%	7,05%	10,58%	6,01%
Income > 2500	14,13%	7,25%	19,64%	7,47%	14,29%	7,05%	25,00%	8,46%
Cinema	**1,15**	**0,32**	**2,07**	**0,31**	**1,32**	**0,32**	**1,85**	**0,31**
Theatre	0,78	0,27	1,04	0,24	0,66	0,26	0,96	0,24
Opera- ballet	0,74	0,31	0,54	0,21	0,54	0,26	0,49	0,18
Classic music concerts	0,53	0,27	0,74	0,26	0,47	0,24	0,78	0,26
Painting exhibitions	0,80	0,30	0,94	0,23	0,68	0,25	0,90	0,22
Museums	1,00	0,29	1,36	0,25	0,94	0,26	1,37	0,25
Cinema d'essai	0,61	0,31	0,58	0,24	0,35	0,23	0,48	0,22

Feature	Poor health (n= 92)		Good health (n = 112)		Distress (n = 98)		Well-being (m = 104)	
	Mean	IC 95%	Mean	IC 95%	Mean	IC 95%	Mean	IC 95%
Novels reading	1,74	0,34	1,94	0,31	1,58	0,32	1,93	0,32
Poetry reading	0,73	0,29	0,53	0,23	0,64	0,27	0,65	0,25
Disco dance	**0,66**	**0,33**	**1,11**	**0,32**	**0,45**	**0,26**	**0,43**	**0,24**
Sport practice	**1,79**	**0,41**	**2,79**	**0,33**	**1,78**	**0,39**	**2,52**	**0,37**
Rock concerts	0,68	0,31	0,70	0,24	0,58	0,25	0,53	0,20
Jazz concerts	0,60	0,32	0,48	0,24	0,41	0,26	0,36	0,20
Watching sports games	0,62	0,32	0,96	0,28	0,51	0,28	0,70	0,25
Volunteering	1,00	0,38	0,87	0,30	0,78	0,32	1,02	0,32
Local community support	0,85	0,33	0,76	0,29	0,65	0,30	0,67	0,27
Overall cultural consumption	81,11	24,69	119,83	23,22	62,54	18,27	136,00	28,73
Class of cultural consumption	**1,59**	**0,23**	**2,26**	**0,16**	**1,51**	**0,20**	**2,16**	**0,19**
Cultural consumption = zero	**18,48%**	**8,08%**	**2,68%**	**3,04%**	**19,39%**	**7,97%**	**4,81%**	**4,18%**
Cultural index 1-25	32,61%	9,76%	16,96%	7,06%	29,59%	9,20%	25,00%	8,46%
Cultural consumption 26-100	20,65%	8,43%	31,25%	8,72%	31,63%	9,37%	19,23%	7,70%
Cultural consumption > 100	**28,26%**	**9,38%**	**49,11%**	**9,40%**	**19,39%**	**7,97%**	**50,96%**	**9,77%**
Number of concomitant diseases	**4,14**	**0,51**	**1,18**	**0,41**	**3,36**	**0,46**	**1,22**	**0,36**

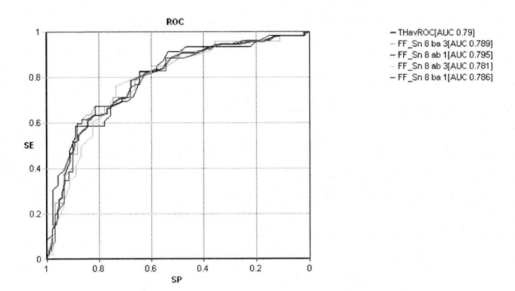

Figure 2a. Performance of neural networks in distinguishing between distress and well-being (PGWBI).

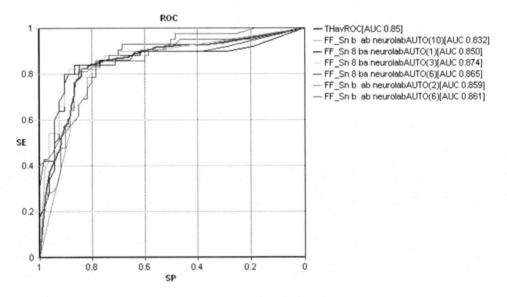

Figure 2b. Performance of neural networks in distinguishing among poor health and very good health (HSP).

During the training phase, it is possible to monitor the complex pattern of the neural network computation, which determines the relative importance of each variable in enabling the system to effectively predict the target variable. In other words, this analysis provides us with what we may call the 'input relevance' of each variable. Input relevance is expressed as a quantity on an arbitrary scale proportional to the importance of the contribution of that variable to the implicit statistical model. Once this analysis is carried out, it is interesting and quite surprising to ascertain that, according to average input relevance (as computed in both A-B and B-A tests), we find that culturally-related variables firmly sit within the top scoring variables; that is to say, certain forms of cultural access prove to be quite important predictors of actual PGWBI and HSP levels. In the case of PGWBI the most important implied variables are: Practicing sport, Novel Reading, Cinema, and Theatre. In the case of HSP these are: Practicing sport, Cinema d'essai, Novel Reading, Cinema, and Theatre.

Table 2. Variables selected by TWIST in the PGWBI and HSP domains

PGWBI domain	HSP domain
Male	Male
Female	Age
Age	Education
Education	Family components
Blue collar	Income < 1000 €
White collar	Concomitant diseases
Single	Volunteering activities
Widower	Watching sport games
Income 1000-1500 €	Cinema
Income 1500-2000 €	Theatre
Cinema	Opera - Ballet
Opera – Ballet	Cultural consumption 26 – 100 year
Rock concert	Practicing sport
Cultural consumption = 0	Cinema d'essai
Cultural consumption 26 – 100 year	
Cultural consumption > 100 year	
Practicing sport	

Evaluation

Only recently has the cultural dimension been advocated as a possible tool for enhancing individual and social development, and has the developmental function of this resource in relation to individual health perception and well-being been endorsed thanks to certain empirical studies undertaken from 2000. Our study has tried to estimate the role of cultural participation in relation to the extent of two specific measures: the influence upon perceived health status and on individual psychological well-being. While previous studies have tried to evaluate the net effect of culture on the two aforementioned dimensions, the strength of this study is based on the statistical representative sample and on the adoption of a predictive approach to data evaluation, which allow research to determine precisely the weight of cultural resources in the bundle of health and well-being determinants as highlighted in the literature. The results show that cultural participation may be considered relevant as a determinant of health-status perception and psychological well-being, if compared also to the total of non-cultural variables that are reported in table 2. This is an important finding arising from this study, which allows the researcher to challenge the approaches of current public health strategies, and to design and implement new welfare policies in a pro-active perspective.

Table 3. Ranking of the major determinants in the PGWBI and HSP domains

Rank	Variable
1	Disease
2	Income
3	Culture
4	Age
5	Education
6	Gender
7	Employment
8	Geography

The relationship between cultural participation, health-status perception and subjective well-being, however, is likely to be quite subtle and elusive, at least when investigated by means of conventional univariate, bivariate or multivariate statistical analyses. Cultural habits are manifold and are rarely reducible to single-channel patterns: People with cultural interests tend to allocate their time, attention and energy to several different activities. Therefore, if one wants to trace how cultural access contributes to improve both elements, there is a great necessity to rely upon tools that allow the researcher to take into account this inextricable multi-dimensional association between variables that translate the typical behavioral patterns of (cultural) choice. The advanced ANN techniques adopted in this paper, allow us to do precisely this and consequently to evaluate which is the best bundle of variables to explain the variability of the target and the internal ranking of such variables in terms of relative predictive power. There is clear evidence that cultural access has a definite impact on individual health-status perception and psychological well-being, and moreover that culture provides some of the most effective predictors of well-being (see table 3).

How can we make sense of these results? As noted in the previous sections, a number of indications suggest that arts in general, but more specifically cultural participation, may greatly affect several realms of our lives. Arts participation in addition to experiencing culture such as behaving in such a way as to be exposed in a active (e.g., playing an instrument) or passive mode (e.g., attending to an exhibition or going to a cinema) on a somewhat methodical basis can have physical, mental and social effects. Our results supply new elements in depicting the individual's health picture, in that the relevance of cultural participation on individual health-status perception and psychological well-being directs policy makers towards the possible establishment of new welfare policies by addressing individual and social issues such as human deprivation and degenerative illnesses, and with the aim of increasing the well-being ecosystem framework. In this perspective, the urban environment will be the privileged context where this hypothesis may be tested, given the density of cultural opportunities and individuals, and which should provide new evidence in relation to the contribution of the cultural dimension in the previously described dimensions. A recent study (Tavano Blessi et al., 2015) has noted that there is direct correlation between the stock of cultural resources, cultural participation and the psychological condition of well-being in urban dwellers.

One of the reason can be ascribed to the social impact of culture, which relates to the mechanism that arts and culture may be considered as an engine of individual and social commitment, fostering new forms of sociability, which is likely to favor emotionally-based effects such as community engagement and empowerment, which impact substantially on subjective well-being.

Our results thus tend to suggest that the quality of cultural participation alone may generate powerful developmental effects, irrespective of the instrumental economic impact of cultural activity and that the public health dimension is of primary importance in this respect. Seen from our perspective, instrumental approaches to cultural development may cause a lack of social sustainability and welfare losses in that they discourage individual, intrinsically motivated participation in favor of opportunistically motivated appropriation of its economic effects (Tavano Blessi et al., 2014).

There are two strengths to this study; one is the sample, which is statistically representative of the population and the second is the predictive approach, which should allow us to continuing reasoning within the stream of research already established in terms of causation and not of simple association. It is also important to stress the limit of this study, which has to do with the fact that this is a cross-sectional piece of research, and not a longitudinal one, thus not allowing for an evaluation of dynamic impacts. Moreover, our analysis is based on individual statements and memories of one's cultural habits, which cannot be checked, for example, through a memory card recording the real participation in culture-related activities, a fact that would allow us a more objective assessment of the relationship between actual cultural access and psychological well-being. Analogous remarks can be made with reference to subjects self-reporting their (perceived) diseases. It is therefore necessary to develop more sophisticated observation tools and devices to capture the required information while minimizing as far as possible informational noise. This would be a much-needed improvement and an exciting challenge for research to come.

CONCLUSION

The construct of subjective well-being is multidimensional and extremely complex, resulting from a dynamic interplay of several physical, social and environmental descriptors. In much the same way, individual health-status perception is related to a number of bio-psycho-social factors. Advanced artificial adaptive systems are able to connect available personal descriptors to low and high subjective well-being and low and high health status, the former being more difficult to predict compared to the latter. Leisure activities and cultural participation play an important role both in psychological general well-being and in health-status perception, offering a net contribution distinct from that related to traditional socio-demographic determinants.

APPENDIX 1. LIST OF DISEASES INCLUDED IN THE QUESTIONNAIRE

Hypertension
Heart Attack
Heart Diseases
Diabetes
Angina
Cancer
Allergy
Arthritis
Low Back Pain
Lung Diseases
Skin Diseases
Deafness
Limited Arms and/or Legs Functionality
Blindness
Psychiatric Disturbances
Depression

REFERENCES

Buscema, M. (2005). *TWIST Software*. Semeion Software #32, Semeion, Rome.

Dupuy, H.J. (1990). The Psychological General Well-being (PGWB) Index. In N.K. Wenger, M.E. Mattson, C.D. Furburg, J. Elinson (Eds.) *Assessment of Quality of Life in Clinical Trials of Cardiovascular Therapies.* (New York: Le Jacq Publishing), 170-83.

Grossi, E., Groth, N., Mosconi, P., Cerutti, R., Pace, F., Compare, A., & Apolone, G. (2006), Development and validation of the short version of the Psychological General Well-Being Index (PGWB-S). *Health Qual Life Outcomes*, 4(1), 88- 96.

Grossi, E., Sacco, P.,L,. Tavano Blessi, G., & Cerutti. R. (2011a) The impact of culture on the individual subjective well-being of the Italian population: An exploratory study. *Applied Research in Quality of Life*, 6(4), 387-410.

Grossi, E., Tavano Blessi, G., Sacco, P.L., & Buscema, M. (2011b). The interaction between culture, health and psychological well-being: Data mining from the Italian Culture and Well-Being Project. *Journal of Happiness Studies* 13(2): 129-148.

Grossi, E., Compare, A., Lonardi, C., Cerutti, R., Callus, E., & Niero, M. (2013). Gender-related effect of cultural participation in psychological well-being: Indications from the well-being project in the Municipality of Milan. *Social indicators research*, *114*(2), 255-271.

Hyppa, M. T. Maki, J. Impivaara, O. Aromaa, A. (2006). Leisure Participation Predicts Survival: A Population-Based Study in Finland. *Health Promotion International*, 21, 5-12.

Koonlaan, B.B. Bygren, L.O. Johansson, S.E. (2000). Visiting the Cinema, Concerts, Museums or Art Exhibitions as Determinant of Survival: A Swedish Fourteen-Year Cohort Follow-up. *Scandinavian Journal of Public Health*, 28, 174-178.

Michalos, A.C. (2005). Arts and the Quality of Life: An Exploratory Study. *Social Indicators Research*, 71, 11-59.

Michalos, A.C. Kahlke, P.M. (2008). Impact of Arts-Related Activities on the Perceived Quality of Life. *Social Indicators Research*, 89, 193-258.

Nummela, O. Sulander, T. Rahkonen, O. Uutela, A. (2008). Associations of Self-Rated Health With Different Forms of Leisure Activities Among Ageing People. *International Journal of Public Health*, 53, 227-235.

Tavano Blessi, G., Tremblay, D.G., Pilati, T., Sandri, M., (2012) 'New trajectories in urban regeneration processes: Cultural capital as source of human and social capital accumulation. Evidence from the case of Tohu in Montreal', *Cities*, 29, pp. 397–407.

Tavano Blessi, G., Grossi, E., Sacco, P. L., Pieretti, G., & Ferilli, G. (2014). Cultural participation, relational goods and individual subjective well-being: some empirical evidence. *Review of Economics & Finance*, 4, 33-46.

Tavano Blessi, G., Grossi, E., Sacco, P. L., Pieretti, G., & Ferilli, G. (2016). The contribution of cultural participation to urban well-being. A comparative study in Bolzano/Bozen and Siracusa, Italy. *Cities*, 50, 216-226.

Väänänen, A., Murray, M., Koskinen, A., Vahtera, J., Kouvonen, A., & Kivimäki, M. (2009). Engagement in cultural activities and cause-specific mortality: prospective cohort study. *Preventive medicine*, 49(2), 142-147.

In: Psychological Well-Being
Editor: Rafael Bowers

ISBN: 978-1-63484-354-6
© 2016 Nova Science Publishers, Inc.

Chapter 5

EMOTIONAL INTELLIGENCE IN ADOLESCENTS FROM 13 TO 16 YEARS: EXPLANATORY VARIABLES

Maite Garaigordobil and Ainize Peña*
Faculty of Psychology, University of the Basque Country,
Donostia-San Sebastián, Spain

ABSTRACT

Emotional Intelligence (EI) is associated with better performance at work, greater well-being, physical health, and higher quality of interpersonal relationships... Given the importance of EI in human life, the study had three main objectives: (1) to analyze sex differences in EI; (2) to explore the concomitant relations between EI and various behavioral, emotional, cognitive, and physical factors (positive and negative social behaviors, behavioral problems, empathy, happiness, cognitive strategies to resolve social situations, ability to analyze feelings, personality traits, state-trait anger, anger expression, and psychosomatic symptoms); and (3) to identify predictors of high EI. This study was conducted with a sample of 148 Spanish adolescents aged between 13 and 16 (45.3% boys and 54.7% girls). The study uses a descriptive, comparative, and correlational cross-sectional methodology. In order to assess the variables, we administered 10 assessment instruments with psychometric guarantees of reliability and validity. The results of the analysis of variance only revealed sex differences in interpersonal emotional intelligence, with significantly higher scores in females. In the rest of the variables (intrapersonal intelligence, stress management, adaptability, and general mood), and in the Emotional Intelligence Quotient (EIQ; global score that includes all the EI variables), the scores were similar in both sexes. Pearson correlation coefficients suggest that boys and girls with high EIQ were significantly more likely to display many positive social behaviors (social conformity, social sensitivity, help-collaboration, and self-assurance-firmness), many feelings of happiness, personality traits such as conscientiousness, openness, extroversion, agreeableness, and emotional stability, few social anxiety behaviors, and few psychosomatic symptoms. In addition, boys with high EIQ showed many prosocial-leadership behaviors, high empathy, high anger

---

* Corresponding author: Maite Garaigordobil, Faculty of Psychology, University of the Basque Country, Avda. de Tolosa 70, 20018 Donostia-San Sebastián, Spain, Phone: 34-943-015634, Fax: 34-943-015670. Email: maite.garaigordobil@ehu.es.

control-out and anger control-in, few aggressive and antisocial behaviors, few anxiety problems, and a low level of state-anger. Girls with high EIQ had high social adaptation/adjustment, a low level of trait-anger, and low anger expression-in. The results of the regression analyses revealed seven predictors of EIQ that explain 63.7% of the variance: high happiness, high agreeableness, low emotional instability, many help-collaboration behaviors, few psychosomatic symptoms, high anger control-out, and few anxiety problems. The results suggest the importance of implementing programs to promote the development of EI during childhood and adolescence, and the study identifies relevant variables to design these programs.

Keywords: emotional intelligence, adolescence, sex differences correlations, predictors

INTRODUCTION

Emotional Intelligence: Definition and Theoretical Framework of the Study

The idea of Emotional Intelligence (EI) has been present for many years; however, it is in the last two decades when more research has been dedicated to this subject. Different theories have thus emerged, and there is currently no single definition of the concept. In fact, researchers who study EI are divided into three groups according to the perspective from which they understand this construct. EI can be understood as an ability, a trait, or a combination of abilities and traits. According to this classification, EI ability is a cognitive skill related to emotions. Mayer and Salovey (1997) define EI as the "*the capacity to perceive and express emotion, to assimilate emotion in thought, to understand and reason with emotions, and regulate emotion in the self and others.*" Further, *t*rait-EI has been defined as a constellation of emotional perceptions at the lowest levels of the personality hierarchy (Petrides & Furnham, 2001). Finally, the mixed models argue that EI involves both socio-emotional skills and personality traits. As an example of this model, Goleman (1995) defines EI as the *'capacity to recognize one's own feelings, the feelings of others, and to motivate oneself to adequately to deal with one's relationships with others and with oneself".*

This study is based on Bar-On's (1997) theoretical framework. The Bar-On model is a mixed model, as it incorporates personality traits, motivation, self-concept, and so on within the skills of perception, expression, and control of emotions. This model is influenced by different theories such as those of Darwin, Thorndike, Wechsler, and Sifneos. Firstly, Darwin's work on the importance of emotional expression for the survival and adaptation of species (1872/1965) influenced Bar-On's model. In fact, Bar-On attaches great importance to emotional expression and takes into account the emotionally and socially intelligent behaviors resulting from the adaptation posited by Darwin. He is also influenced by Thorndike (1920) and his theory of social intelligence, by Wechsler (1940) and intelligent behavior, and by Sifneos (1967) and alexithymia.

The Bar-On (1997, 2000) model is founded on the competences that attempt to explain how individuals relate to the people around them and to their environment. EI is therefore a set of emotional, personal, and social factors that influence people's ability to adapt to the pressures and demands of their environment (Bar-On, 1997, 2000, 2006). EI influences people's emotional well-being and is related to success in life. Emotionally intelligent people are able to recognize and express their emotions, understand themselves, actualize their potential, lead a healthy, happy life, understand how other people feel, and establish and maintain satisfactory, responsible interpersonal relations without becoming dependent. These people are generally optimistic, flexible, and realistic. They are successful in solving their problems and dealing with stress without losing control.

The Bar-On model is made up of 5 components: (1) *Intrapersonal Component:* the ability to be aware of and understand one's own emotions, feelings, and ideas. This component covers the following aspects: self-regard, emotional self-awareness, assertiveness, independence and self-actualization; (2) *Interpersonal Component:* the ability to be aware of and understand other people's emotions, feelings, and ideas. This component includes the following abilities: empathy, interpersonal relations, and social responsibility; (3) *Adaptability Component:* the ability to be open to changes of feelings depending on the situation. This component takes in the following aspects: problem-solving, reality testing, and flexibility; (4) *Stress Management Component:* the ability to handle stress and control one's emotions. This component involves stress tolerance and impulse control; and (5) *General Mood Component:* the ability to feel and express positive emotions and to be optimistic. This component covers the aspects of happiness and optimism.

According to Bar-On, these 5 components involve 15 factors: (1) *Self-regard:* the ability to look within and perceive, understand, and accept oneself; (2) *Emotional self-awareness:* the ability to be aware of, identify, and understand one's own emotions, which involves recognizing and differentiating emotions; (3) *Assertiveness/Self-expression:* the ability to express one's feelings and beliefs and to stand up for one's rights; (4) *Independence:* the ability to be self-reliant and free from emotional dependency on others; (5) *Empathy:* the ability to be aware of, understand, and be sensitive to how others feel; (6) *Social responsibility:* the ability to identify with ones' social group and cooperate constructively with others; (7) *Interpersonal relations:* the ability to establish and maintain mutually satisfying relationships and relate well with others; (8) *Stress tolerance:* the ability to manage emotions effectively and constructively; (9) *Impulse control:* the ability to control emotions effectively and constructively (i.e., the ability to resist or delay an impulse); (10) *Reality testing:* the ability to objectively validate one's and feelings and thinking with external reality; (11) *Flexibility:* the ability to adapt and adjust one's feelings and thinking to new situations; (12) *Problem solving:* the ability to effectively solve problems of a personal and interpersonal nature; (13) *Self-actualization:* the ability to strive to achieve personal goals and actualize one's potential; (14) *Optimism:* the ability to be positive and look at the brighter side of life; and (15) *Happiness/Well-being:* the ability to feel content with oneself, with others, and with life in general.

Emotional Intelligence: Sex Differences

Despite its growing relevance, results about the existence and magnitude of sex differences in EI have been contradictory, and the underlying explanations for the existence of such differences are still unclear. A review of the literature suggests that women obtain higher scores in EI (Day & Carroll, 2004; Extremera, Fernández-Berrocal, & Salovey, 2006; Joseph & Newman, 2010). Hence, women possess greater emotional knowledge, better emotional awareness, and more interpersonal competencies (Ciarrochi, Hynes, & Crittenden, 2005; Hall & Mast, 2008). However, there are also studies finding no sex effect on EI (Fernández-Berrocal, Extremera, & Ramos, 2004; Saklofske, Austin, Galloway, & Davidson, 2007).

Biological as well as social factors have been invoked to explain these sex-based differences. On the one hand, the biological explanation proposes that women's biochemistry is better prepared to consider their own emotions and those of others as an important element for survival (Fernández-Berrocal, Cabello, Castillo, & Extremera, 2012). Likewise, the "extreme male brain theory of autism" proposed by Baron-Cohen (2002) confirms that men and women's brains are structured differently. According to this theory, the female brain is predominantly structured to feel empathy, whereas the male brain predominantly seeks to understand and construct systems. However, the social perspective states that whereas women receive an education biased towards emotional aspects, men are taught to minimize certain emotions related to sadness, guilt, vulnerability, and fear (Sánchez-Núñez, Fernández-Berrocal, Montañés, & Latorre, 2008).

Emotional Intelligence: Correlations with Behavioral, Emotional, Cognitive, and Physical Variables

Many studies have shown that EI is related to *social behavior*. In fact, EI is positively related to positive social behaviors like self-leadership (Furtner, Rauthmann, & Sachse, 2010), prosocial behaviors (Schokman et al., 2014), social attitudes (social sensitivity, help and collaboration, prosocial leadership, and self-assurance-firmness) (Jiménez & López-Zafra, 2013), more peer nominations for prosocial behaviors (Mavroveli & Sánchez-Ruiz, 2011)… and it is negatively related to negative social behaviors like antisocial behavior (Garaigordobil et al., 2013), disruptive behaviors (Esturgó-Deu & Sala-Roca, 2010), peer nominations for antisocial behavior, as well as self-reported bullying behaviors (Mavroveli & Sánchez-Ruiz, 2011).

Other studies have also shown an inverse relationship between EI and *behavioral problems*. A study carried out by Downey, Johnson, Hansen, Birney, and Stough (2010), for example, confirmed that EI was negatively related to aggressive behavior, thought problems, attention problems, anxiety/depression, withdrawal/depression, rule-breaking, somatic behavior, and internalizing and externalizing behaviors. Likewise, in the study conducted by Liau, Liau, Teoh, and Liau, (2003), lower levels of EI were linked with higher levels of internalizing problem behaviors such as stress, depression, and somatic complaints, as well as with higher levels of externalizing problem behaviors such as aggression and delinquency. The results obtained in the study of Poulou (2014) point in the same direction as the others, confirming that students with higher trait-EI were less likely to present emotional and behavioral difficulties. Concerning the *psychosomatic symptoms*, a meta-analysis carried out by Martins, Ramalho, and Morin (2010) confirmed that EI was positively related to better psychosomatic health.

In addition, several studies have evidenced that EI is positively correlated with *empathy* (King, Mara, & DeCicco, 2012; Kokkinos & Kipritsi, 2012) as well as with *happiness* (Chamorro-Premuzic, Bennett & Furnham, 2007; Furnham & Christoforou, 2007; Ruiz-Aranda, Extremera, & Pineda-Galán, 2014; Vergara, Alonso-Alberca, San-Juan, Aldás, & Vozmediano, 2015), and life satisfaction (Di Fabio & Saklofske, 2014).

Likewise, EI is associated with *conflict resolution styles*. In fact, EI is positively related to constructive conflict management (Zeidner & Kloda, 2013), enabling people with high EI to respond appropriately to different problems (Hopkins & Yonker, 2015). In this way, EI positively correlates with collaborative and compromising solution styles and negatively with accommodating and forceful ways of dealing with conflict (Salami, 2010).

Regarding *personality traits*, the vast majority of the studies agree on the fact that EI is positively related to extroversion, openness, agreeableness and conscientiousness, and negatively to neuroticism and emotional instability (Chamorro-Premuzic et al., 2007; Di Fabio & Saklofske, 2014; Petrides et al., 2010; Van der Linden, Tsaousis, & Petrides, 2012). As for *angry feelings*, two studies have proved that EI correlates negatively with anger, that is to say, people with lower levels of EI reported more hostility and angry feelings (Inglés et al., 2014; Şahin-Baltaci & Demir, 2012).

Emotional Intelligence: Predictors

Despite the scarcity of research on the predictors of EI, some works have confirmed that personality traits and sociodemographic characteristics can predict it. Among the sociodemographic characteristics, it was found that being female explains EI (Harrod & Scheer, 2005). Previous research has shown that the level of EI is a significant predictor of well-being (Augusto-Landa, Pulido-Martos, & López-Zafra, 2010) and physical health (Mikolajczak et al., 2015). Kumar and Bhushan (2008) showed that personality (adaptability, sociability, openness, agreeableness, and conscientiousness) predicted self-awareness and self-management within EI. However, when the five personality dimensions were analyzed separately, only conscientiousness predicted EI. In the same vein, the regression analysis conducted by Schulte, Ree, and Carretta (2004) showed that personality (neuroticism, extroversion, openness, agreeableness and conscientiousness) predicted EI.

EI is associated with better performance at work, greater well-being, physical health, higher quality of interpersonal relationships... Given the importance of EI in human life, we need to identify the factors that help to predict it. The identification of explanatory variables will be useful for the designing of programs to promote the development of EI.

Objectives and Hypotheses

With this contextualization, the study had three main objectives: (1) to analyze sex differences in EI; (2) to explore the concomitant relations between EI and various behavioral, emotional, cognitive, and physical factors (positive and negative social behaviors, behavioral problems, empathy, happiness, cognitive strategies to resolve social situations, ability to analyze feelings, personality traits, state-trait anger, anger expression, and psychosomatic symptoms); and (3) to identify predictors of high EI.

Taking into account the results obtained in previous works, three hypotheses are postulated: H1) There will be sex differences in EI, with significantly higher scores in females; H2) Adolescents with high scores in Emotional Intelligence Quotient (EIQ) will display many positive social behaviors (social conformity, social sensitivity, help-collaboration, self-assurance-firmness, prosocial-leadership), high happiness, high empathy, adaptive personality traits (agreeableness and emotional stability), and high anger control, as well as few negative social behaviors (aggressiveness-stubbornness, antisocial behavior, and social anxiety), low levels of trait-anger, and few psychosomatic symptoms; and H3) The following variables will predict high EI: many positive social behaviors and few negative social behaviors, many feelings of happiness, adaptive personality traits (agreeableness and emotional stability), high anger control, and physical health.

METHOD

Participants

This study was conducted with a sample of 148 Spanish adolescents aged between 13 and 16 years. The initial sample included 161 participants, but due to experimental mortality, 13 were excluded (for incorrect completion of instruments). Of these 148 participants, 45.3% were boys ($n = 67$) and 54.7% were girls ($n = 81$). The adolescents studied the third course of Compulsory Secondary Education (equivalent to Grade 9 in American highschool). The socio-demographic characteristics (sex, age, type of school, and parents' level of education) can be seen in Table 1.

There are no significant differences between the number of boys and girls, a greater percentage of 14-year-old participants is confirmed (which is logical because all students are enrolled in third course of secondary education), with a higher percentage of public schools than of private ones (which is also consistent with the population of public and private schools in the Basque Country). Regarding the fathers' studies, the largest percentage has secondary (up to age 16) and primary studies (up to age 12), whereas the mothers mainly have university diplomas (a three-year course of university education), and primary and secondary studies.

Table 1. Socio-demographic characteristics of the sample

		F (%)	χ^2	p
Sex	Males	67 (45.3)	1.32	.250
	Females	81 (54.7)		
Age	13	30 (20.3)	162.32	.000
	14	102 (68.9)		
	15	13 (8.8)		
	16	3 (2.2)		
Type of school	Public	103 (69.6)	22.73	.000
	Private/Subsidized	45 (30.4)		
Father's educational level	Primary level studies	6 (4.4)	45.10	.000
	Secondary level studies	41 (30.1)		
	Higher Secondary studies	49 (36.0)		
	Qualified/diploma	22 (16.2)		
	Bachelor's degree	18 (13.2)		

		F (%)	χ^2	p
Mother's educational level	Primary level studies	8 (5.8)	38.15	.000
	Secondary level studies	37 (26.8)		
	Higher Secondary studies	30 (21.7)		
	Qualified/diploma	48 (34.8)		
	Bachelor's degree	15 (10.9)		

F = frequency; (%) = percentage; χ^2 = Pearson chi square; p = significance.

The selection of schools was random, incorporating public and private centers that represent different socio-economic-cultural levels. The list of schools Bizkaia (Basque Country, northern Spain) of the Education Department of the Basque Government was used to select the sample. The centers on the list were categorized according to the socio-economic-cultural level (low-medium-high). Using a simple random design, one center from each category was selected, and a letter was sent to the headmaster, inviting the collaboration of the school. When the headmaster of a center declined to participate, another center of the same category was randomly selected and the procedure was repeated.

Design and Procedure

The study uses a descriptive, comparative, and correlational cross-sectional methodology. A letter was sent to the headmasters of randomly selected schools from the list of centers in Bizkaia (northern Spain) with an explanation of the project and a request for their collaboration. With those who agreed to collaborate, we conducted an interview to present the project and deliver the informed consent forms for the parents. Informed consent of the parents and teenagers was then requested, the collective administration of the assessment instruments in the classroom followed, and two evaluation sessions were subsequently undertaken by research team members. The study respected the ethical values required in research with human beings (informed consent, confidentiality, etc.), having received a favorable report from the Ethics Committee of the University of the Basque Country (CEISH/146/2012).

Chart 1. Assessment instruments and measured variables

Assessment Instruments	Measured Variables
Emotional Quotient Inventory: Youth Version (EQ-i:YV; Bar-On & Parker, 2000; Spanish adaptation Ferrándiz, Hernández, Bermejo, Ferrando, & Prieto, 2012)	Emotional Intelligence Factors: • Intrapersonal intelligence • Interpersonal intelligence • Stress management • Adaptability • General mood Emotional Intelligence Quotient (global score that includes all the variables)
The "Cuestionario de Actitudes y Estrategias Cognitivas Sociales" (AECS; in English, *Attitudes and Social Cognitive Strategies Questionnaire;* Moraleda, González, & García-Gallo, 2004)	Positive Social Behaviors: • Social conformity • Social sensitivity • Help-collaboration • Self-assurance-firmness • Prosocial leadership Negative Social Behaviors: • Aggressiveness-stubbornness • Dominance • Apathy-withdrawal • Social anxiety

Chart 1. (Continued)

Assessment Instruments	Measured Variables
"Escala de Problemas de Conducta" (EPC; in English, *Behavioral Problems Scale*; Navarro, Peiró, Llácer, & Silva, 1993)	Behavioral Problems • School-academic problems • Antisocial behavior • Shyness-withdrawal • Psychopathological disorders • Anxiety problems • Psychosomatic disorders Positive Social adaptation/adjustment
The Questionnaire Measure of Emotional Empathy (QMEE; Mehrabian & Epstein, 1972)	Empathy
The Oxford Happiness Questionnaire (OHQ; Hills & Argyle, 2002)	Happiness (psychological well-being)
"Cuestionario de Estrategias Cognitivas de Resolución de Situaciones Sociales" (EIS; in English, *Cognitive Strategies for Resolution of Social Situations Questionnaire*; Garaigordobil, 2008)	Social Interaction Strategies: • Assertiveness • Passivity • Aggressiveness
"Cuestionario de Evaluación de la Capacidad de Análisis de Sentimientos" (CECAS; in English, *Questionnaire for the Assessment of the Ability to Analyze Feelings*; Garaigordobil, 2008)	Cognitive ability of analysis of 4 negative emotions (sadness, envy, anger, and fear). It identifies: • Causes • Consequences • Ways to resolve negative emotions
Big Five Questionnaire for Children and Adolescents (BFQ-CA; Barbaranelli, Caprara, & Rabasca, 1998; Spanish adaptation Del Barrio, Carrasco, & Holgado, 2006)	Big Five Personality Factors • Conscientiousness • Openness • Extroversion • Agreeableness • Emotional Instability
State-Trait Anger Expression Inventory in Children and Adolescents (STAXI-NA; Del Barrio, Aluja, & Spielberger, 2005)	Anger Feelings • State-Anger • Trait-Anger • Anger Expression-Out • Anger Expression-In • Anger Control-Out • Anger Control-In
Patient Health Questionnaire (PHQ-15; Kroenke, Spitzer, & Williams, 2002; Spanish adaptation by Ros, Comas, & García-García, 2010)	15 possible physical problems (psychosomatic symptoms)

Assessment Instruments

In order to measure the variables, we administered 10 assessment instruments with psychometric guarantees of reliability and validity (see Chart 1).

Emotional Quotient Inventory: Youth Version (EQ-i:YV; Bar-On & Parker, 2000; Spanish adaptation: Ferrándiz, Hernández, Bermejo, Ferrando, & Prieto, 2012). The EQ-i:YV assesses the level of emotional and social functioning in adolescents and children aged 7 to 18. It is based on the conceptual model of Bar-On and consists of 60 items across five dimensions: (1) *Intrapersonal Intelligence* (the ability to be aware of and understand one's own emotions, feelings, and ideas): Self-Regard (to have a precise perception, understanding, and acceptance of one's emotions), Assertiveness (to express one's emotions and oneself effectively and constructively), Emotional Self-Awareness (to be aware of and understand one's own feelings), Independence (to be self-reliant and free of emotional dependency on others), and Self-Actualization (to strive to achieve personal goals and actualize one's potential); (2) *Interpersonal Intelligence* (the ability to be aware of and understand other people's emotions, feelings, and ideas): Social Responsibility (to identify and cooperate with one's social group), Interpersonal Relationship (to establish mutually satisfying relationships and relate well with others), and Empathy (to be aware of and understand how others feel); (3) *Stress Management* (the ability to handle stress and control one's emotions): Stress Tolerance (to constructively and effectively manage one's emotions), and Impulse Control (to constructively and effectively control emotions); (4) *Adaptability* (the ability to be open to changes of feelings depending on the situation): Problem-Solving (to effectively solve personal and interpersonal problems), Reality-Testing (to objectively validate one's feelings and thinking with external reality), and Flexibility (to adapt and adjust one's thinking and feelings to new situations); and (5) *General Mood* (the ability to feel and express positive emotions and to be optimistic): Optimism (to be positive and look on the brighter side of life), and Happiness (to be content with oneself, with others, and with life in general). From these dimensions the *Emotional Intelligence Quotient* is obtained (Total score). The responses to the questionnaire are given on a Likert-type scale (1 = *rarely happens to me or isn't true*, 4 = *frequently happens to me or is true*). For example, "It is easy to tell people how I feel," "I am good at understanding the way other people feel," "I can stay calm when I am upset," "I try to use different ways of answering hard questions," and "I enjoy having fun." Data from various studies show that the different scales have adequate internal consistency ranging from $\alpha = .84$ for the Intrapersonal Intelligence Scale to $\alpha = .89$ for the total scale (Bar-On & Parker, 2000; Parker et al., 2004). The internal consistency obtained in the sample of our study was very good both for the test as a whole ($\alpha = .89$) and for all the scales (Intrapersonal Intelligence $\alpha = .81$, Interpersonal Intelligence $\alpha = .77$, Adaptability $\alpha = .78$, General Mood $\alpha = .80$, and Stress Management $\alpha = .79$). The five-factor internal structure has been confirmed, and the reliability was $\alpha = .88$ for the entire scale (Ferrándiz, Ferrando, Bermejo, & Prieto, 2006). As for concurrent validity, correlational analyses were carried out between the total EI score and the scores of intelligence, personality, self-concept, academic achievement and trait-EI. The results confirm the validity of the EQ-i:YV (Ferrándiz et al., 2012).

The "*Cuestionario de Actitudes y Estrategias Cognitivas Sociales*" (AECS; in English, *Attitudes and Social Cognitive Strategies Questionnaire;* Moraleda, González, & García-Gallo, 2004). This measures various social behaviors: *Social Conformity* (conforming to what is socially correct); *Social Sensitivity* (a willingness to understand others' feelings and value other people); *Help-Collaboration* (a tendency to share with others, reinforce them, and to collaborate at work); *Self-Assurance-Firmness* (confidence in one's own possibilities to achieve the goals of an interaction, firmness in the defense of one's rights); *Prosocial Leadership* (a tendency to propose ideas to the group, to unite the members around common goals); *Aggressiveness-Stubbornness* (a tendency to violent expressions against people or things, to use threats and intimidation); *Dominance* (a tendency to dominate and manipulate others to achieve benefits); *Apathy-Withdrawal* (a lack of interest in groups or in participating in their activities, a tendency to be reserved, isolated); *Social Anxiety* (a tendency towards shyness, fear of expressing oneself and of relating with others). Adolescents rate their degree of agreement with the contents of the items on a 7-point Likert scale. For example, " I respect my classmates' things and try not to spoil them," " I like to be generous with others and lend them my things if they need them," " I am rather shy and submissive," " I think the most important thing in life is to gain power in any way and to order other people about." The scales of the original study provided the following consistency indexes (Cronbach's alpha): Social Conformity α = .59, Social Sensitivity α = .70, Help-Collaboration α = .70, Self-Assurance-Firmness α = .62, Prosocial Leadership α = .61, Aggressiveness-Stubbornness α = .66, Dominance α = .54, Apathy-Shyness α = .57, and Social Anxiety α = .62. The internal consistency in our study was low for Prosocial Leadership (α = .55) and Aggressiveness-Stubbornness (α = .65) and adequate for the rest of the variables: Social Conformity α = .72, Social Sensitivity α = .72, Help-Collaboration α = .70, Self-Assurance-Firmness α = .71, Dominance α = .77, Apathy-Shyness α = .76 and Social Anxiety α = .76. With regard to the composite reliability (FC) and average variance extracted (AVE) obtained with the data of the study, the results of the confirmatory factor analysis with the maximum likelihood method for the total scale indicate a high level of reliability (*FC* = .98), and an adequate level of AVE (46.69%).

The "*Escala de Problemas de Conducta*" (EPC; in English, *Behavioral Problems Scale*; Navarro, Peiró, Llácer, & Silva, 1993). This 99-item scale is filled in by the parents to assess their children's behavioral problems. The items are grouped in 7 scales: *School-Academic Problems* (related to low academic performance), *Antisocial Behavior* (behaviors that can be classified as aggressive, and other behaviors that are not aggressive but could impair social relationships), *Shyness-Withdrawal* (a tendency to solitude and susceptibility in social relationships), *Psychopathological Disorders* (serious problems which generally have a depressive component), *Anxiety Problems* (behaviors that express fear and/or anxiety, generalized form), *Psychosomatic Disorders* (physical disorders without a medical cause), and a positive scale of *Social Adaptation/Adjustment* (adjustment to social rules). Parents report whether or not their children engage in these behaviors. As regards the reliability of the scale, information about the internal consistency of the entire EPC has been gathered (α = .88). To test criterion validity, the EPC was applied to different samples of children and adolescents (referred by the school psychologist for problems at school, referred to a clinical psychologist, and prison inmates due to criminal problems), and multiple regression analysis showed that belonging to different criterion groups was the variable that presented the highest level of relations with the EPC scores. The internal consistency obtained with the sample of our study was high (α = .87). As for the scales, School-Academic Problems (α = .87), Antisocial Behavior (α = .84), Shyness-Withdrawal (α = .73) and Psychopathological Disorders (α = .70) have better internal consistency than Anxiety Problems (α = .64), Psychosomatic Disorders (α = .64) and Social Adaptation/Adjustment (α = .67).

The Questionnaire Measure of Emotional Empathy (QMEE; Mehrabian & Epstein, 1972; Spanish adaptation: Garaigordobil, 2008). This consists of 22 sentences referring to empathic feelings by means of which the ability for empathy is measured. The empathy concept includes a cognitive and an emotional perspective. In terms of the cognitive role-taking approach, an empathic person can assume the other's role and understand and accurately predict that person's thoughts, feelings and actions. From another perspective, empathy is defined as a vicarious emotional response to the perceived emotional experiences of others. The inventory's task consists of reading a series of statements and indicating whether one usually does, thinks, or feels what the sentence states. For example, "Seeing someone cry makes me feel like crying", "When I see someone is ill, I feel sad", and so on. A global empathy score is based on adolescents' agreement (= 1) or disagreement (= 0) with items tapping attributes including emotional expression and attitudes (e. g., "Sometimes I cry when I watch TV"), sympathy (e.g., "It make me sad to see a boy who is rejected by group"), and empathy (e.g., "Seeing a girl crying makes me feel like crying"). Cronbach's alpha verified the good reliability of this scale (α = .74), and in this sample, Cronbach's alpha reached .71, indicating good internal consistency. In two experiments, highly empathic subjects were less aggressive toward slow-learning students. Mediational analysis showed that helping behavior was a function of the empathic tendency (β = .31).

The Oxford Happiness Questionnaire (OHQ; Hills & Argyle, 2002; Spanish adaptation: Garaigordobil & Durá, 2006). The OHQ was derived from the Oxford Happiness Inventory (OHI), which—reduced to 29 items— attempts to measure the happiness of a general nature of each individual, that is, psychological well-being. For example, "I am not particularly optimistic about the future,""I am well satisfied about everything in my life," "I am very happy," "Life is good," and "I always have a cheerful effect on others"... The person expresses his or her degree of agreement with the statements on a 6-point Likert scale (1 = *strongly disagree*; 6 = *strongly agree*). The studies carried out with a sample of people aged between 13 and 68 verified the good reliability of this scale (α = .91) based on standardized items. In this sample, Cronbach's alpha reached .84, indicating good internal consistency. The construct validity of the OHI was assessed through its associations with different measures of individual differences in cognitive traits and variables (extroversion, neuroticism, self-esteem, satisfaction with life, depression, happiness). In the original study, the associations of the OHI and the OHQ were compared, obtaining significant correlations.

The *"Cuestionario de Estrategias Cognitivas de Resolución de Situaciones Sociales"* (EIS; in English, *Cognitive Strategies for Resolution of Social Situations Questionnaire*; Garaigordobil, 2008) was used to explore the cognitive strategies to solve 6 conflictive social situations in which respondents should: address a moral conflict, respond to an aggression, make friends, cope with others' rejection, recover an object that has been taken away by another peer, and resist pressure (e.g., refuse drugs). The adolescents report all the resolution strategies that the protagonist can perform in each situation. The test assesses assertive, passive, and aggressive social interaction strategies. Assertive strategies are those in which the problem situation is directly faced, and effective behaviors are proposed to achieve the goal nonaggressively (developing skills, asking, expressing one's feelings, asserting one's rights, dialogue and reasoning with the other, etc.). Passive strategies do not directly address the problem situation and include responses of inhibition (there is no action), submission, avoiding the situation, or seeking help from others to resolve the situation. Aggressive strategies include responding with behavior that is negative or aggressive for the interaction (threats, physical and verbal aggression, insults, blackmail, reporting others so they will be punished, etc.) The reliability of the questionnaire is acceptable both in the original (α = .72, .74, and .68, for assertive, passive, and aggressive strategies, respectively) and in the present study (α = .72, .72, and .68). The results support the convergent and divergent validity of the instrument, showing that adolescents who use many assertive cognitive strategies as social conflict resolution techniques have a positive self-concept and capacity for empathy, displaying few withdrawal behaviors and few antisocial behaviors.

The *"Cuestionario de Evaluación de la Capacidad de Análisis de Sentimientos"* (CECAS; in English, *Questionnaire for the Assessment of the Ability to Analyze Feelings*; Garaigordobil, 2008) is used to explore the cognitive ability of analysis of four negative emotions: sadness, envy, anger, and fear. The task requests respondents to identify causes (factors, situations, or stimuli that generate these emotions), consequences (the impact of these emotions at the behavioral, cognitive, and emotional level), and ways to resolve these emotions (behavioral, cognitive, and emotional coping strategies to constructively resolve negative emotions). For example, with regard to sad feelings, they suggest as causes "the death of a close friend or relative or failing exams," as consequences "isolation or aggressiveness," and as ways of dealing with them "talking to friends or studying more for the next exam." The reliability of the test is good both in the original study (α = .77) and in the sample of our study (α = .92) and in the scales of Analysis of Causes (α = .83), Analysis of Consequences (α = .86) and Resolution of Negative Emotions (α = .87). In addition, validation studies found that adolescents who were able to provide a large number of answers about the causes of feelings showed few withdrawal behaviors, many prosocial behaviors, had a good self-concept, high capacity of empathy, etc. Likewise, adolescents who listed many positive ways of resolving negative emotions also displayed many hetero-assertive behaviors, many cognitive strategies to resolve problematic social situations, and they were nominated by their peers as prosocial individuals.

Big Five Questionnaire for Children and Adolescents (BFQ-CA. Barbaranelli, Caprara, & Rabasca, 1998; Spanish adaptation: Del Barrio, Carrasco, & Holgado, 2006). The BFQ-CA assesses in children and adolescents aged 8-15 the Big Five personality factors: *Conscientiousness* (autonomy, order, precision and complying with norms and commitments), *Openness* (intellectual aspects, creativity, cultural interests), *Extroversion* (activity, enthusiasm, assertiveness, and self-confidence), *Agreeableness* (concern and sensitivity towards others and their needs), and *Emotional Instability* (anxiety, depression, discontent, or anger). The questionnaire consists of 65 items with five possible responses rated from 1 (*always never*) to 5 (*almost always*). For example, "I get very involved in the things I do and I do them to the best of my ability," "I understand things immediately," "I like to spend time with other people," "I am polite when I talk to others," and "I get nervous for silly things." The works that until now have studied the internal consistency (Cronbach's alpha) of the different scales of the BFQ-CA have discovered appropriate coefficients which oscillate between .78 in Emotional Instability and .88 in Conscientiousness. The internal consistency obtained in the sample of our study was high in all the scales (Conscientiousness α = .84, Openness α = .77, Extroversion α = .80, Agreeableness α = .78, Emotional Instability α = .84). The validity studies carried out in other studies revealed an adequate concurrent and predictive validity.

State-Trait Anger Expression Inventory in Children and Adolescents (STAXI-NA; Del Barrio, Aluja, & Spielberger, 2005). The STAXI-NA allows us to obtain a precise assessment of the various components of anger (experience, expression, and control) and its facets as state and trait. It assesses state-trait anger, its expression (internal and external), and control (external and internal). *State-Anger*: level of feelings of anger at the time of assessment; *Trait-Anger*: feelings of anger and frustration habitually experienced, tendency to react frequently with rage and fury. *Anger Expression-Out:* expression of anger toward other persons or objects; *Anger Expression-In:* holding in or suppressing angry feelings; *Anger Control-Out:* controlling angry feelings by preventing their expression towards persons or objects; and *Anger Control-In:* controlling feelings of anger by calming down or cooling off. The STAXI-NA is self-applicable. It consists of 32 elements divided into 6 scales. For example, "I feel irritated/I am furious," "I get angry very quickly," "I control my angry feelings," "I do something that relaxes me," "I express my anger," and "I hold my anger in." The reliability of the test is very good, with the alpha coefficient ranging between .78 and .89 for the scale of State-Anger, between .75 and .82 for the scale of Trait-Anger and between .64 and .84 for the scales of Anger-Expression and Anger-Control. The internal consistency obtained in the sample of our study was adequate both in terms of the overall test (α = .74) and in terms of the majority of the scales. The internal consistency of the State-Anger scale (α = .90) is the highest together with the scales of Trait-Anger (α = .74), Anger Control-Out (α = .77) and Anger Control-In (α = .76). The scales of anger expression have a lower internal consistency (Anger Expression-Out α = .57; Anger Expression-In α = .50). Analyses confirmed the convergent and discriminant validity of the STAXI-NA, finding that feelings of anger have high correlations with aggressiveness, whereas consideration for others and self-control correlate positively with anger control, and withdrawal correlates positively with state-anger and trait-anger.

Patient Health Questionnaire (PHQ-15; Kroenke, Spitzer, & Williams, 2002; Spanish adaptation: Ros, Comas, & García-García, 2010). The PHQ-15 is made up of 15 items referring to 15 possible physical problems (psychosomatic symptoms) that the participant might have suffered in the past month: stomach-ache, back-ache, pain in the arms, pain in legs or joints, menstrual pain, headaches, chest pain, dizziness or fainting, feeling one's heartbeats go faster, pains or problems during sex, constipation or diarrhea, feeling tired or having little energy, and trouble sleeping. The subject has to choose between the scores 0 (*no pain*), 1 (*a little pain*) and 2 (*a lot of pain*) for each of the 15 items, taking the last month as a reference. The reliability of the questionnaire was assessed as internal consistency, obtaining a Cronbach alpha coefficient of .78 in the Spanish validation, a Cronbach alpha of .80 in the original study, and of .67 in the present study. Regarding validity, its correlations between the Montgomery-Asberg Depression Rating Scale (MADRS) and the PHQ-15 were studied, finding moderate to high correlations (r > .30 and < .70, respectively). The 15 items showed moderate associations with each other. The majority of the item-item correlations are between .20 and .29. Only 6% of the item-item correlations were lower than .10, and 9% were above .40, the highest correlation being that between "trouble sleeping" and "tiredness".

RESULTS

Emotional Intelligence: Sex Differences

First, we explored the existence of sex differences in EI. After confirming the basic assumptions (homogeneity, homoscedasticity, etc.), we performed descriptive analysis and analysis of variance, the results of which are presented in Table 2.

Table 2. Mean, standard deviation, analysis of variance and effect size (Eta-squared) in Emotional Intelligence in boys and girls

	Boys (n = 67)	Girls (n = 81)	$F(1, 146)$	p	η^2
	M (SD)	M (SD)			
Intrapersonal Intelligence	13.76 (4.18)	14.35 (3.98)	0.75	.387	.005
Interpersonal Intelligence	32.19 (5.17)	35.15 (3.80)	15.99	.000	.099
Stress Management	32.55 (5.91)	32.36 (6.24)	0.03	.848	.000
Adaptability	24.55 (4.08)	23.38 (4.44)	2.72	.101	.018
General Mood	43.73 (6.80)	42.59 (6.23)	1.12	.290	.008
Emotional Intelligence Quotient	146.79 (17.29)	147.83 (12.98)	0.17	.678	.001

The results of the analysis of variance (see Table 2) revealed sex differences only in Interpersonal Emotional Intelligence, with significantly higher scores in females. In the rest of the variables (Intrapersonal Intelligence, Stress Management, Adaptability and General Mood), and in the Emotional Intelligence Quotient (EIQ), the scores were similar in both sexes.

Correlations between Emotional Intelligence and Behavioral, Emotional, Cognitive, and Physical Variables

Pearson correlations between scores on the EQi-YV with the rest of the variables under study were calculated to analyze the concomitant relationships between IE and various behavioral, emotional, cognitive, and physical variables (positive and negative social behaviors, behavioral problems, empathy, happiness, social situation resolution cognitive strategies, ability to analyze feelings, personality traits, state-trait anger, anger expression, and psychosomatic symptoms). The correlation coefficients obtained with the total sample are presented in Table 3. Moreover, as in Interpersonal Intelligence, sex differences were found. The correlations obtained by differentiating boys and girls in all variables are also presented.

Firstly, he correlation coefficients (see Table 3) show significant positive correlations ($p < .05$) in both sexes between *Intrapersonal Emotional Intelligence* and social behaviors of self-assurance-firmness and the personality trait of agreeableness, and a significant negative correlation with psychosomatic symptoms. In addition, in the sample of boys, significant positive correlations were found with behaviors of social sensitivity, prosocial-leadership, and with anger expression-out. In the sample of girls, the coefficient showed significant negative correlations with anger expression-in.

Table 3. Pearson correlations between Emotional Intelligence and behavioral, emotional, cognitive, and physical variables

	Intrapersonal Intelligence			Interpersonal Intelligence			Stress Management		
	Total	Boys	Girls	Total	Boys	Girls	Total	Boys	Girls
AECS Social Behavior									
Social Conformity	-.10	-.04	-.16	.23**	.29*	.13	.23**	.25*	.21*
Social Sensitivity	.18*	.25*	.07	.53***	.48***	.47***	-.03	.14	-.18
Help-Collaboration	.02	.15	-.10	.50***	.52***	.46***	.05	.21	-.06
Self-Assurance-Firmness	.28***	.33**	.24*	.25***	.21	.28*	-.18*	-.07	-.26*
Prosocial-Leadership	.03	.25*	-.13	.23**	.18	.34**	-.11	.03	-.22*
Aggressiveness	.15	.16	.17	-.13	-.28*	.09	-.47***	-.56***	-.43***
Dominance	.04	-.00	.15	-16*	-.14	.03	-.23**	-.29*	-.22*
Apathy-Withdrawal	-.01	.01	-.00	-.18*	-.13	-.11	-.05	-.04	-.07
Social Anxiety	-.16*	-.15	-.20	-.14	-.27*	-.19	.05	.07	.05
EPC. Behavioral Problems									
School-Academic Problems	.10	.13	.09	-.11	-.11	-.06	-.30***	-.37**	-.25*
Antisocial Behavior	.10	.03	.15	-.08	-.26*	.05	-.45***	-.49***	-.41***
Shyness/Withdrawal	-.13	-.23	-.03	-.07	-.10	-.04	-.08	-.14	-.03
Psychopathological Disorders	-.00	-.06	.03	.11	.01	.22	-.20*	-.26*	-.16
Anxiety Problems	-.11	-.17	-.08	-.04	-.21	.00	-.16	-.25	-.09
Psychosomatic Disorders	.04	-.02	.09	.11	.11	.02	-.30***	-.35**	-.26*
Social Adaptation/Adjustment	-.03	.01	-.08	.20*	.30*	.07	.29***	.39**	.21
QMEE Empathy									
Empathy	.10	.21	-.03	.47***	.39***	.40***	-.07	-.04	-.09
OHQ Happiness									
Happy feelings	.13	.17	.07	.34***	.31**	.32**	.25**	.46***	.03
EIS. Social Interaction Strategies									
Passive	-.10	-.09	-.10	.02	.11	-.02	.28***	.39***	.20
Assertive	-.09	-.13	-.09	.08	.01	.03	.22**	.26*	.19

Table 3. (Continued)

	Intrapersonal Intelligence			Interpersonal Intelligence			Stress Management		
	Total	Boys	Girls	Total	Boys	Girls	Total	Boys	Girls
Aggressive	.03	.06	.03	-.03	.11	-.07	-.09	-.05	-.13
CECAS. Analysis of Emotions									
Causes	-.13	-.22	-.11	.20*	.16	.15	.02	.13	-.03
Consequences	-.07	-.20	-.00	.20*	.17	.11	.17*	.24*	.13
Resolution	.02	.00	.02	.15	.15	.09	.16*	.12	.20
BFQ-CA. Personality Traits									
Conscientiousness	-.08	.02	-.17	.24**	.27*	.29**	.17*	.39***	-.00
Openness	-.09	-.01	-.16	.11	.16	.16	.25**	.40***	.12
Extroversion	.07	.15	-.06	.44***	.32**	.51***	-.05	.11	-.24*
Agreeableness	.23**	.23*	.22*	.49***	.44***	.50***	.10	.25**	-.03
Emotional Instability	.00	-.01	.02	-.11	-.27*	.05	-.62***	-.60***	-.64***
STAXI-NA. Anger									
State-Anger	.05	.01	.14	-.09	-.14	.14	-.19*	-.25*	-.15
Trait-Anger	-.02	.06	-.09	-.11	-.15	-.05	-.53***	-.48***	-.57***
Expression-Out	.20*	.27*	.12	.11	.19	.01	-.48***	-.37**	-.56***
Expression-In	-.28***	-.17	-.37***	.02	.00	.01	-.05	-.00	-.08
Control-Out	-.00	.03	-.02	-.01	.16	-.09	.51***	.47***	.56***
Control-In	.09	.13	.06	.15	.24*	.02	.12	.17	.09
PHQ-15 Physical Problems									
Psychosomatic Symptoms	-.42***	-.43***	-.41***	-.25**	-.34**	-.20	-.07	-.18	.01

	Adaptability			General Mood			Emotional Intelligence Quotient		
	Total	Boys	Girls	Total	Boys	Girls	Total	Boys	Girls
AECS Social Behavior									
Social Conformity	.18*	.18	.22*	.13	.19	.11	.24**	.28*	.22*
Social Sensitivity	.17*	.21	.27*	.14	.25*	.12	.31***	.40***	.22*
Help-Collaboration	.31***	.43***	.26*	.32***	.48***	.20	.41***	.56***	.26*
Self-Assurance-Firmness	.23**	.30*	.21	.35***	.40***	.32**	.30***	.35**	.25*
Prosocial-Leadership	.35***	.32**	.37***	.29***	.31**	.27*	.26**	.32**	.21
Aggressiveness	-.03	-.15	.00	-.00	-.20	.12	-.20*	-.35**	-.06
Dominance	.05	-.02	.03	.03	-.12	.15	-.10	-.20	.03
Apathy-Withdrawal	-.08	-.09	-.14	-.14	-.29*	-.02	-.16*	-.18	-.13
Social Anxiety	-.25**	-.15	-.28**	-.37***	-.41***	-.33**	-.30***	-.29*	-.34**
EPC. Behavioral Problems									
School-Academic Problems	-.08	-.20	.00	-.04	-.01	-.08	-.17*	-.17	-.15
Antisocial Behavior	-.10	-.20	-.02	-.13	-.11	-.14	-.26**	-.32**	-.21
Shyness/Withdrawal	-.04	-.10	.00	-.15	-.05	-.25*	-.16	-.17	-.16
Psychopathological Disorders	.02	-.13	.14	-.15	-.17	-.13	-.11	-.19	-.01
Anxiety Problems	-.17*	-.22	-.12	-.16	-.14	-.17	-.23**	-.29*	-.19
Psychosomatic Disorders	.13	.07	.20	-.10	-.11	-.08	-.08	-.11	-.06
Social Adaptation/Adjustment	.10	.14	.07	.10	-.02	.23*	.24***	.24	.23*
QMEE Empathy									
Empathy	.14	.27*	.18	.13	.27*	.10	.24**	.32**	.17
OHQ Happiness									
Happy feelings	.29***	.39***	.25*	.53***	.57***	.53***	.56***	.61***	.48***
EIS. Social Interaction Strategies									
Passive	-.03	.06	-.13	.06	.03	.07	.11	.17	.04
Assertive	.02	.08	.02	.05	.21	-.11	.15	.16	.03
Aggressive	.11	.07	.10	.12	.01	.20	.04	.05	.05
CECAS. Analysis of Emotions									
Causes	.01	.00	.06	-.07	.06	-.14	.01	.06	-.05
Consequences	.03	.10	.03	-.06	.03	-.11	.09	.12	.05
Resolution	-.02	.09	-.08	-.05	.08	-.14	.09	.14	.03

Table 3. (Continued)

	Intrapersonal Intelligence			Interpersonal Intelligence			Stress Management		
	Total	Boys	Girls	Total	Boys	Girls	Total	Boys	Girls
BFQ-CA. Personality Traits									
Conscientiousness	.42***	.38***	.44***	.24**	.29*	.18	.34***	.42***	.26*
Openness	.41***	.34**	.47***	.26***	.26*	.25*	.34***	.36**	.34**
Extroversion	.27***	.30*	.35***	.30***	.41***	.26*	.34***	.41***	.25*
Agreeableness	.29***	.36**	.30**	.28***	.35***	.25*	.46***	.50***	.42***
Emotional Instability	-.14	-.25*	-.05	-.26***	-.38***	-.15	-.44***	-.50***	-.38***
STAXI-NA. Anger									
State-Anger	-.05	-.09	-.07	-.13	-.29*	.04	-.16*	-.26*	.01
Trait-Anger	-.11	-.05	-.17	-.05	-.00	-.10	-.31***	-.21	-.43***
Expression-Out	.06	.15	.01	.12	.16	.08	-.03	.10	-.18
Expression-In	-.01	.08	-.08	-.14	-.15	-.12	-.15	-.08	-.24*
Control-Out	.02	.22	-.17	.10	.21	-.02	.25**	.35**	.16
Control-In	.09	.23	.02	.12	.05	.19	.20**	.24*	.17
PHQ-15 Physical problems									
Psychosomatic symptoms	-.15	-.28*	-.04	-.36***	-.43***	-.29**	-.42***	-.50***	-.33**

Note: * $p < .05$, ** $p < .01$, *** $p < .001$

Secondly, the coefficients showed (see Table 3) positive significant correlations ($p < .05$) in both sexes between *Interpersonal Emotional Intelligence* and social behaviors of social sensitivity, help-collaboration, empathy, happiness, and with personality traits such as conscientiousness, extroversion, and agreeableness. In addition, in the sample of boys, positive correlations were found between interpersonal intelligence and social behaviors of social conformity, social adaptation/adjustment and anger control-in, as well as negative correlations with aggressive behavior, social anxiety, anti-social behavior, emotional instability, and psychosomatic symptoms. In the sample of girls, positive correlations were found between interpersonal intelligence and social behaviors of self-assurance-firmness and prosocial leadership.

Thirdly (see Table 3), significant positive correlations ($p < .05$) were found in both sexes between *Stress Management* and behaviors of social conformity and anger control-out, as well as negative correlations between stress management and aggressive social behavior, dominance, school-academic problems, antisocial behavior, psychosomatic disorders, emotional instability, trait-anger, and anger expression-in. In addition, significant positive correlations were found in boys between stress management and happiness, use of passive and assertive social interaction strategies, capacity to analyze the consequences of negative emotions, personality traits such as conscientiousness, openness, and agreeableness, as well as negative correlations with psychopathological symptoms and state-anger. Significant negative correlations were found in girls between stress management and social behaviors of self-assurance-firmness, prosocial leadership, and extroversion.

Fourthly, the correlations (see Table 3) in both sexes revealed significant positive relationships between *Adaptability* and social behaviors of help-collaboration, prosocial leadership, feelings of happiness, and personality traits such as conscientiousness, openness, extroversion, and agreeableness. Significant positive correlations were found in boys between adaptability, social behavior of self-assurance-firmness and empathy, as well as negative correlations between adaptability, emotional instability, and psychosomatic symptoms. Positive correlations were found in girls between adaptability and social behaviors of social conformity, social sensitivity, whereas negative correlations were found with social anxiety behaviors.

Fifthly, the results (see Table 3) confirmed significant positive correlations in both sexes between *General mood* and social behaviors of self-assurance-firmness, prosocial leadership, happiness, and personality traits such as openness, extroversion, and agreeableness, as well as negative correlations of general mood with social anxiety behaviors and psychosomatic symptoms. In addition, in the sample of boys, positive correlations were found between general mood and social behaviors of social sensitivity, help-cooperation, empathy, and the personality trait of conscientiousness, and negative correlations with social behaviors of apathy-withdrawal, emotional instability, and state-anger. Positive correlations were found in girls between general mood and social adaptation/adjustment, and negative correlations with shyness-withdrawal behaviors.

Finally, Pearson coefficients confirmed in both sexes (see Table 3) significant positive correlations between the *Emotional Intelligence Quotient* (EIQ) and positive social behaviors such as social conformity, social sensitivity, help-collaboration, and self-assurance-firmness, feelings of happiness, personality traits such as conscientiousness, openness, extroversion, and agreeableness, as well as significant negative correlations with social anxiety behaviors, emotional instability, and psychosomatic symptoms. Also, in the sample of boys, positive correlations were found between EIQ and prosocial leadership behaviors, empathy, anger control-out, and anger control-in, as well as negative correlations with aggressive and antisocial behaviors, anxiety problems, and state-anger. And in the sample of girls, positive correlations were found between EIQ and social adaptation/adjustment, as well as negative correlations with trait-anger and anger expression-in.

Predictor variables of Emotional Intelligence Quotient

To identify the variables that predict a high *Emotional Intelligence Quotient* (EIQ), we performed stepwise multiple linear regression analysis, including all the variables. The results are presented in Table 4.

Table 4. Predictor variables of Emotional Intelligence Quotient

	R	R²	ΔR²	B	SE	Constant	β	t
Total Sample								
Happiness	.611	.373	.368	.227	.069	75.20	.231	3.28***
Agreeableness	.688	.473	.465	.716	.191	56.56	.247	3.74***
Emotional Instability	.730	.532	.521	-.509	.121	84.07	-.265	-4.22***
Help-Collaboration Behaviors	.766	.587	.574	.537	.130	72.82	.247	4.12***
Psychosomatic Symptoms	.791	.626	.611	-1.071	.335	91.85	-.186	-3.20**
Anger Control-Out	.802	.643	.626	.949	.390	79.91	.134	2.43*
Anxiety Problems	.810	.657	.637	-.649	.296	89.96	-.118	-2.19*
Boys								
Happiness	.664	.440	.430	.182	.107	69.06	.186	1.70*
Help-Collaboration Behaviors	.765	.585	.570	.798	.207	33.84	.321	3.85***
Anger Control-Out	.808	.653	.633	1.888	.657	23.13	.217	2.87**
Emotional Instability	.830	.688	.664	-.864	.219	55.85	-.398	-3.94***
Conscientiousness	.853	.728	.701	.443	.138	51.04	.259	3.20**
Passive Interaction Strategies	.869	.755	.725	-1.313	.511	52.13	-.190	-2.57*
Self-Assurance-Firmness Behaviors	.881	.775	.743	.427	.204	45.05	.165	2.08*
Girls								
Happiness	.529	.280	.271	.200	.094	84.58	.202	2.12*
Trait-Anger	.621	.385	.368	-.879	.372	106.95	-.214	-2.36*
Agreeableness	.669	.448	.425	.446	.258	90.62	.170	1.72*
Emotional Instability	.700	.489	.461	-.405	.153	98.00	-.243	-2.64**
Psychosomatic Symptoms	.723	.523	.489	-1.113	.431	118.23	-.232	-2.58*
Help-Collaboration Behaviors	.744	.554	.515	.429	.168	111.99	.227	2.54*
Social Anxiety Behaviors	.761	.580	.536	-.265	.130	121.41	-.170	-2.03*

Note: SE = Standard Error (unstandardized coefficients); * *p* < .05, ** *p* < .01, *** *p* < .001.

From the set of variables (see Table 4), seven were significant predictors of EIQ: Happiness (β = .231), Agreeableness (β = .247), Emotional Instability (β = -.265), Help-Collaboration Behaviors (β = .247), Psychosomatic Symptoms (β = -.186), Anger Control-Out (β = .134), and Anxiety Problems (β = -.118). The standardized regression coefficients (Beta) indicated that these variables had considerable weight on the criterion variable, EIQ. The percentages of variance explained (adjusted coefficients of determination) for each one of these predictor variables were of large size (36.8%, 46.5%, 52.2%, 57.4%, 61.1%, 62.6%, and 63.7%). *Seven variables, which explain 63.7% of the variance, were EIQ predictors: high happiness, high agreeableness, low emotional instability, many help-collaboration behaviors, few psychosomatic symptoms, high anger control-out, and few anxiety problems.*

Although no sex differences were found in EIQ, regression analyses were also conducted separately with the sample of boys and girls. The results (see Table 4) confirmed that three variables predict a high level of EI in both sexes: high happiness, low emotional instability, and many help-collaboration behaviors. Furthermore, high anger control-out, high conscientiousness, few passive interaction strategies, and many self-assurance-firmness behaviors were predictors of EI in boys, whereas low levels of trait-anger, high agreeableness, few psychosomatic symptoms, and few social anxiety behaviors predicted high EI in girls.

CONCLUSION

The study had three objectives: (1) to analyze sex differences in Emotional Intelligence (EI); (2) to explore the concomitant relations between EI with various behavioral, emotional, cognitive, and physical factors; and (3) identify variables that predict high EI.

First, the results only yielded sex differences in interpersonal emotional intelligence, with significantly higher scores in females. In the rest of the variables (intrapersonal intelligence, stress management, adaptability, and general mood), and in the Emotional Intelligence Quotient (EIQ), the scores were similar in both sexes. Hence, the results do not confirm Hypothesis 1, and point in the same direction as other studies finding no sex differences in EI (Fernández-Berrocal et al., 2004; Saklofske et al., 2007), or as studies finding that women have more interpersonal competencies (Hall & Mast, 2008). However, these results contradict those obtained in other studies in which women obtain higher scores in EI (Day & Carroll, 2004; Extremera et al., 2006; Joseph & Newman, 2010). These discrepancies may be explained by the different assessment instruments used, as well as by the differences in the ages of the samples of the diverse investigations.

Second, results of correlational analysis showed that:

(1) Boys and girls with high *intrapersonal emotional intelligence* are significantly more likely to display many social behaviors of self-assurance-firmness, they are agreeable, and they have significantly few psychosomatic symptoms. In addition, boys with high intrapersonal emotional intelligence show many behaviors of social sensitivity, prosocial-leadership, and anger expression-out, whereas girls have low anger expression-in.

(2) Boys and girls with high *interpersonal emotional intelligence* are significantly more likely to display many social sensitivity and help-collaboration behaviors, they have

high empathy, many feelings of happiness, as well as the personality traits of conscientiousness, extroversion and agreeableness. Besides, boys display many social behaviors social conformity, high social adaptation/adjustment, high anger control-in, emotional stability, few aggressive, antisocial and social anxiety behaviors, and few psychosomatic symptoms; whereas girls show many self-assurance-firmness and prosocial leadership behaviors.

(3) Boys and girls with high *stress management* are significantly more likely to display many social behaviors of social conformity, high anger control-out, few aggressive, antisocial and dominance behaviors, few academic problems, few psychosomatic symptoms, emotional stability as a personality trait, low trait-anger and anger expression-out. In addition, boys with high stress management have many feelings of happiness, use many strategies of passive and assertive social interaction, a high ability to analyze the consequences of negative emotions, and personality traits such as conscientiousness, openness, and agreeableness, few psychopathological symptoms, and low level of state-anger; whereas girls with high stress management have few self-assurance-firmness and prosocial leadership behaviors, and low extroversion.

(4) Boys and girls with high *adaptability* are significantly more likely to display many positive social behaviors (help-collaboration and prosocial leadership), many feelings of happiness, personality traits such as conscientiousness, openness, extroversion, agreeableness, and emotional stability. Furthermore, boys with high adaptability display social behaviors of self-assurance-firmness, high empathy, and few psychosomatic symptoms. Girls show many positive social behaviors (social conformity and social sensitivity), and few social anxiety behaviors.

(5) Boys and girls with high *general mood* are significantly more likely to display many positive social behaviors (self-assurance-firmness and prosocial-leadership), many feelings of happiness, and personality traits such as openness, extroversion and agreeableness, few social anxiety behaviors, and few psychosomatic symptoms. Besides, boys with high general mood display many social sensitivity and help-collaboration behaviors, high empathy, and conscientiousness and emotional stability as personality traits, few apathy-withdrawal behaviors, and low level of state-anger; whereas girls with high general mood show high social adaptation/adjustment and few shyness-withdrawal behaviors.

(6) Boys and girls with high *Emotional Intelligence Quotient* (EIQ, including all the above subscales) are more likely to display many positive social behaviors (social conformity, social sensitivity, help-collaboration, and self-assurance-firmness), many feelings of happiness, personality traits such as conscientiousness, openness, extroversion, agreeableness, and emotional stability, few social anxiety behaviors, and few psychosomatic symptoms. In addition, boys with high EIQ show many prosocial-leadership behaviors, high empathy, high anger control-out and anger control-in, few aggressive and antisocial behaviors, few anxiety problems, and a low level of state-anger. Girls with high EIQ show high social adaptation/adjustment, a low level of trait-anger and low anger expression-in.

Therefore, Hypothesis 2 is confirmed almost entirely, as it has been shown that boys and girls adolescents with high scores in EIQ have many positive social behaviors (social conformity, social sensitivity, help-collaboration, and self-assurance-firmness), many feelings of happiness, adaptive personality traits (agreeableness and emotional stability), as well as few social anxiety behaviors, and few psychosomatic symptoms. Also boys with high scores in EIQ have many prosocial-leadership behaviors, few aggressiveness-stubbornness and antisocial behaviors, high empathy, and high anger control, and girls with high EIQ have a low level of trait-anger.

Our results confirm those of other studies finding that EI correlated positively with positive social behaviors (Schokman et al., 2014; Jiménez & López-Zafra, 2013), empathy (King et al., 2012; Kokkinos & Kipritsi, 2012), happiness (Chamorro-Premuzic et al., 2007; Furnham & Christoforou, 2007; Ruiz-Aranda et al., 2014; Vergara et al., 2015), life satisfaction (Di Fabio & Saklofske, 2014), personality traits such as extroversion, openness, agreeableness, and conscientiousness; and negatively with emotional instability (Chamorro-Premuzic et al., 2007; Di Fabio & Saklofske, 2014; Petrides et al., 2010; Van der Linden et al., 2012), aggressive and antisocial behavior (Downey et al., 2010; Garaigordobil et al., 2013; Liau et al., 2003), angry feelings (Inglés et al., 2014; Şahín-Baltraci & Demir, 2012), and psychosomatic symptoms (Downey et al., 2010; Liau et al., 2003; Martins et al., 2010).

Thirdly, with the whole sample, the results of the regression analyses revealed seven predictors of EI (EIQ), which explain 63.7% of the variance. The variables that predict high EI (EIQ) were: high happiness, high agreeableness, low emotional instability, many help-collaboration behaviors, few psychosomatic symptoms, high anger control-out, and few anxiety problems. The results confirmed that in both sexes, the three variables that predict a high level of EI (EIQ) were: high happiness, low emotional instability, and many help-collaboration behaviors. Moreover, anger control-out, high conscientiousness, few passive interaction strategies and many self-assurance-firmness behaviors were predictors of EI in boys. Complementarily, in girls, the variables that predicted high EI (EIQ) were: low level of trait-anger, high agreeableness, few psychosomatic symptoms, and few social anxiety behaviors.

These results confirm Hypothesis 3 and those obtained by other studies identifying well-being (Augusto-Landa et al., 2010), physical health (Mikolajczak et al., 2015), adaptive personality traits such as agreeableness and emotional stability (Schulte et al., 2004) as predictors of EI. However, they do not confirm that being female is a predictor of high EI, as found by Harrod and Scheer (2005).

The results suggest the importance of implementing programs to promote the development of EI during childhood and adolescence, and the study identifies relevant variables to design such programs. As limitations of the study, we note its correlational and cross-sectional nature, which does not allow establishing causal relations between the variables. As a future line of research, we recommend designing intervention programs that contain activities related to the variables identified in this study. These programs should include activities to increase positive social behaviors (social conformity, social sensitivity, help-collaboration, self-assurance-firmness, and prosocial-leadership), promote adaptive personality traits (conscientiousness, openness, extroversion, agreeableness, and emotional stability), stimulate feelings of happiness, the capacity of empathy for other human beings... as well as activities to reduce negative social behaviors (aggressive and antisocial behaviors and social anxiety) and activities to learn how to control feelings of anger, regulate negative emotions.... These programs should be implemented consistently throughout the school course, and their effects should be assessed, especially their effects on EI, but also on other variables of social and affective-emotional development.

ACKNOWLEDGMENTS

The Spanish Ministry of Economics and Competitiveness (MINECO) (PSI2012-30956), the Department of Education, Language Policy and Culture of the Basque Government (IT638-13) (BFI-2012-10), and the University of the Basque Country (UFIPSIXXI-11/04) financed the study.

REFERENCES

Augusto-Landa, J. M., Pulido-Martos, M. & López-Zafra, E. (2010). Emotional intelligence and personality traits as predictors of psychological well-being in Spanish undergraduates. *Social Behavior and Personality*, *38*(6), 783-794. doi:10.2224/ sbp.2010.38.6.783.

Barbaranelli, C., Caprara, G. V. & Rabasca, A. (1998). *Manuale del BFQ-C. Big Five Questionnaire Children* [*Manual of the BFQ-C. Big Five Questionnaire -Children*]. Florence, Italy: Organizzaaioni Speciali.

Bar-On, R. (1997). *The Emotional Quotient Inventory (EQ-I): Technical manual*. Toronto, Canada: Multi-Health Systems.

Bar-On, R. (2000). Emotional and social intelligence: Insights from the Emotional Quotient Inventory (EQ-i). In R. Bar-On & J. D. A. Parker (Eds.), *Handbook of emotional intelligence: Theory, development, assessment and application at home, school and in the workplace* (pp. 363-388). San Francisco: Jossey-Bass.

Bar-On, R. (2006). The Bar-On model of emotional-social intelligence. *Psicothema*, *18*, 13-25.

Bar-On, R. & Parker, J. D. A. (2000). *Emotional Quotient Inventory: Youth Version (EQ-i:YV): Technical manual*. Toronto, Canada: Multi-Health Systems.

Baron-Cohen, S. (2002). The extreme male brain theory of autism. *Trends in Cognitive Science*, *6*, 248-254.

Chamorro-Premuzic, T., Bennett, E. & Furnham, A. (2007). The happy personality: Mediational role of trait emotional intelligence. *Personality and Individual Differences*, *42*, 1633–1639. doi:10.1016/j.paid.2006. 10. 029.

Ciarrochi, J. V., Hynes, K. & Crittenden, N. (2005). Can men do better if they try harder? Sex and motivational effects on emotional awareness. *Cognition and Emotion*, *19*, 133-141.

Darwin, C. (1965). *The expression of the emotions in man and animals*. Chicago: University of Chicago Press. (Original work published 1872).

Day, A. L. & Carroll, S. A. (2004). Using an ability-based measure of emotional intelligence to predict individual performance, group performance, and group citizenship behaviours. *Personality and Individual Differences*, *36*, 1443-1458. doi:10.1016/S0191-8869 (03)002 40-X.

Del Barrio M. V., Aluja, A. & Spielberger, C. D. (2005). *STAXI-NA. Inventario de Expresión de Ira Estado-Rasgo en niños y adolescentes. [STAXI-NA. The State-Trait Anger Expression Inventory in Children and Adoelscents]*. Madrid: TEA Ediciones.

Del Barrio, M. V., Carrasco, M. A. & Holgado, F. P. (2006). *BFQ-NA Cuestionario de los Cinco Grandes para niños y adolescentes (adaptación a la población española) [BFQ-NA -Big Five Questionnaire for Children and Adolescents]*. Madrid: TEA Ediciones.

Di Fabio, A. & Saklofske, D. H. (2014). Promoting individual resources: The challenge of trait emotional intelligence. *Personality and Individual Differences, 65,* 19-23. doi:10.1016/j.paid.2014.01.026

Downey, L. A., Johnson, P. J., Hansen, K., Birney, J. & Stough, C. (2010). Investigating the mediating effects of emotional intelligence and coping on problem behaviours in adolescents. *Australian Journal of Psychology, 62*(1), 20-29. doi:10.1080/00049530903312873.

Esturgó-Deu, M. E. & Sala-Roca, J. (2010). Disruptive behaviour of students in primary education and emotional intelligence. *Teaching and Teacher Education, 26,* 830-837. doi:10.1016/j.tate.2009.10.020.

Extremera, N., Fernández-Berrocal, P. & Salovey, P. (2006). Spanish version of the Mayer-Salovey-Caruso Emotional Intelligence Test (MSCEIT). Version 2.0: Reliabilities, age and gender differences. *Psicothema, 18,* 42-48.

Fernández-Berrocal, P., Cabello, R., Castillo, R. & Extremera, N. (2012). Gender differences in emotional intelligence: The mediating effect of age. *Behavioral Psychology/Psicología Conductual, 20*(1), 77-89.

Fernández-Berrocal, P., Extremera, N. & Ramos, N. (2004). Validity and reliability of the Spanish modified version of the Trait Meta-Mood Scale. *Psychological Reports, 94,* 751–755.

Ferrándiz, C., Ferrando, M., Bermejo, M. R. & Prieto, M. D. (2006, September). *Emotional intelligence and personality*. Paper presented at the Annual Meeting of the British Educational Research Association (BERA). Conventry, UK: Warwick University.

Ferrándiz, F., Hernández, D., Bermejo, R., Ferrando, M. & Prieto, M. D. (2012). La inteligencia emocional y social en la niñez y adolescencia: validación castellana de un instrumento para su medida [Social and emotional intelligence in childhood and adolescence: Spanish validation of a measurement instrument]. *Revista de Psicodidáctica, 17*(2), 309-318. doi:10.1387/Rev.Psicodidact.2814.

Furnham, A. & Christoforou, I. (2007). Personality traits, emotional intelligence, and multiple happiness. *North American Journal of Psychology, 9*(3), 439-462.

Furtner, M. R., Rauthmann, J. F. & Sachse, P. (2010). The socioemotionally intelligent self-leader: Examining relations between self-leadership and socioemotional intelligence. *Social Behavior and Personality, 38*(9), 1191-1196. doi:10.2224/sbp.2010.38.9.1191.

Garaigordobil, M. (2008). *Intervención psicológica con adolescentes. Un programa para el desarrollo de la personalidad y la educación en derechos humanos.* (2nd ed.) [*Psychological intervention in adolescence. A program to develop personality and human rights*]. Madrid: Pirámide. (Original work published in 2000).

Garaigordobil, M., Aliri, J., Martínez-Valderrey, V., Maganto, C., Bernarás, E. & Jaureguizar, J. (2013). Conducta antisocial: conexión con emociones positivas y variables predictoras [Antisocial behavior: Connection with positive emotions and predictors]. *Apuntes de Psicología, 31*(2), 123-133.

Garaigordobil, M. & Durá, A. (2006). Relaciones del autoconcepto y la autoestima con sociabilidad, estabilidad emocional y responsabilidad en adolescentes de 14 a 17 años [Relationships between self-concept and self-esteem with sociability, emotional stability and responsibility in adolescents aged 14 to 17]. *Análisis y Modificación de Conducta, 32* (141), 37-64.

Goleman, D. (1995). *Emotional intelligence*. New York: Bantam Books.

Hall, J. A., & Mast, M. S. (2008). Are women always more interpersonally sensitive than men? Impact of goals and content domain. *Personality and Social Psychology Bulletin, 34*, 144-155. doi:10.1177/0146167207309192.

Harrod, N. R. & Scheer, S. D. (2005). An exploration of adolescent emotional intelligence in relation to demographic characteristics. *Adolescence, 40*(159).

Hills, P. & Argyle, M. (2002). The Oxford Happiness Questionnaire: A compact scale for the measurement of psychological well-being. *Personality and Individual Differences, 33*, 1073-1082. doi:10.1016/S0191-8869(01)00213-6.

Hopkins, M. M. & Yonker R. (2015). Managing conflict with emotional intelligence: Abilities that make a difference. *Journal of Management Development, 34*(2), 226-244. doi:10.1108/JMD-04-2013-0051.

Inglés, C. J., Torregrosa, M. S., García-Fernández, J. M., Martínez-Monteagudo, M. C., Estévez, E. & Delgado, B. (2014). Conducta agresiva e inteligencia emocional en la adolescencia [Aggressive behavior and emotional intelligence in adolescence]. *European Journal of Education and Psychology, 7*(1), 29-41. doi:10.1989/ejep.v7i1.150.

Jiménez, M. I. & López-Zafra, E. (2013). The impact of students' perceived emotional intelligence, social attitudes and teacher expectations on academic performance. *Electronic Journal of Research in Educational Psychology, 11*(1), 075-098.

Joseph, D. L. & Newman, D. A. (2010). Emotional Intelligence: An integrative meta-analysis and cascading model. *Journal of Applied Psychology, 95*(1), 54-78. doi:10.1037 /a0017286.

King, D. B., Mara, C. A. & DeCicco, T. L. (2012). Connecting the spiritual and emotional intelligences: Confirming an intelligence criterion and assessing the role of empathy. *International Journal of Transpersonal Studies, 31*(1), 11-20.

Kokkinos, C. M. & Kipritsi, E. (2012). The relationship between bullying, victimization, trait emotional intelligence, self-efficacy and empathy among preadolescents. *Social Psychology of Education, 15*, 41-58. doi:10.1007/s11218-011-9168-9.

Kroenke, K., Spitzer R. L. & Williams, J. B. (2002). Patient Health Questionnaire. *Psychosomatic Medicine, 64*, 258-266.

Kumar, N. & Bhushan, B. (2008). Can personality dimensions predict emotional intelligence and interpersonal communication? *Journal of Psychiatric Research, 3*(2), 205-214.

Liau, A. K., Liau, A. W. L., Teoh, G. B. S. & Liau, M. T. L. (2003). The case for emotional literacy: The influence of emotional intelligence on problem behaviours in Malaysian secondary school students. *Journal of Moral Education, 32*(1). doi:10.1080/ 0305724022000073338.

Martins, A., Ramalho, N. & Morin, E. (2010). A comprehensive meta-analysis of the relationship between emotional intelligence and health. *Personality and Individual Differences, 49*, 554–564. doi:10.1016/j.paid.2010.05.029.

Mavroveli, S. & Sánchez-Ruiz, M. J. (2011). Trait emotional intelligence influences on academic achievement and school behavior. *British Journal of Educational Psychology*, *81*, 112-134. doi:10.1348/2044-8279.002009.

Mayer, J. D. & Salovey, P. (1997). What is emotional intelligence? In P. Salovey & D. J. Sluyter (Eds.), *Emotional development and emotional intelligence: Educational implications* (pp. 3-11). New York: Harper Collins.

Mehrabian, A. & Epstein, A. (1972). A measure of emotional empathy. *Journal of Personality*, *40*, 525-543.

Mikolajczak, M., Avalosse, H., Vancorenland, E., Verniest, R., Callens, M., van Broeck, N., Fantini-Hauwel, C. & Mierop, A. (2015). A nationally representative study of emotional competence and health. *Emotion*, *15*(5), 653-667. doi:10.1037/emo0000034.

Moraleda, M., González, J. & García-Gallo, J. (2004). AECS. *Actitudes y Estrategias Cognitivas Sociales. [CSAS. Cognitive-Social Attitudes and Strategies]*. Madrid: TEA (Original work published in 1998).

Navarro, A. M., Peiró, R., Llácer, M. D. & Silva, F. (1993). EPC. Escala de problemas de conducta [SBP. Scale of behavioural problems]. In F. Silva & M. C. Martorell (Eds.), *EPIJ. Evaluación Infanto-Juvenil* [CYE. Child-Youth Evaluation] (pp. 31-81). Madrid: MEPSA.

Parker, J. D. A., Creque, R. E., Barnhart, D. L., Harris, J. I., Majeski, S. A., Wood, L. M., Bond, B. J. & Hogan, M. J. (2004). Academic achievement in high school *Personality and Individual Differences*, *37*, 1321-1330. doi:10.1016/j.paid.2004.01.002.

Petrides, K. V. & Furnham, A (2001) Trait emotional intelligence: Psychometric investigation with reference to established trait taxonomies. *European Journal of Personality*, *15*, 425-448.

Petrides, K. V., Vernon, P. A., Schermer, J. A., Ligthart, L., Boomsma, D. I. & Veselka, L. (2010). Relationships between trait emotional intelligence and the Big Five in the Netherlands. *Personality and Individual Differences*, *48*, 906–910. doi:10.1016/j.paid.2010.02.019.

Poulou, M. S. (2014). How are trait emotional intelligence and social skills related to emotional and behavioural difficulties in adolescents? *Educational Psychology: An International Journal of Experimental Educational Psychology*, *34*(3), 354-366, doi:10.1080/01443410.2013. 785062.

Ros, M., Comas, A. & García-García, M. (2010). Validación de la versión española del cuestionario PHQ-15 para la evaluación de síntomas físicos en pacientes con trastornos de depresión y/o ansiedad: estudio DEPRE-SOMA [Validation of the Spanish version of the PHQ-15 Questionnaire for the evaluation of physical symptoms in patients with depression and/or anxiety disorders: DEPRE-SOMA study]. *Actas Españolas de Psiquiatría*, *38*(6), 345-357.

Ruiz-Aranda, D., Extremera, N. & Pineda-Galán, C. (2014). Emotional intelligence, life satisfaction and subjective happiness in female student health professionals: The mediating effect of perceived stress. *Journal of Psychiatric and Mental Health Nursing*, *21*, 106-113. doi:10.1111/jpm.12052.

Şahin-Baltaci, H. & Demir, K. (2012). Pre-service classroom teachers' emotional intelligence and anger expression styles. *Educational Sciences: Theory & Practice*, *12*(4), 2422-2428.

Saklofske, D. H., Austin, E. J., Galloway, J. & Davidson, K. (2007). Individual difference correlates of health-related behaviours: Preliminary evidence for links between emotional intelligence and coping. *Personality and Individual Differences, 42*, 491–502.

Salami, S. O. (2010). Conflict resolution strategies and organizational citizenship behavior: The moderating role of trait emotional intelligence. *Social Behavior and Personality, 38*(1), 75-86. doi:10.2224/sbp.2010. 38.1.75.

Sánchez-Núñez, M. T., Fernández-Berrocal, P., Montañés, J. & Latorre, J. M. (2008). Does emotional intelligence depend on gender? The socialization of emotional competencies in men and women and its implications. *Electronic Journal of Research in Educational Psychology, 15*, 455-474.

Schokman, C., Downey, L. A., Lomas, J., Wellhamc, D., Wheaton, A., Simmons, N. & Stougha, C. (2014). Emotional intelligence, victimisation, bullying behaviours and attitudes. *Learning and Individual Differences, 36*, 194–200. doi:10.1016/ j.lindif.2014.10.013.

Schulte, M. J., Ree, M. J. & Carretta, T. R. (2004). Emotional intelligence: Not much more than g and personality. *Personality and Individual Differences, 37*, 1059–1068.

Sifneos, P. E. (1967). Clinical observations on some patients suffering from a variety of psychosomatic diseases. *Acta Medicina Psychosomatica, 7*, 1-10.

Thorndike, E. L. (1920). Intelligence and its uses. *Harper's Magazine, 140*, 227-235.

Van der Linden, D., Tsaousis, I. & Petrides, K. V. (2012). Overlap between general factors of personality in the Big Five, Giant Three, and trait emotional intelligence. *Personality and Individual Differences, 53*, 175-179. doi:10.1016/j.paid.2012.03.001.

Vergara, A. I., Alonso-Alberca, N., San-Juan, C., Aldás, J. & Vozmediano, L. (2015). Be water: Direct and indirect relations between perceived emotional intelligence and subjective well-being. *Australian Journal of Psychology, 67*, 47-54. doi: 10.1111/ ajpy.12065.

Wechsler, D. (1940). Non-intellective factors in general intelligence. *Psychological Bulletin, 37*, 444-445. doi:10.1037/h0060613.

Zeidner, M. & Kloda, I. (2013). Emotional intelligence (EI), conflict resolution patterns, and relationship satisfaction: Actor and partner effects revisited. *Personality and Individual Differences, 54*, 278-283. doi:10.1016/j.paid.2012.09.013.

In: Psychological Well-Being
Editor: Rafael Bowers

ISBN: 978-1-63484-354-6
© 2016 Nova Science Publishers, Inc.

Chapter 6

FACTORS AFFECTING THE FORMATION AND REFORMATION OF ETHNIC IDENTITY: A STUDY OF THE PSYCHOLOGICAL WELL-BEING OF CHINESE IMMIGRANT ADOLESCENTS

Jennifer J. Chen
Kean University, NJ, US

ABSTRACT

As the number of Chinese immigrants grows exponentially, our public school system has subsequently faced massive influxes of Chinese immigrant students. While adjusting to living in a vastly different sociocultural milieu, these immigrant students are also simultaneously adapting to a different educational system and learning a new language. All of these new academic, sociocultural, and linguistic demands can incur stress and other negative consequences that intrude on Chinese immigrant students' psychological well-being. This phenomenon, in turn, portends particular challenges to the teachers and educators working with them. It is, thus, imperative that we understand Chinese immigrant students' post-immigration experience to better address their psychological needs. This study investigated particularly three first-generation Chinese immigrant adolescents' meaning making of the factors contributing to their shaping and reshaping of their ethnic identity vis-à-vis their cultural adaptation as a means to understand their psychological well-being. To this end, I conducted individual interviews with these adolescents. The results revealed that the three Chinese immigrant adolescents' meaning making of their formation and reformation of their ethnic identity was influenced by four major factors: (1) ethnic background; (2) cultural valuation of filial piety; (3) friendship network; and (4) English proficiency. These contributing factors are interpreted from both the cultural and contextual perspectives. Educational implications and directions for future research are also discussed.

INTRODUCTION

In the last decade, immigration to the United States has been at a record high. According to the 2010 American Community Survey of the U.S. Census Bureau, the foreign-born population was estimated to be nearly 40 million, representing 13 percent of the total U.S. population (Grieco et al., 2012a). Within this unprecedented foreign-born population, the increased statistical prominence of Asians, particularly Chinese immigrants, can be hardly ignored. According to the 2010 U.S. Census[3], between 2000 and 2010, the Asian population was the fastest growing racial group in the United States, increasing at a rate (43%, from 10.2 million to 14.7 million) that was more than four times the total U.S. population (9.7%, from 281.4 million to 308.7 million) (Hoeffel, Rastogi, Kim, & Shahid, 2012). Of all Asian groups in the United States in 2010, immigrants from China (including Hong Kong and Taiwan) were the largest, with a total of 2.2 million (constituting approximately 19% of the foreign-born population from Asia and 5% of the entire foreign-born population) (Grieco et al., 2012b).

As the number of Chinese immigrants grows exponentially, our public school system has subsequently faced massive influxes of Chinese immigrant students. While adjusting to living in a vastly different sociocultural milieu, these immigrant students are also simultaneously adapting to a different educational system and learning a new language. All of these new academic, sociocultural, and linguistic demands can incur stress and other negative consequences that intrude on Chinese immigrant students' psychological well-being. This phenomenon, in turn, portends particular challenges to the teachers and educators working with them. It is, thus, imperative that we understand Chinese immigrant students' post-immigration experience to better address their psychological needs.

In the last four decades, numerous scholars have examined how immigrant students adjust socially and psychologically to a new country. It was found that transitioning to a new culture and adapting to a different educational environment are generally disruptive and stressful for children and adolescents (Kwong, 1987; Lynch, 1992; Sung, 1987). It has been reported that immigrant children and adolescents experience a variety of negative psychological consequences, including "cultural shock" (Garza-Guerrero, 1974), linguistic discontinuities (LaFromboise, Coleman, & Gerton, 1998; Sung, 1987; Wong-Fillmore, 1991), cultural discontinuities (C. Suárez-Orozco & M. M. Suárez-Orozco, 2001), and difficulties in adapting to a new culture (Lynch, 1992), and challenges in forming friendships (Goodenow & Espin, 1993). Compounding these psychological challenges further is the fact that many of these immigrants, especially adolescents, also engage in the process of identity formation and reformation. Particularly, adolescence is characterized as a period of heightened identity development (Erikson, 1968). It is in this theoretical context that I focused my study on identifying the contributors to the shaping and reshaping of ethnic identity among three first-generation Chinese immigrant adolescents as a means to understand the quality of their psychological well-being in the new culture. To this end, the current study endeavored to address this core research question: *How do Chinese immigrant adolescents make meaning of the factors affecting their formation and reformation of their ethnic identity in the new cultural context?*

---

[3] At the time of this writing, the latest U.S. census was conducted in 2010.

THEORETICAL PERSPECTIVE ON IDENTITY DEVELOPMENT

Identity development is not a new concept. Early theoretical perspectives on identity development can be traced back to psycho-dynamic theorists, particularly Erik Erikson. Erikson (1964) theorized that the process of identity development in children begins by associating with the people in their immediate environment and then gradually broadening their circle to include others (e.g., friends, teachers). Particularly, the process of identity development in adolescents involves bridging the psychosocial stages of an egocentric self in childhood and a responsible, matured self in adulthood (Erikson, 1968). Furthermore, the Western psychological expectation of what categorizes as "normal" adolescent identity formation is described as involving the psychological separation of oneself from his or her parents during adolescence and the acceptance of one's social roles (Erikson, 1964). This psychological expectation is promoted in individualist-oriented Western societies. However, in stark contrast, in collectivist-oriented Chinese societies (e.g., Bond, 1996; Hofstede, 1991; Triandis, 1989), Chinese adolescents are expected to form their self-identities that reflect collectivistic values, including sensitivity and conformity to familiar expectations. For instance, filial piety to one's parents is an essential characteristic of collectivism emphasized in Chinese culture (Hofstede, 1991). Chinese children demonstrate filial piety to their parents in many ways, notably by achieving educational excellence and engaging in culturally desirable behaviors. One prevalent motivation for a Chinese child to excel academically is the acute cognition that his success brings honor to his parents, whereas failure incurs shame that he must avert (Yao, 1985).

Identity formation is particularly a complex process for adolescents (Erikson, 1968). It is even doubly complex and challenging for immigrant children and adolescents who juggle two different cultures (Ekstrand, Foster, Olkiewicz, & Stankovski, 1981; Goodenow & Espin, 1993; C. Suárez-Orozco, 2000; C. Suárez-Orozco & M. M. Suárez-Orozco, 2001). Given differences between the Chinese and Western cultures, it would be interesting to explore how Chinese immigrant adolescents interpret as the factors influencing the formation and reformation of their ethnic identity vis-à-vis their psychological adaptation in the new cultural context.

ETHNIC IDENTITY

Rotherham and Phinney (1987) defined ethnic identity as related to the enculturation of immigrant groups, including the individual's sense of affiliation to an ethnic group and the adoption of associated behaviors, attitudes, and feelings. One notable example of such a cultural and social behavior is speaking the heritage language of one's ethnic group (De Vos, 1995; Fishman, 1999; Giles, Bourhis, & Taylor, 1977; Isajiw, 1990). Furthermore, immigrants are faced with a multitude of other post-immigration changes in the new country, especially acculturation.

Identity Formation and Reformation in the Context of Acculturation

Immigrating to a new country entails acculturation, a concept that is defined as a process involving cultural and psychological changes as a result of intercultural interaction (Berry, 2003). Cultural changes include shifts in orientations, such as customs, language, and values, while psychological changes include shifts in the individual's attitudes, such as those concerning the acculturation process and the new culture (Phinney, 2003). Language is an important alternation in the acculturation process, especially for immigrant students who must learn the language of schooling to succeed academically. Furthermore, immigration and ensued acculturation collectively necessitate alternations in the individual's self-identity as he or she must learn to negotiate and navigate the two different cultural terrains (Bornstein & Bohr, 2011). Consequently, the quality of cultural adaptation for the individual can affect his or her psychological well-being (Berry, 2003).

Acculturation Strategies

Acculturating individuals are faced with issues involving "the distinction between (1) a relative preference for maintaining one's heritage culture and identity, and (2) a relative preference for having contact with and participating in the larger society along with other ethnocultural groups" (Berry, 2005, p. 704). In this connection, Berry (2005) proposed four acculturation strategies to capture one's cultural preference:

(1) *Assimilation:* Individuals prefer to relinquish their heritage culture and instead immerse into the dominant society.
(2) *Separation:* Individuals embrace their native culture, while avoiding to interact with others in the new culture.
(3) *Integration:* Individuals desire to maintain one's heritage culture, while also welcoming daily interactions with those from other groups in the larger society where cultural diversity is celebrated. Integration involves respecting and accepting the rights and values of all groups (non-dominant and dominant) to live as culturally diverse people in a pluralistic society. Berry (2005) found that, "The largest number of youth fell into the integrated cluster (defined by a preference for integration, positive ethnic and national identities, use of both languages, and a friendship network that included youth from both cultures)" (p. 707).
(4) *Marginalization:* Individuals show little interest in either maintaining their heritage culture or relating to people from other cultural groups in the larger society.

FACTORS AFFECTING THE FORMATION AND REFORMATION OF ETHNIC IDENTITY

Ethnic Background and Ethnic Identity

An immigrant's ethnic background is likely to influence the crafting and recrafting of his or her ethnic identity. Of particular importance are ethnic background characteristics and circumstances surrounding one's immigration including country of birth and citizenship, length of residence in the host country, age of immigration, and physical features (Doucet & C. Suárez-Orozco, 2006; Perez & Hirschman, 2009). For instance, despite uprooting to a new country, first-generation immigrants who retain strong connections to people in their country of origin tend to continue upholding a strong ethnic identity rooted in these ethnic ties (Doucet & C. Suárez-Orozco, 2006). In the case of new immigrant adolescents who are faced with linguistic barriers and cultural differences in adjusting to life in the host country, it is possible that they may continue to form and reform their ethnic identity in relation to their ethnic background.

Ethnic Identity and Heritage Language

For immigrants, the continued use of their heritage language serves more than a necessary vehicle for verbal communication; it symbolizes their ethnic identity (Fishman, 1977; Isajiw, 1990; Padilla, 1999; C. Suárez-Orozco & M. M., Suárez-Orozco, 2001), because it defines their belonging to a distinct group (Giles et al., 1977; Padilla, 1999). Thus, language is viewed as constituting a distinct characteristic feature in the development and maintenance of a separate ethnic identity (De Vos, 1995). It does not only provide a sense of social group solidarity, but also operates as a means for transmitting heritage cultural values (Giles et al., 1977), especially from parents to children (Chen, Chen, & Zhang, 2012).

However, heritage language fluency may be viewed as a double-edged sword. In the case of Chinese immigrants, although heritage language fluency may render a sense of ethnic identity, it may also pose as a source of hindrance to their educational success, especially when the heritage language is perceived to be less valued than the dominant language of English (Ryan, Giles, & Sebastian, 1982). In this context, Chinese immigrant adolescents may place an importance on achieving a high level of English proficiency for academic success.

METHOD

Participants

To investigate factors affecting Chinese immigrant adolescents' own perceptions of their formation and reformation of their ethnic identity post-immigration, I conducted individual interviews with three Chinese immigrant adolescents attending public schools in a northeastern city with a large Chinese population. The three participants were recruited from their respective schools. They were assigned the pseudonyms of Ming and Lei (both from Mainland China) and May (from Hong Kong). At the time of this study, Ming was a 19 year-old male who was a senior in high school. The only child in the family, Ming immigrated to the United States with his parents two years ago. A 17 year-old female, May was also a senior in high school. She immigrated to the United States with her parents and an older sister a year ago. A 13-year-old 7th grader in a middle school, Lei was the youngest of all three participants. He immigrated to the United States with his parents and a younger sister a year ago. Having lived in the United States only for a year or two, these participants could be considered relatively new immigrants.

Procedure

Prior to their participation in the research, all three Chinese immigrant adolescents and their parents were all well informed in writing about the purpose of the study, procedures, the participant's involvement and rights. A signed consent letter was obtained from Ming who had already reached the legal age for self-consent and from the parents of May and Lei, respectively. For data collection, I interviewed each of the three adolescents individually once, lasting approximately an hour and half to two hours. All three interviews were conducted at a mutually agreed upon time and location. At the time of the interview, I reiterated to each participant what was already written in the consent letter, including the purpose of my study, their participation, and their rights as participants. On the basis of the adolescents' language preference, the interview with Ming was conducted in English, and the one with May in Cantonese Chinese. However, the interview with Lei was first conducted in English as requested, but shortly after, he agreed to switch to Cantonese Chinese due to his limited English facility. All interviews were audiotaped and later transcribed for analysis.

Data Collection

To address the research question, which reflected my interest in understanding factors affecting the three Chinese immigrant adolescents' formation and reformation of their ethnic identity from their own perspectives, I employed interviewing as an appropriate method of data collection. As Seidman (2006) asserted that: "At the heart of interviewing research is an interest in other individuals' stories because they are of worth" (p. 9). Specifically, I adopted the "interview guide approach" with "open-ended" interviews (Patton, 1990), a methodological design which ensured that I would ask each participant a standard set of pre-formulated questions, while having the flexibility to adjust wording and sequencing of these questions to reflect the interview context with each individual. In addition, the interviews were semi-structured (Strauss & Corbin, 2015) to ensure that I would be able to ask clarification and follow-up questions as well as other relevant emerging questions during the interview. Guided by these methodological considerations, I developed an interview protocol and formulated a list of interview questions arranged in the order from the most important to the least important. These questions aimed at eliciting the three adolescents' own understanding of the factors affecting their ethnic identity development in the new culture.

Data Analysis

My data analysis involved several steps. First, all three interviews were transcribed in English. The interviews conducted in Chinese were translated to English. With all the transcripts in hand, I first read through them to obtain a general sense of the data, noting general themes that cut across the data. I then conducted a preliminary analysis of the data, focusing on these general themes and trying to understand how the three adolescents made sense of their identity development in the new culture.

Second, I employed open coding and axial coding strategies as described by Strauss and Corbin (2015). My analysis of the data using open coding led to the formation of core categories and concepts as well as subcategories. I grouped conceptually similar experiences into categories. Next, I conducted axial coding to discover potential relationships among these categories.

Third, I further examined each interview transcript for material pertaining to the research question. To identify certain key segments, I conducted what Strauss and Corbin (2015) described as the "microanalysis," which entails a detailed study of the data "line-by-line."

Finally, after applying all these analytic strategies, I began to notice salient themes/concepts. After identifying these concepts, I color coded the contexts or statements that would support them. As my data were segmented into categories, I began prioritizing them and selecting the core ones to present as the major results of the study. Figure 1 illustrates the four core categories or major themes as factors that the three Chinese immigrant adolescents interpreted as influencing their formation and reformation of their own ethnic identity.

FINDINGS

Acculturation and Ethnic Identity

An important finding from the study revealed that the three Chinese immigrant adolescents desired to acculturate by employing what Berry (2005) described as the *integration* strategy. Despite living in a different cultural context, they have reformed their identity to represent a positive Chinese ethnic identity that they have previously formed. However, their efforts to integrate both their heritage and host cultures were thwarted by their realization that they lacked proficiency in English (which was the language of the dominant society) and developed only a limited social network that included mostly ethnic peers. Given these contextual challenges to cultural integration, the three adolescents have instead continued to cultivate a strong Chinese ethnic identity, influenced by four major factors: (1) ethnic background; (2) cultural valuation of filial piety; (3) friendship network; and (4) proficiency in English.

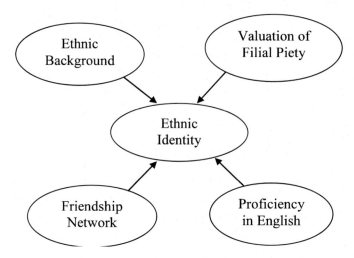

Figure 1. Factors affecting the Chinese immigrant adolescents' formation and reformation of their ethnic identity.

Ethnic Background

The three Chinese immigrant adolescents perceived their ethnic background characteristics, notably country of birth and citizenship, as well as native language proficiency, as playing a pivotal role in their embracing a strong Chinese ethnic identity. For instance, May considered herself Hong Kongnese because as she asserted, "I was born in Hong Kong. I think where you were born, that is where you are a person of." Even when asked if she would still feel the same way upon becoming a U.S. citizen, May was quick with her reasoning: "It is still the same because I was born in Hong Kong. So I should still be a Hong Kongnese. You can consider yourself American. There are two views on this. I think I will choose to identity myself based on my birthplace." In May's case, it is clear that her birth origin was the main source of her crafting and recrafting of a strong Chinese ethnic identity. Similarly, Lei considered himself Chinese even if he were a U.S. Citizen. When asked why he would perceive himself that way, Lei emphasized the fact that he was born in China. Furthermore, his physical features were also influential in his maintenance of a strong Chinese ethnic identity, as Lei declared that he was Chinese because "I have black hair." Like Lei, Ming also perceived himself to be Chinese because of his ethnically identifiable physical features that included "yellow skin and black hair."

While May and Lei identified themselves ethnically as Chinese by their country of birth, Ming further emphasized language and citizenship as sources of his formation and reformation of a strong Chinese ethnic identity. Ming believed that "I think I am still Chinese. My English is poor and I am still not a citizen in the United States." In addition, all three adolescents considered maintaining their Chinese culture to be important in their reformation of their ethnic identity in the new cultural context. For instance, May perceived that, "Because….we are Chinese, we should maintain our Chinese culture." Ming was also proud of his Chinese heritage affirming that, "we have many good cultural values."

Cultural Valuation of Filial Piety

Filial piety as a cultural value in a collectivist Chinese society emerged as a salient theme in the three adolescents' preservation of a strong Chinese ethnic identity. Although they are different in many ways including biographic histories and family configurations, the three adolescents all concurred that they had to be respectful of their parents for their love and gift of life. Specifically, Lei believed that as a person, "no matter what you do, do your best. And more importantly, respect your parents." As a demonstration of filial piety to his parents, Lei aspired to be "a person who knows a lot of things, finds a good job, and lives a good life, so that [his] parents do not have to work so hard."

Espousing the idea of filial piety, Ming also repeatedly stressed the importance of being a "filial son" by maintaining a positive, respectful relationship with his parents. He was adamant about the importance of "being nice to [his] parents," as he reasoned that "because they are my parents. They are the only parents that I will ever have." To show his filial piety to his parents, Ming endeavored to make his parents proud by excelling at school including "being a good student," "studying very hard," and "earning good grades at school." Both May and Lei also perceived that pursuing academic excellence is an essential aspect of maintaining a positive Chinese ethnic identity tied to being filial to their parents. In addition to striving for academic success, Ming also perceived spending quality time and engaging in family activities with his parents as essential filial behaviors. For instance, one family activity Ming did frequently with his parents was going to Chinatown for Dim Sum, a style of traditional Cantonese Chinese food.

Friendship Network

All three Chinese immigrant adolescents believed strongly about the significance of having friends in their lives. As explained by Ming, "it is important because in society, you need friends to help you and you help them. You can't live by yourself." They spoke with introspection about their friendship network with respect to: (1) the ways in which they have maintained contact with their friends "back home," (2) the kinds of friends they have had and why, and (3) the difficulty of expanding their friendship network to include having friends in the new culture.

First, despite geographic distance, all three adolescents were still keeping in contact with friends in their homeland via emails, a technological vehicle through which they used often. As May explained, "I usually write emails to my friends. Most of the times, I write email to send a file, chat, and play games. And now I am in America, I still write emails to friends in Hong Kong."

Second, while all three adolescents expressed that they did have friends who were not Chinese, they felt more comfortable interacting with peers who were Chinese due to their shared language and culture. For instance, Ming lamented his desire to talk to American friends but his lack of English proficiency presented a hurdle. Third, all three adolescents found it much more challenging to make friends in the United States than "back home" due to class arrangements and the language barrier. For instance, May analyzed that, "In Hong Kong, it is better because you stay with the same classmates in all the classes. So you became more familiar with them. When I came here, I had to move from class to class so I was not too familiar with my classmates to befriend them." Furthermore, May lamented the difficulty of making friends here in this way:

> In Hong Kong, you know more friends and make friends very fast. Here, you have to wait for a while before you become familiar with them. And in Hong Kong, Hong Kong has Hong Kongnese, and they are similar to me. It is easier.

Proficiency in English

All three Chinese immigrant adolescents variously considered language to be an integral part of their Chinese ethnic identity. In particular, language stood out as playing a central role in Ming's own perceptions of his ethnic identity. First and foremost, Ming believed that if he was proficient in English, he "would consider himself American." Important too was how English proficiency has contributed to his psychological well-being in terms of feeling happy, confident, and competent. For instance, Ming repeatedly lamented his scarce English proficiency as making him feel inadequate, while expressing how knowing English would make him happy "because I can speak with someone in English. Right now, I want to say some words in English, but I don't know how to say them. I would be happy if I could communicate with other people in English." Asserting that achieving proficiency in the new language was essential to his happiness in living in the United States, Ming expressed a strong desire to master English.

While Ming linked English mastery to his state of happiness, May believed that it would affect people's perceptions of who she was and why she was here. Specifically, May expressed how knowing English or not would affect the way people might treat her and question her motivation for being in the United States as she was adamant that, "if you don't know English and you came to an English-speaking country, people might look down on you. They would question why you came here." Lei further elaborated on the importance of knowing English in this way:

> If you live in the United States, you must know English. If not, you can't work and you can't do anything. If you don't know English, your social circle will be very small. If you know English, you will have more choices ... For example, if you don't know English, you can only work in a Chinese place. Then you can't enter the American society. If you know English, you can try to communicate with Americans and work for Americans ... If you know English, you can get to know more people and understand what they say.

DISCUSSION

This study investigated three Chinese immigrant adolescents' meaning making of the factors affecting their own perceptions of their formation and reformation of their ethnic identity. The results revealed four major influencing factors: (1) ethnic background; (2) cultural valuation of filial piety; (3) friendship network; and (4) English proficiency. These findings can be interpreted from both the cultural and contextual perspectives. First and foremost, although the three Chinese immigrant adolescents desired to acculturate by integration of both their native and host cultures, they perceived their scarcity of English proficiency as a major impediment to their efforts in integrating into the dominant society. In addition to being influenced by the contextual circumstance of language limitation, the adolescents' reformation of a strong Chinese ethnic identity in the new culture was also shaped by ethnic and cultural characteristics, notably native language proficiency, an ethnic-friendship network, and the endorsement of filial practices. This finding is not surprising, especially considering that contextually, these Chinese adolescents have only been living in the United States for a short amount of time (one to two years), which did not seem to have given them enough time to acquire high levels of English proficiency needed to interact successfully with their English-speaking peers and integrate into the dominant society. Cummins (1981) pointed out that it is likely for second language learners to take at least two years to achieve proficiency even in basic interpersonal communication skills, and five to seven years to acquire cognitive academic language proficiency.

Furthermore, from a contextual perspective, the Chinese ethnic background characteristics, including country of birth, physical features, and citizenship, served as factors contributing to their formation and reformation of their ethnic identity, a finding that is consistent with previous observations of immigrants (Doucet & C. Suárez-Orozco, 2006; Perez & Hirschman, 2009). It is even more reasonable to expect that new immigrants would identify themselves by their ethnic background attributes, especially given their unfamiliarity with the new culture due to their short amount of time for cultural exposure.

The findings of the valuation of filial piety and the maintenance of an ethnic-friendship network may be interpreted from a cultural perspective. The fact that the three adolescents placed a high premium on filial piety demonstrated their preservation of certain Chinese cultural values. As filial piety is a prominent value in the collectivist-oriented Chinese culture (Hofstede, 1991), it is not surprising that these adolescents would still perceive it as playing a vital role in their reformation of a strong Chinese ethnic identity in the new culture. Furthermore, considering that ethnic-friendship network has been found to contribute to one's formation of ethnic identity (Xu, Shim, Lotz, & Almeida, 2014), it is also not surprising that the three Chinese immigrant adolescents continued to maintain a positive sense of ethnic identity, as they were still keeping contact with friends in their homeland and socializing with ethnic peers sharing the same Chinese language and culture.

Finally, the finding, that low levels of proficiency in English coupled with high levels of Chinese proficiency were significant factors in the Chinese immigrant adolescents' ethnic orientation, may also be interpreted from a cultural perspective. It has been reported that language affects ethnic identity (Fishman, 1977; Isajiw, 1990; Padilla, 1999; C. Suárez-Orozco & M. M. Suárez-Orozco, 2001), group membership (Giles et al., 1977; Padilla, 1999), and transmission of heritage cultural values (Giles et al., 1977). We may reasonably conjecture that proficiency in their heritage language is an essential constitution of a strong ethnic identity for the Chinese immigrant adolescents in this study.

However, recognizing that English is the language used in school for academic learning and for social interaction, these Chinese adolescents desired to master English so that they could succeed academically and socially. We may expect that over time, the Chinese immigrant adolescents may be able to acquire higher levels of sophistication in the English language to enable them to communicate and befriend peers from other ethnic and cultural groups socially and be better positioned to excel academically. They may also be able to finally adopt what Berry (2005) characterized as the *integration* strategy in acculturating successfully into the dominant society, while simultaneously retaining their ethnic, cultural values. We may conjecture that such fulfillment of cultural integration in the future may enhance the three Chinese immigrant adolescents' psychological well-being. In the meantime, immigrating to the new country has resulted in their reformation and cementation of a strong sense of ethnic identity, which seemed to have contributed to their current psychological adjustment.

Educational Implications

The factors found to be significant in influencing the three Chinese immigrant adolescents' formation and reformation of their Chinese ethnic identity while adjusting to the new culture suggests that to help Chinese immigrant students achieve optimal psychological well-being, it is imperative that educators engage in practices that acknowledge and validate these students' prior cultural and linguistic knowledge, capitalize on their motivation to succeed academically and socially, as well as address their socio-emotional consequences associated with their transition from one culture to another due to immigration. Particular attention should be paid to the language challenges that thwart Chinese immigrant students' efforts to successfully make new friends and integrate into the host country.

Limitations of the Study and Directions for Future Research

This study represents a humble beginning toward understanding Chinese immigrant adolescents' meaning making of their Chinese ethnic identity as influenced by four salient factors. However, it has methodological limitations. First, the small sample size of three participants limits the generalizability of the findings. Second, as is true of qualitative research, the validity of the interpretations needs to be attended to. In this study, I sought to minimize threats to the validity of my conclusions by exploring possible discrepant evidence, a method that was suggested by Maxwell (1996). For instance, I examined words, phrases, and statements that may be inconsistent with my conclusions. Furthermore, to verify and test the validity of my research conclusions, I explored alternative interpretations. To increase descriptive and interpretative validity, I conducted what Maxwell (1996) described as 'member checks,' but only with one participant to "check" the accuracy of my interpretations. Conducting member checks with all participants in future interview studies would be helpful.

The findings of the current study provide important implications for future research. For instance, given that in this study, I focused only on three recent immigrant adolescents (within two years of arrival), future research interviewing a larger sample of Chinese immigrant adolescents with more varied lengths of residence in the United States may reveal insights not captured in this study. Furthermore, as identity development is dynamic and changes over time, a longitudinal study investigating whether and how Chinese immigrant adolescents may perceive their formation and reformation of their ethnic identity differently over time would help yield important insights.

REFERENCES

Berry, J. W. (2003). Conceptual approaches to acculturation. In K. Chun, P. Balls-Organista, & G. Marin (Eds.), *Acculturation: Advances in theory, measurement and applied research* (pp. 17-37). Washington, DC: APA Press.

Berry, J. W. (2005). Acculturation: Living successfully in two cultures. *International Journal of Intercultural Relations, 29*(6), 697-712.

Bond, M. H. (1996). Chinese values. In M. H. Bond (Ed.), *The handbook of Chinese psychology* (pp. 208-226). Hong Kong: Oxford University Press.

Bornstein, M. H., & Bohr, Y. (2011). Immigration, acculturation, and parenting. In R. E. Tremblay, M. Boivin, & R. deV. Peters (Eds.), *Encyclopedia of Early Childhood Development* (pp. 1-8). Ottawa, Canada: Center of Excellence for Early Childhood Development.

Chen, J. J. L., Chen, T., & Zheng, X. X. (2012). Parenting styles and practices among Chinese immigrant mothers with young children. *Early Child Development and Care, 182*(1), 1-21.

Cummins, J. (1981). The role of primary language development in promoting educational success for language minority students. In California State Department of Education (Ed.), *Schooling and language minority students: A theoretical framework* (pp. 3-49). Los Angeles: Evaluation, Dissemination and Assessment Center California State University.

De Vos, G. A. (1995). Ethnic pluralism: Conflict and accommodation. In L. Romanucci-Ross & G. A. De Vos (Eds.), *Ethnic identity: Creation, conflict, and accommodation* (3rd ed., pp. 15-47). Walnut Creek, CA: Alta Mira Press.

Doucet, F. & Suárez-Orozco, C. (2006). Ethnic identity and schooling: The experiences of Haitian immigrant youth. In L. Romanucci-Ross & G. DeVos (Eds.), *Ethnic identities: Problems and prospects for the twenty-first century* (4th ed., pp. 163-188). Walnut Creek, CA: Alta Mira Press.

Ekstrand, L. H., Foster, S., Olkiewicz, E., & Stankovski, M. (1981). Interculture: Some concepts for describing the situation of immigrants. *Journal of Multilingual and Multicultural Development, 2*(4), 269-296.

Erikson, E. (1964). *Childhood and society*. New York: W. W. Norton & Company.

Erikson, E. H. (1968). *Identity: Youth and crisis*. New York: Norton.

Fishman, J. A. (1977). Language and ethnicity. In H. Giles (Ed.), *Language, ethnicity, and intergroup relations* (pp. 15-57). New York: Academic Press.

Fishman, J. A. (1999). *Handbook of language and ethnic identity*. New York: Oxford University Press.

Garza-Guerrero, A. C. (1974). Culture shock: Its mourning and the vicissitudes of identity. *Journal of the American Psychoanalytic Association, 22*(2), 408-429.

Giles, H., Bourhis, R. Y., & Taylor, D. M. (1977). Towards a theory of language in ethnic group relations. In H. Giles (Ed.), *Language, ethnicity, and intergroup relations* (pp. 307-348). New York: Academic Press.

Goodenow, C., & Espin, O. M. (1993). Identity choices in immigrant adolescent females. *Adolescence, 28*(109), 173-184.

Grieco, E. M., Acosta, Y. D., Cruz, G. P., de la, Gambino, C., Gryn, T., Larsen, L. J., et al. (2012a). *The foreign-born population in the United States: 2010 (No. ACS-19).* Washington, DC: United States Census Bureau. Retrieved from http://www.census.gov/prod/2012pubs/acs-19.pdf.

Grieco, E. M., Trevelyan, E., Larsen, L., Acosta, Y. D., Gambino, C., de la Cruz, P., Gryn, T. & Walters, N. (2012b). *The size, place of birth, and geographic distribution of the foreign-born population in the United States: 1960 to 2010.* Washington, DC: United States Census Bureau. Retrieved from https://www.census.gov/population/foreign/files/WorkingPaper96.pdf.

Hoeffel, E. M., Rastogi, S., Kim, M. O., & Shahid, H. (2012). *The Asian population: 2010 (Census 2010 Briefs, No. C2010BR-11).* Washington, DC: United States Census Bureau. Retrieved from https://www.census.gov/prod/cen2010/briefs/c2010br-11.pdf.

Hofstede, G. (1991). *Culture and organisations.* London, England: McGraw-Hill.

Isajiw, W. W. (1990). Ethnic-identity retention. In R. Breton, W. W. Isajiw, W. E. Kalbach, & J. G. Reitz (Eds.), *Ethnic identity and equality.* Toronto: University of Toronto Press.

Kwong, P. (1987). *The new Chinatown.* New York: Hill and Wang.

LaFromboise, T., Coleman, H. L. K., & Gerton, J. (1998). Psychological impact of biculturalism. In P. B. Organista, K. M. Chun, & G. Marin (Eds.), *Readings in ethnic psychology* (pp. 123-155). New York: Routledge.

Lynch, E. W. (1992). From culture shock to cultural learning. In E. W. Lynch & M. J. Hanson (Eds.), *Developing cross-cultural competence: A guide for working with young children and their families* (pp. 19-34). Baltimore, MD: Paul H. Brooke.

Maxwell, J. A. (1996). *Qualitative research design: An interactive approach.* Thousand Oaks, CA: Sage Publications.

Padilla, A. (1999). Psychology. In J. A. Fishman (Ed.), *Handbook of language and ethnic identity* (pp. 109-121). New York: Oxford University Press.

Patton, M.Q. (1990). *Qualitative evaluation and research methods* (2nd ed.). Newbury Park, CA: Sage.

Perez, A. D., & Hirschman, C. (2009). The changing racial and ethnic composition of the US population: Emerging American identities. *Population and Development Review*, *35*(1), 1-51.

Phinney, J. (2003). Ethnic identity and acculturation. In K. Chun, P. Organista, & G. Marin (Eds.), *Acculturation: Advances in theory, measurement, and applied research* (pp. 63-81).Washington, DC: American Psychological Association.

Rotherham, M. J., & Phinney, J. S. (1987). Introduction: Definitions and perspectives in the study of children's ethnic socialization. In J. S. Phinney & M. J. Rotherham (Eds.), *Children's ethnic socialization: Pluralism and development* (pp. 10-28). Newbury Park, CA: Sage.

Ryan, E. B., Giles, H., & Sebastian, R. J. (1982). An integrative perspective for the study of attitudes towards language variation. In E. B. Ryan & H. Giles (Eds.), *Attitudes towards language variation: Social and applied contexts* (pp. 1-19). London: E. Arnold.

Seidman, I. (2006). *Interviewing as qualitative research: A guide for researchers in education and the social sciences* (3rd ed.). New York: Teachers College Press.

Strauss, A., & Corbin, J. (2015). *Basics of qualitative research: Techniques and procedures for developing grounded theory* (4th ed.) Thousand Oaks, CA: Sage.

Suárez-Orozco, C. (2000). Identities under siege: Immigration stress and social mirroring among the children of immigrants. In A. Robben & M. Suárez-Orozco (Eds.), *Cultures under siege: Social violence and trauma* (pp. 194-226). New York: Cambridge University Press.

Suárez-Orozco, C., & Suárez-Orozco, M. M. (2001). *Children of immigration.* Cambridge, MA: Harvard University Press.

Sung, B. L. (1987). *The adjustment experience of Chinese immigrant children in New York City.* New York: The Center for Migration Studies.

Triandis, H. C. (1989). The self and social behavior in different cultural contexts. *Psychological Review, 96*(3), 506-520.

Wong-Fillmore, L. (1991). When learning a second language means losing the first. *Early Childhood Research Quarterly, 6*(3), 323-346.

Xu, J., Shim, S., Lotz, S., & Almeida, D. (2004). Ethnic identity, socialization factors, and culture-specific consumption behavior. *Psychology and Marketing, 21*(2), 93-112.

Yao, E. L. (1985). A comparison of family characteristics of Asian American and Anglo-American high achievers. *International Journal of Comparative Sociology, 26*(34), 198-207.

In: Psychological Well-Being
Editor: Rafael Bowers

ISBN: 978-1-63484-354-6
© 2016 Nova Science Publishers, Inc.

Chapter 7

PSYCHOLOGICAL WELL-BEING AT ADOLESCENCE AND IMPROVING STRATEGIES

F. Ebru Ikiz[1,], Firdevs Savi Cakar[2] and Esra Asici[3]*

[1]Assoc. Prof., Dokuz Eylül University, Izmir, Turkey
[2]Asst. Prof., Mehmet Akif Ersoy University, Burdur, Turkey
[3]Res. Asst., Dokuz Eylül University, Izmir, Turkey

ABSTRACT

Adolescence is a physical, sexual, cognitive, emotional and social development period. Adolescents may experience difficulties about meeting their psychological needs, adapting themselves to changing life conditions. Psychological counseling and guidance services not only focus on identifying and treating psychological disorders, but also they should focus on the positive developmental aspects of mental health. By doing so, they may contribute youths to attain better understanding about their strong aspects and sources they have, to develop effective strategies against life difficulties, to set realistic targets about future, and eventually to obtain psychological well-being (PWB). Adolescents' positive characteristics may be improved with school-based applications long before problem emerges and before adolescents' psychological well-being is not ruined, their live skills may be strengthened, and their positive coping skills and self-esteem may be increased. In this chapter we propose to introduce the concept of PWB, to explain variables related to PWB, to discuss the importance of PWB in the field of psychological counseling and guidance.

INTRODUCTION

In the age of changing and innovation which we live in, adolescents, especially, may experience many difficulties about meeting their psychological needs, adapting themselves to life changing conditions. Adolescence is a physical, sexual, cognitive, emotional and social development period. In this period, adolescents may be faced with multidimensional and

---

* Corresponding author: E-mail address: esra.asici@deu.edu.tr

numerous problems developmentally, and other challenges such as low socio-economic status, unsuitable social conditions, poor health conditions, and limited educational opportunities, may adversely affect this period. As a result of the interaction between compelling characteristics of adolescence and changing innovation age, adolescents' life quality may reduce and they may need professional help.

Although, psychological counseling and guidance services are for all peoples, in the adolescence period the importance and responsibilities increase. One of the basic aims of psychological counseling and guidance services for adolescents is to help youths to develop healthy personality. To fulfill this aim, psychological counseling and guidance services not only focus on identifying and treating psychological disorders, but also they should focus on the positive developmental aspects of mental health. By doing so, they may contribute youths to attain better understanding about their strong aspects and sources they have, to develop effective strategies against life difficulties, to set realistic targets about future, and eventually to obtain psychological well-being (PWB).

PWB, having studied intensively in field of counseling currently, is seen as a positive aspect of mental health. PWB is related to the actualization of human potentials. According to multidimensional PWB model which integrates mental health, clinical and life span developmental theories, PWB consists of six dimensions. First dimension is *self-acceptance*, emphasizing positive evaluation of oneself and one's past life. Second dimension is having positive *relations with others*, emphasizing the possession of quality relations with others. Third is *autonomy*, emphasizing a sense of self-determination. Fourth is *environmental mastery*, emphasizing the capacity to manage effectively one's life and surrounding world. Fifth is having a *purpose in life*, emphasizing the belief that one's life is purposeful and meaningful. Sixth dimension is *personal growth*, emphasizing a sense of continued growth and development as a person. We can say that high PWB is a sign of successful self-development and the adolescents having high PWB may have more productive and happier life.

THE FACTORS INFLUENCING PSYCHOLOGICAL WELL BEING OF ADOLESCENTS

The demands about enhancing and supporting mental health, personality development, life quality and satisfaction of adolescents led researchers to concern on identifying factors which are related to PWB. The following part explains the factors affecting PWB of adolescents according to results of studies.

The Effect of Gender

Gender differences always become an issue getting attention of researchers. The researchers focused on whether or not there are differences between PWB level of males and females too. Findings generally showed that females had higher PWB level than males (Cooper, Okamura, & McNeil 1995; Ryff, 1989; 1995; Ryff & Singer, 2008; Ziskis, 2010). In terms of adolescents, generally females have higher PWB level too, however it is seen that there are some different findings in literature. For instance, while Vleioras and Bosma (2005) found that Greek adolescent females had higher scores than adolescent males' positive relations with others, in personal growth and in purpose in life facets of PWB; Goldbeck, Schmitz, Besier, Herschbach and Henrich (2007) found that German adolescent girls had lower general and health-related life satisfaction than adolescent boys. Visani, Albieri, Offidani, Ottolini, Tomba and Ruini (2011) found that although there were no significant differences between total PWB of Northern Italian adolescent males and females, self-acceptance of females statistically lower than males and females showed higher symptoms of anxiety, depression, somatization and hostility. According to Lin, Chou, Wu and Lin (2014), females living in Northern Taiwan had higher psychological symptoms than males at early, middle and late adolescents. Contrary to Shah's (2014) and Akhter's (2015) findings demonstrated that Indian females had higher PWB level than males, Pawar and Adsul's (2015) research showed that males had higher PWB level than females among Indian adolescents. Besides, in literature there are studies showed that gender was not effective on PWB of adolescence living in southwestern Nigeria (Salami, 2011).

In conclusion, it can be said that adolescent females have indices of higher PWB level, however depending on country, this situation may demonstrate changing. It can be thought that the contrast findings related to gender differences among countries arise from cultural differences. In different cultures, the life conditions of adolescent males and females differ. Moreover, the parental and the societal attitudes towards adolescent male and female changing.

The Effect of Family

Although it is well known that children's dependency on their families decrease and their interests direct their peers in the adolescence period which is a physical, mental, and psychological changing (Santrock, 2012), families still maintain to having important impacts on their children's development and emotional, social or academic attainments. Such that, adolescents' perceived attachment to peers doesn't compensate for a low attachment to parents in regard to their mental ill-health (Raja, McGee & Stanton, 1991). Because, the quality of approaches to their children of parents impacts multiple areas of adolescents' development (Cripps & Zyromski, 2009), the families have power to negatively or positively affect PWB of adolescents.

PWB of adolescents primarily is based on their self-evaluations and interactions with others. Adolescents' initial source of self-evaluations and the quality of relationships is personal experiences arising from the parent-adolescent relationship. Adolescents determine their personal self-worth, self-efficacy, and self-esteem depending on their perception about parental involvement (Cripps & Zyromski, 2009). Even though, parent-adolescent relationship is rather important factor, there can be differences between the effects of mother-adolescent relationship and father-adolescent relationship on PWB of adolescence. For example, according to the results of a study which was conducted by Flouri and Buchanan (2003), although both mother and father involvement contributed to happiness of adolescents; the effect of father involvement was more powerful. Similarly, it was found that parent-adolescent conflict (Shek,1998) and parenting characteristics (Shek 1999) were associated with PWB including indices of hopelessness, life satisfaction, self-esteem, purpose in life and general psychiatric morbidity, and father-adolescent conflict (Shek,1998) and paternal parenting (Shek 1999) had more stronger effect on PWB of adolescent. The adolescents who experience more parent-adolescent conflict show more mental health problems (Shek, 1997a). Raja et al. (1991) indicated that in early adolescence, PWB was more strongly correlated with the perceived level of attachment to parents rather than peers. Low perceived attachment to parents was related to greater problems of conduct, inattention, depression and frequent experience of negative life events. Moreover, PWB of adolescents is related to parental psychological control and when both parents exert considerable psychological control, PWB level of adolescent becomes the lowest (Shek, 2007).

The family functioning style has a direct or indirect impact on adolescents PWB, the adolescents in families with better functioning show better mental health and lower levels of symptoms (Shek, 1997b). While, the undesirable parental qualities are correlated with psychological difficulties (Maynard &Harding, 2010), the more favorable parental qualities are related to better indices of adolescents PWB such as existential well-being, life satisfaction, mastery, self-esteem and general psychiatric morbidity (Shek, 2002). It must be note that the important thing in here is perceptions of adolescents, not their parents' perceptions about family functioning, parental qualities, parent-adolescent conflict etc.

Finally, according to Telzer and Fuligni, (2009) family assistance enhances the happiness level of adolescents. Adolescents who assist their parents in household works, taking care of siblings or official business have a sense of role fulfillment and as a result, they feel happier, even the adolescents don't feel close to their parents. Family assistance positively supports PWB of adolescents by serving as a meaningful activity in adolescents' lives.

The Effect of Identity Status

According to Erikson (1963) the major developmental task in adolescence is identity formation and a successful identity formation is related to being psychologically well. Marcia (1996) defined four identity statuses: achievement, moratorium, foreclosure, and diffusion. Generally, the youths who have achievement identity status are seen as psychologically healthier. The adolescents who are at moratorium have high anxiety, depression and experiences many conflicts about autonomy issues. The individuals who have foreclosure status direct the roles which are identified by parents or authority figures and adopt them; they are in need of social approval. The youths who have diffusion identity have inconsistent, discrete and uncompleted sense of self and they generally experience psychological and interpersonal problems (Steinberg, 2013).

Philips and Pittman (2007) indicated that adolescents with a diffuse-avoidant style who pay little attention to future or the long term consequences of actions, make emotion-based decisions, and tend to procrastinate until consequences determine a course of action show decreased well-being and a less hopeful outlook toward future. They are less optimistic, have lower self-esteem, greater hopelessness and higher delinquent attitude. According to Abu-Rayya (2006) the adolescents with achievement and moratorium identity status have higher PWB that adolescents with foreclosure, diffusion identity status. Vleioras and Bosma (2005) conducted a study examining the relationships between identity style and PWB in late adolescents and found that the diffuse/avoidant orientation was a significant predictor of environmental mastery, positive relations with others, purpose in life, and personal growth facets of PWB. The information and normative orientations were significant predictors of personal growth facet of PWB. The identity styles didn't predict autonomy facet of PWB.

Moreover, the sense of having an ethnic identity affects PWB of adolescence. The adolescents who have high regard and sense of belonging to an ethnic group have high PWB (Abu-Rayya, 2006; Chae &Foley, 2010; Kiang, Gonzales-Backen, Fuligni, Yip & Witkow, 2006; Smith & Silva, 2011).

The Other Factors Related to PWB of Adolescents

In addition to factors which are explained in above, in literature there are many different variables related to PWB of adolescents. One of these factors is personality traits. Personality is seen as a major determinant of adolescents' well-being. PWB of adolescents is positively correlated with extraversion, conscientiousness (Anglim & Grant, 2014; Garcia, 2011; Ziskis, 2010), agreeableness (Anglim & Grant, 2014; Salami, 2011; Ziskis, 2010) and openness to experiences (Salami, 2011) and is negatively related with neuroticism (Anglim & Grant, 2014; Garcia, 2011; Salami, 2011; Trainor, et.al., 2010; Ziskis, 2010). The adolescents who are extravert, conscientious, agreeable and open to experiences have high PWB level, who are neurotic have low PWB level. Besides, while self-directedness predicts high PWB level, harm avoidance predict low PWB level of adolescents (Garcia, 2011). Also, the adolescent with high PWB level are assertive individuals (Sarkova, Bacikova-Sleskova, Orosova, Geckova, Katreniakova, Klein, et al. 2013).

Another variable is obesity. Adolescents intensively interest in their body and their perceptions of body image affect their psychological health. In adolescence, body dissatisfaction is greatly shown, especially in girls. Obesity can be lead to body dissatisfaction and social rejection, discrimination and negative stereotyping. As a result, negative consequences about of self- image, self-esteem and mood may appear, so it is suggested that obesity is linked to PWB of adolescents (Wardle & Cooke, 2005). The results of Yuan (2010) demonstrated that while PWB of female adolescents decrease depending on their perceptions of being larger or more developed, being larger or more developed don't affect PWB of male adolescents. It seems that the impact of obesity on PWB of adolescents changes depending on gender. During adolescents, body perceptions may disadvantage PWB of females relative to males. Also, Wardle and Cooke (2005) indicated that although there are adverse social and interpersonal consequences of obesity, obese adolescents may have only moderate levels of body dissatisfaction and few may be depressed or have low self-esteem.

Among other variables; income, perceived stress level, self-efficiency, a meaningful life, emotional intelligence, interpersonal relations, loneliness, assertiveness, sexual activity, emotion focused coping, social skills, social support may be lined up.

The adolescents with low PWB level have higher perceived stress level (Cripps and Zyromski, 2009; Moeini, Shafii, Hidarnia, Babaii, Birashk & Allahverdipour, 2008; Segrein, Hanzal, Donnerstein, Taylor, & Domschke, 2007), sense of loneliness (Corsano, Majorano, & Champretavy, 2006) and use emotion focused coping strategies in difficulties times (Trainor, Delfabbro, Anderson, &Winefield, 2010). If an adolescent, especially female adolescent, is sexually active may have low PWB level (Sabia & Rees, 2008).

The adolescent with high PWB level have higher self-efficiency (Moeini et.al, 2008) good interpersonal relations (Corsano, Majorano, & Champretavy, 2006), social support system (Detrie & Lease, 2007; Sen Chu, Saucier & Hafner, 2010) and developed social skills (Segrin, et al., 2007). They think their live to be meaningful and purposeful life (Rathi & Rastogi, 2007) and perceive themselves as being in touch with their emotions and able to regulate them (Mavroveli, Petrides, Rieffe, & Bakker, 2007; Salami, 2011).

According to Archontaki, Lewis and Bates (2013) genetic factors may influence PWB of adolescents. And, Shek (2005) indicated that the adolescent who comes from economic disadvantage group has weaker PWB than who not comes from economic disadvantage group, however findings of Lin et al. (2014) showed that family income has not a significant influence on PWB of adolescents.

Moreover, there may be differences among countries and ethnic groups in PWB of adolescents. For instance, the study compared youth well-being in OECD countries found that Korean children are at the lowest subjective well-being level among OECD countries (20th out of 20 countries). In terms of material well-being (10th out of 25 countries), family and peer relationships (12th out of 22 countries), and health-related behaviors, they were in the middle level range (Park, Seo, & Youm, 2010). Another study conducting by National Youth Policy Institute compared the youth of South Korea, Japan and Chine found that South Korean youth had lowest happiness level among the three countries (Choi, Kim, Lim, & Kang, 2011). Chae and Foley (2010) demonstrated that Japanese Americans had the highest PWB level among Chinese, Korean and Japanese Americans. Finally, in her study compared English and Turkish late adolescents' PWB level Kuyumcu (2012) found that English college students had higher PWB level rather than Turkish college students.

PSYCHOLOGICAL COUNSELING AND PSYCHOLOGICAL WELL BEING OF ADOLESCENTS

Today, instead of focusing on the negative trend in psychology and pathology, it can be seen that there is a change into improving existing situations; making lives of human beings more meaningful; ensuring enjoyment in a person's life; accepting human as a talented being and improving these talents; and seeing human as living beings who can stand strong against various negative living conditions and who can cope with these negativities (Seligman and Csikszentmihalyi, 2000; Sheldon and King, 2001). It is certain that this perspective brings in very important meaning and point of view to psychology.

Positive psychology is a discipline that focuses on the development of positive properties of individuals and protecting their mental health by means of programs increasing their subjective wellbeing and making them live positive experiences (Seligman ve Csikszentmihalyi, 2000). There are a number of assumptions of positive psychology. One of these assumptions is that individuals are active entities who are capable of directing their own developments. The second one is that individuals have necessary inherent power to change their behaviors and regulate them. The third one is that changing behavior dependent of psychology creates motivation in individuals towards connecting to life (Akın-Little and Little, 2004).

Among the concepts of positive psychology, psychological well-being refers to more than being stress-free or the absence of other psychological problems. Psychological well-being includes positive self-perception, good relations with people, environmental sovereignty, autonomy and emotions towards the meaning of life and a healthy growth (Ryff, 1995). In psychological wellbeing, it is necessary for the individual to improve his/her capacity and abilities to function completely (Ryff, 1989). This approach is important in various fields of development, particularly regarding the developmental period during adolescence.

According to positive psychology understanding, psychological counseling service is an important tool for normal people in both solving their adaptation problems and improving their capacities (Terjesen et al., 2004). During adolescence, while their various developmental duties that adolescents must achieve in this change and development period, there are also problematic fields to be dealt with such as academic and career planning and regulating interpersonal relationships. In this process, it is apparent that adolescents can be at risk in terms of psychological well-being. That is because there are a large number of defined problem fields that children and young people may experience. For example, psychological counseling applications are required towards problems such as suicide, substance abuse, familial conflicts, unable to make contact, career and value confusion, depression, school problems, risky behaviors, low self-esteem etc. In this respect, focusing of individual and group psychological counseling works may contribute to adolescents' well-being.

Psychological counselors can realize individual and group psychological counseling, group guidance and psycho-education programs towards revealing individuals' positive feelings. Individual psychological counseling will provide significant contributions in adolescents' process of recognition of themselves, developing positive perception of ego, developing effective decision-making skills and making realistic decisions about themselves. Group psychological counseling, one the other hand, may help solving conflicts and individual and interpersonal needs of the young in teaching coping skills with problems (Dinkmeyer & Muro, 1979). Counseling groups provide an environment of courage and confidence in accepting new behaviors. Therefore, the group can be readily used for psychological education (Seligman, 1982). In addition, since peers influence each other quite a lot, group counseling increases the chance of applying behaviors shown by peers and other important people and taking as example (Gazda, 1989).

Besides all these facts, psychological counselors may prepare psycho-education programs that increase psychological well beings not only for normal adolescents but also for those within risk group. In context of preventive and developmental approach, improving individuals' capacities based on positive psychology and developing from various aspects will also prevent experiencing possible problems (Akın-Little and Little, 2004). In forming contents of these programs, concepts and knowledge of positive psychology may be employed. Among these concepts, there are factors such as establishing supportive relationship with the surrounding, planning activities that improve individuals' skills and interests, improving individuals' communication and problem solving skills, determining live goals that will make their lives meaningful (Benard, 2004; Benard and Slade, 2009).

Protecting and improving adolescents' psychological well-being is an important concept in terms of psychological counseling. Adolescents' positive characteristics may be improved with school-based applications long before problem emerges and before adolescents' psychological wellbeing is not ruined, their live skills may be strengthened, and their positive coping skills and self-esteem may be increased. All these applications may contribute to adolescents' psychological wellbeing in a positive way.

REFERENCES

[1]   Abu-Rayya, HM. Ethnic identity, ego identity, and psychological well-being among mixed-ethnic Arab-European adolescents in Israel. *British Journal of Developmental Psychology*, 24(4), 669-679 (2006).

[2]   Akhter, MS. Psychological well-being in student of gender difference. *The International Journal of Indian Psychology*, 2(4), 253-161 (2015).

[3]   Akın-Little, KA; Little, SG. A preventative model of school consultation: Incorporating perspectives from positive psychology. *Psychology in the Schools*, 41(1), 155-162. (2004).

[4]   Anglim, J; Grant, S. Predicting psychological and subjective well-being from personality: Incremental prediction from 30 facets over the big 5. *Journal of Happiness Studies*, 1-22 (2014).

[5]   Benard, B. *Resiliency: What we have learned*. San Francisco: West Ed. (2004).

[6]   Benard, B; Slade, S. *Listening to students: Moving from resilience research to youth development practice and school connectedness*. (R. Gilman, E. S. Huebner, & M. J. Furlong (Eds.), Handbook of positive psychology in the schools (pp.353-370). New York: Routledge (2009).

[7]   Chae, MH; Foley, PF. Relationship of ethnic identity, acculturation, and psychological well-being among Chinese, Japanese, and Korean Americans. *Journal of Counseling & Development*, 88(4), 466-476 (2010).

[8]   Choi, IJ; Kim, JK; Lim, HJ; Kang, HC. *2010 International comparison of   youth worldview*. Seoul: Ministry of Gender Equality and Family (2011).

[9]   Chu, PS; Saucier, DA; Hafner, E. Meta-analysis of the relationships between   social support and well-being in children and adolescents. *Journal of Social and Clinical Psychology*, 29(6), 624-645 (2010).

[10]   Cooper, H; Okamura, L; McNeil, P. Situation and personality correlates of psychological well-being: Social activity and personal control. *Journal of Research in Personality*, 29, 395-417 (1995).

[11]   Corsano, P; Majorano, M; Champretavy, L. Psychological well-being in adolescence: The contribution of interpersonal relations and experience of being alone. *Adolescence*, 41(162), 341-353 (2006).

[12]   Cripps, K; Zyromski, B. Adolescents' psychological well-being and perceived parental involvement: Implications for parental involvement in middle schools. *RMLE Online: Research in Middle Level Education*, 33(4), 1-13 (2009).

[13]   Detrie, PM; Lease, SH. The relation of social support, connectedness, and collective self-esteem to the psychological well-being of lesbian, gay, and bisexual youth. *Journal of Homosexuality*, 53(4), 173-199 (2007).

[14]   Dinkmeyer, DC; Muro, JJ. *Group counselling*: Theory and practice. (2nd ed.), Boston: Allyn and Bacon (1979).

[15]   Erikson, EH. Youth: Fidelity and diversity. In Erikson, E. H. (Ed.), *Youth: Change and challenge* (pp. 1–23). New York & London: Basic Books, Inc., Publishers (1963).

[16]   Flouri, E; Buchanan, A. The role of father involvement in children's later mental health. *Journal of Adolescence*, 26(1), 63-78 (2003).

[17] Garcia, D. Two models of personality and well-being among adolescents. *Personality and Individual Differences*, 50(8), 1208-1212 (2011).

[18] Gazda, GM. Group counseling: A developmental approach (4th ed.). Boston: Allyn & Bacon (1989).

[19] Goldbeck, L; Schmitz, TG; Besier, T; Herschbach, P; Henrich, G. Life satisfaction decreases during adolescence. *Quality of Life Research*, 16(6), 969-979 (2007).

[20] Kiang, L; Yip, T; Gonzales-Backen, M; Witkow, M; Fuligni, AJ. Ethnic identity and the daily psychological well-being of adolescents from Mexican and Chinese backgrounds. *Child Development*, 77(5), 1338-1350 (2006).

[21] Kuyumcu, B. Investigation of psychological well-being emotional awareness and expression of emotion of Turkish and English university students with respect to country and gender. *The Journal of Erzincan Education Faculty*, 14(2), 1-24 (2012).

[22] Lin, FG; Chou, YC; Wu, CH; Lin, JD. Short-term and long-term influences of family arguments and gender difference on developing psychological well-being in Taiwanese adolescents. *Research in Developmental Disabilities*, 35(11), 2735-2743 (2014).

[23] Marcia, J. Development and validation of ego identity status. *Journal of Personality and Social Psychology*, 3, 551-558 (1996).

[24] Mavroveli, S; Petrides, KV; Rieffe, C; Bakker, F. Trait emotional intelligence, psychological well-being and peer-rated social competence in adolescence. *British Journal of Developmental Psychology*, 25(2), 263-275 (2007).

[25] Maynard, MJ; Harding, S. Perceived parenting and psychological well-being in UK ethnic minority adolescents. *Child: Care, Health and Development*, 36(5), 630-638 (2010).

[26] Moeini, B; Shafii, F; Hidarnia, A; Babaii, GR; Birashk, B; Allahverdipour, H. Perceived stress, self-efficacy and its relations to psychological well-being status in Iranian male high school students. *Social Behavior and Personality: An International Journal*, 36(2), 257-266 (2008).

[27] Park, CU; Seo, HJ; Youm, YS. Collection of Korean child well-being index and its international comparison with other OECD countries. *The Korean Journal of Sociology*, 44(2), 121–154 (2010).

[28] Pawar, PR; Adsul, RK. Influence of gender and nature of family on psychological well-being among adolescents. *Indian Journal of Health and Wellbeing*, 6(6), 631(2015).

[29] Phillips, TM; Pittman, JF. Adolescent psychological well-being by identity style. *Journal of Adolescence*, 30(6), 1021-1034 (2007).

[30] Rathi, N; Rastogi, R. Meaning in life and psychological well-being in pre-adolescents and adolescents. *Journal of the Indian Academy of Applied Psychology*, 33(1), 31-38 (2007).

[31] Raja, SN; McGee, R; Stanton, WR. Perceived attachments to parents and peers and psychological well-being in adolescence. *Journal of Youth and Adolescence*, 21(4), 471-485 (1992).

[32] Ryff, CD. *Psychological well-being in adult life*. Current Directions in Psychological Science, 4(4), 99-104 (1995).

[33] Ryff, CD; Singer, B. Know thyself and become what you are: A eudaimonic approach to psychological well-being. *Journal of Happiness Studies*, 9, 13-39 (2008).

[34] Sabia, JJ; Rees, DI. The effect of adolescent virginity status on psychological well-being. *Journal of Health Economics*, 27(5), 1368-1381(2008).

[35] Salami, SO. Personality and psychological well-being of adolescents: The moderating role of emotional intelligence. *Social Behavior and Personality: An International Journal*, 39(6), 785-794 (2011).

[36] Santrock, JW. *Life-span development*. McGraw-Hill (2012).

[37] Sarkova, M; Bacikova-Sleskova, M; Orosova, O; Madarasova Geckova, A; Katreniakova, Z; Klein, D; et al., Associations between assertiveness, psychological well-being, and self-esteem in adolescents. *Journal of Applied Social Psychology*, 43(1), 147-154. (2013).

[38] Segrin, C; Hanzal, A; Donnerstein, C; Taylor, M; Domschke, TJ. Social skills, psychological well-being, and the mediating role of perceived stress. *Anxiety, Stress, And Coping*, 20(3), 321-329 (2007).

[39] Seligman, M. Authentic happiness: Using the new positive psychology to realize your potential your potential for lasting fulfillment. New York, NY: Free Press (2002).

[40] Seligman, MEP; Csikszentmihalyi, M. Positive psychology: An introduction. *American Psychologist*, 55(1), 5-14 (2000).

[41] Shah, N. A comparative study of psychological-well-being among girls and boys. *Indian Journal of Health and Wellbeing*, 5(8), 976 (2014).

[42] Shek, DT. The relation of parent-adolescent conflict to adolescent psychological well-being, school adjustment, and problem behavior. *Social Behavior and Personality: An International Journal*, 25(3), 277-290 (1997a).

[43] Shek, DT. The relation of family functioning to adolescent psychological well-being, school adjustment, and problem behavior. *The Journal of Genetic Psychology*, 158(4), 467-479 (1997b).

[44] Shek, DT. A longitudinal study of the relations between parent-adolescent conflict and adolescent psychological well-being. *The Journal of Genetic Psychology*, 159(1), 53-67 (1998).

[45] Shek, DT. Parenting characteristics and adolescent psychological well-being: A longitudinal study in a Chinese context. *Genetic, Social, and General Psychology Monographs*, 125(1), 27 (1999).

[46] Shek, DT. The relation of parental qualities to psychological well-being, school adjustment, and problem behavior in Chinese adolescents with economic disadvantage. *American Journal of Family Therapy*, 30(3), 215-230 (2002).

[47] Shek, DT. Perceived parental control processes, parent—child relational qualities, and psychological well-being in Chinese adolescents with and without economic isadvantage. *The Journal of Genetic Psychology*, 166(2), 171-188 (2005).

[48] Shek, DT. A longitudinal study of perceived parental psychological control and pychological well-being in Chinese adolescents in Hong Kong. *Journal of Clinical Psychology*, 63(1), 1-22 (2007).

[49] Sheldon, KM; King, L. Why positive psychology is necessary. *American Psychologist*, 56, 216 – 217 (2001).

[50] Smith, TB; Silva, L. Ethnic identity and personal well-being of people of color: A meta-analysis. *Journal of Counseling Psychology*, 58(1), 42 (2011).

[51] Steinberg, L. *Adolescence*. (Translation ed. Figen Cok), Ankara: Imge Publication (2013).

[52] Telzer, EH; Fuligni, AJ. Daily family assistance and the psychological well-being of adolescents from Latin American, Asian, and European backgrounds. *Developmental Psychology*, 45(4), 1177-1189 (2009).

[53] Terjesen, MD; Jacofsky, M; Froh, J; Digiuseppe, R. Integrating positive psychology into schools: Implications for practice. *Psychology in the Schools*, 41(1), 163-172 (2004).

[54] Trainor, S; Delfabbro, P; Anderson, S; Winefield, A. Leisure activities and adolescent psychological well-being. *Journal of Adolescence*, 33(1), 173-186 (2010).

[55] Wardle, J; Cooke, L. The impact of obesity on psychological well-being. *Best Practice & Research Clinical Endocrinology & Metabolism*, 19(3), 421-440 (2005).

[56] Visani, D; Albieri, E; Offidani, E; Ottolini, F; Tomba, E; Ruini, C. Gender differences in psychological well-being and distress during adolescence. In *The Human Pursuit of Well-Being* (pp. 65-70). Springer Netherlands (2011).

[57] Vleioras, G; Bosma, HA. Are identity styles important for psychological well-being? *Journal of Adolescence*, 28(3), 397-409 (2005).

[58] Yuan, ASV. Body perceptions, weight control behavior, and changes in adolescents' psychological well-being over time: a longitudinal examination of gender. *Journal of youth and adolescence*, 39(8), 927-939 (2010).

[59] Ziskis, AS. *The relationships between personality, gratitude, and psychological well-being*. Rutgers The State University of New Jersey-New Brunswick (2010).

In: Psychological Well-Being   ISBN: 978-1-63484-354-6
Editor: Rafael Bowers   © 2016 Nova Science Publishers, Inc.

Chapter 8

MARRIAGE AND PSYCHOLOGICAL WELL-BEING: EXAMINING THE ROLE OF MARITAL RELATIONS AND COMMUNICATION STYLES AMONG POLISH COUPLES

Dariusz Krok[*]
Opole University, Poland

ABSTRACT

Social sciences have shown recurrent interest in the associations between marriage and its psychological outcomes. Marriage may provide numerous psychological benefits by offering meaning and purpose, facilitating interactions between spouses, sharing financial resources, and generating emotional and social support. Although previous research has demonstrated clear links between marital quality and well-being (Musick & Bumpass, 2012; Carr, Freedman, Cornman, & Schwarz, 2014), the role of specific marital relations and communication styles in psychological well-being remains not fully discovered. The quality of marital interactions and the ways in which partners communicate with each other appear to be linked to their well-being.

The aim of this chapter is to examine the predictive role of marital relations and communication styles in psychological well-being within a model proposed by Ryff (1989, 2014). One hundred and five couples (105 women and 105 men) participated in this study. Their ages ranged from 23 to 62 years ($M = 41.83$; $SD = 11.16$). The group was a representative sample of Polish couples in terms of social status and age. They completed three measures: The Matched Marriage Questionnaire, The Marital Communication Questionnaire, and The Psychological Well-being Scale. Findings showed that couples tended to experience numerous psychological benefits through marital interactions and communication skills. Yet, their overall psychological well-being depend on the quality of marital relations and communication styles. The marital relations which were based on intimacy, self-realization, and similarity were positively associated with psychological well-being dimensions, while the marital relations characterized by disappointment were negatively linked to psychological well-being. The relative contribution of marital relations and communication styles to psychological well-being was different for wives and husbands. The results lead to the conclusion that a

---

[*] dkrok@uni.opole.pl.

better understanding of marital relations and communication styles is likely to improve partners' well-being.

INTRODUCTION

Marriage has long been recognized as an important factor in contributing to the psychological well-being of both spouses. In spite of the recent changes in the demographics and meanings of marriage, the impact of marital quality and communication styles on psychological well-being has remained a vital topic of interest among researchers, practitioners, and the public (Musick & Bumpass, 2012; Carr, Freedman, Cornman, & Schwarz, 2014). Married couples may experience numerous psychological benefits by accepting a stable and officially established character of their union and by trusting that their marital bonds hold legal meaning and significance. Marriage may strengthen spouses' well-being by offering meaning and purpose, facilitating interactions between spouses, sharing financial resources, and generating emotional and social support.

Two of the most important factors in marriage are the quality of marital relations and communication styles. Both factors significantly contribute to spouses' psychological well-being, influencing their cognitive and emotional processes, and behavior (Vanassche, Swicegood, & Matthijs, 2013; Segrin & Flora, 2014). The main reason lies in the well-established observation that marriage is a specific type of interpersonal relationships that is characterized by spouses' long and deep contact in many areas of common life.

The first factor marital relations can be examined in terms of marital quality which is defined as a global evaluation of the marriage along several dimensions, including positive and negative aspects of marriage (e.g., support and strain, conflict and reconciliation), attitudes, and reports of behaviors and interaction patterns (Robles, Slatcher, Trombello, & McGinn, 2014). Therefore, high marital quality is characterized by high self-reported satisfaction with the relationship, predominantly positive attitudes towards one's partner, and low levels of negative and adverse behavior. Low marital quality is reflected by low satisfaction, predominantly negative attitudes towards one's partner, and high levels of negative and adverse behavior. This understanding of marital relations emphasizes partners' subjective satisfaction with their relationships and focuses on the attitudes and behavior which determine the overall quality of marriage. The components of marital relations do not only comprise basic interactions between spouses, but also thoughts and feelings that they express towards each other. The nature of their relationship is very important, because it has a strong impact on the spouses' psychological functioning and the individual development of each of them. The quality of mutual relations can also determine the durability or breakup of a marriage.

Another approach to marital relations was proposed by Plopa (2008), who developed the concept of the well-matched marriage, which is similar to the concept of marital quality in terms of satisfaction with the relationship. What distinguishes the concept of the well-matched marriage is, however, a multidimensional character of marital relations, a stronger emphasis on interpersonal communication, and highlighting the qualitative and functional aspects of marital relations.

Marital quality is understood as a specific process whose results are determined by an appropriate degree of intimacy, self-realization, similarity, and satisfaction (Plopa, 2005).

Intimacy reflects a high level of satisfaction with being in close relations with the spouse which is based on mutual trust, openness, and the willingness to form a loving union. Self-realization expresses the overall satisfaction with marriage, which comes from fulfilling one's potential, values, and goals. Similarity is characterized by partners' compatibility in reaching goals related to their marriage and family which, in turn, enables the partners to develop mature relations. Disappointment represents the feelings of existential failures which destroy marital relations by generating negative thoughts, emotions and reactions. Those four factors are formed during interactions between partners and are influenced by their personality traits, attitudes, behaviors, and communication styles.

The second factor examined in the current research is communication styles. Many authors consider interpersonal communication an essential part of married life (Strong & Cohen, 2013; Segrin & Flora, 2014). In everyday conversations partners use numerous communication patters in order to convey ideas and thoughts, make important decisions or solve conflicts. Plopa (2008) distinguished three major communication styles used by spouses in daily interactions: support, engagement, and deprecation. The support style consists in showing the partner genuine respect and interest, and it also embraces active participation in solving his/her problems. The engagement style reflects an attitude of creating mutual closeness and understanding between partners by showing one's feelings, emphasizing the uniqueness of the spouse, and avoiding potential conflicts. The depreciation style is characterized by aggressive behavior towards the partner, domination, control, and the lack of respect for the partner's dignity. Research examining those styles demonstrated that the support and engagement styles were linked to the secure attachment style, parents' acceptance and autonomy, and emotional stability, whereas the deprecation style was connected with the insecure avoidant and insecure ambivalent/resistant styles, parents' rejection, anxiety, and neuroticism (Plopa, 2008).

The frequency and styles of communication are regarded as one of the most important factors determining the overall level of satisfaction with marriage. Specific communication behaviors can either enrich the quality of marital interactions or reduce their value. Research has demonstrated that acquiring new communication skills turns out to be very useful in developing marital relations and strengthening mutual bonds (Du Rocher Schudlich, Papp, & Cummings, 2011; Guerrero, Andersen, & Afifi, 2013). Couples who can communicate in a constructive and mature way tend to experience fulfilled relationships, empathy and true intimacy with their spouses. Effective communication is also considered a significant strategy in preventing and solving marital conflicts.

In the relational model of communication, which has been successfully applied to marital relations, sender and receiver do not focus as much on themselves as on the message and on what they can do together. This approach provides a good chance to go beyond the current behavior through forming activities and relationships, which can enrich marriage (Stewart, 2005; Krok, 2007). According to the model, communication styles describe the process of determining who the sender and receiver are and what roles they play in everyday interactions. The relational model of communication also raises the question of guilt and responsibility for the process of communication as both the sender and receiver are accountable for the outcomes of their interactions. Two important factors determining the process of communication between partners are motivation and individual predispositions. They enable partners to recognize their personal needs and respond effectively to their spouses' cognitive and emotional reactions.

A very promising area of research on marriage and well-being lies within the model of psychological well-being (PWB) that is explicitly concerned with the development and self-realization of the individual (Ryff, 1989; Ryff, Keyes, 1995). Marriage is often perceived as a process of building mutual relations between spouses, which can enable them to develop their potential and discover personal characteristics. The PWB model developed by Ryff (1989) is based on a eudaimonic approach that perceives life in terms of virtue defined as finding the middle ground between excess and deficiency, and conditioned upon self-truth and self-responsibility (Ryff & Singer, 2008). According to Ryff (1989, 2014) this model of well-being includes 6 constructs: (1) self-acceptance, (2) positive relations with others, (3) autonomy, (4) environmental mastery, (5) purpose in life and (6) personal growth. Taken together they offer a multidimensional, eudaimonic vision of human life, which is noticeably connected to other areas of individual and social functioning (Krok, 2015; Ryff, 2014).

Substantial research has supported links between the quality of marital relations, communication styles, and well-being. For example, Horowitz, McLaughlin, and White (1998) revealed that perceived relationship quality (or satisfaction) was one of the strongest predictors of marriage stability and duration, as well as a robust predictor of psychological health. Plopa (2008) showed that spouses characterized by positive marital relations had lower levels of stress-related outcomes (e.g., fatigue, worries, tensions) than those with negative marital relations. Taking into account the fact that stress-related outcomes are inversely linked to well-being, it is justifiable to expect similar results between marital relations and psychological well-being.

The connections between marital relations, communication styles, and psychological well-being can be better understood within the social role perspective that focuses on how marriage arranges men's and women's understandings of what is expected of them (Ferree, 1990). This perspective posits that marital roles provide a source of meaning and purpose, and facilitate interactions between spouses by offering them guidelines concerning gender expectations, social norms and standards, and the sharing of financial resources. As a result, the patterns of social roles, which are also embedded in marital relations and communication styles may foster a sense of commitment and obligation to the relationship, further prompting behavior conducive to psychological well-being.

Studies examining the links between spouses' demanding and withdrawing and their subjective well-being have found the detrimental effects of these negative communication styles on life satisfaction. Women's, as well as men's, demands were directly associated with men's subjective well-being. Moreover, the individual conflict behavior was indirectly linked with both spouses' subjective well-being via their own marital satisfaction (Siffert & Schwarz, 2011). The results clearly indicate that communication styles used by spouses affect their life satisfaction.

Yet, the effects of marital relations on well-being also depend on the attributions made by partners in the context of the relationship. A longitudinal study of newlywed couples revealed that even though benevolent attributions of a partner's undesirable behaviors were positively associated with marital satisfaction initially, the effects of such attributions on changes in marital satisfaction depended on the severity of the problems that partners faced in their marriages (McNulty, O'Mara, & Karney, 2008). The differences may be likely an outcome of changes in the severity of the problems themselves. Spouses who made benevolent attributions while facing severe problems experienced declines in satisfaction because their problems remained severe, whereas spouses who made less benevolent attributions in the context of severe problems had higher satisfaction because their problems improved.

There also seem to be differences between women's and men's quality of marital relations and their well-being. Results demonstrated that marriage is more advantageous for men than women (Bernard, 1972; Gove, 1972), although recent investigations have shown that both men and women experience gains in psychological well-being from marriage, with some variation in the particular emotional response (Waite, 2000; Williams, 2003). Women tended to derive more advantages in well-being from emotional support than men. The differences may result from different patterns of cognitive and emotional interactions or responses to stresses among women and men, which can change the chances of satisfaction/dissolution, influencing gains to well-being.

Studies examining associations between interpersonal communication in marriage and well-being showed that spouses' interactions predict marital satisfaction and stability. The use of constructive conversation and direct conflict resolution strategies tended to enhance intimacy among partners (Christensen & Shenk, 1991). By contrast, less adaptive strategies (e.g., avoiding problem discussions, demand-withdrawal communication) led to marital dissatisfaction and dissolution (Noller & Feeney, 2002). The results prove that for partners interpersonal communication skills in identifying, understanding, and regulating their own cognitive and emotional reactions are crucial to shaping marriage life successfully and enhancing well-being.

However, the role of communication in influencing spouses' well-being strongly depends on the type of communication styles. Examining marital communication and satisfaction with marriage Plopa (2008) showed positive associations between satisfaction with marriage and partner's support and partner's engagement among both wives and husbands. In contrast, there were negative associations between satisfaction with marriage and partner's depreciation with both spouses. In a study conducted on a community sample of married individuals, Uebelacker, Courtnage, and Whisman (2003) found the associations among perceptions of marital communication styles (i.e., self-silencing and the demand–withdraw communication pattern), marital dissatisfaction, and depression symptoms. For men and women, depression symptoms were correlated with self-silencing and wife-demand and husband-withdraw communication. Depression symptoms were more highly associated with being in the demanding role for women than for men. The researchers concluded that the perceptions of interactions with one's spouse, as well as gender-related expectations of how both husband and wife should communicate with each other, may be important factors to depression and marital dissatisfaction in both men and women. There is also extensive research demonstrating close links between communication styles used in various domains of social life (e.g., clinicians, employers) and well-being (Ong, Visser, Lammes, & De Haes, 2000; Zapf, 2002).

A major concern regarding previous studies is that none of them directly investigated relationships between marital relations, communication styles, and psychological well-being. Although they tried to examine marital quality and communication, and well-being, their results did not reveal the complexity of relationships underlying different facets of these factors. Furthermore, the significant effects in the relationship between marital variables and psychological well-being may be accounted for by common variance in both marital relations and spouses' communication styles. To date, research has shown that different dimensions of marital relations and communication styles are related to different facets of well-being (Noller

& Feeney, 2002; Siffert & Schwarz, 2011; Robles et al., 2014). Given the multidimensional character of marital relations, communication styles, and psychological well-being, the current study was to assess how dimensions of marital relations and communication styles predict spouses' levels of psychological well-being. In addition, the relative contribution of marital relations and communication styles to psychological well-being was tested both for wives and husbands, independently.

Based on the above studies, the following hypotheses were tested: (1) marital relations which reflect positive attitudes towards the spouse are related to psychological well-being; (2) Constructive communication styles used by spouses are beneficial to psychological well-being; (3) The total psychological well-being depends on the relative contribution of both marital relations and communication styles; (4) The relative contribution of marital relations and communication styles to psychological well-being is different for wives and husbands.

METHOD

Participants and Procedure

A total of one hundred and five couples (105 women and 105 men) participated in this study. Their ages ranged from 23 to 62 years ($M = 41.83$; $SD = 11.16$). The duration of marriage ranged from 1 month to 35 years ($M = 17.34$; $SD = 12.65$). The participants were randomly recruited via private persons, various organizations, and work places located in Poland with the aim to be a representative sample of Polish couples in terms of social status and age. There were no statistically significant differences in terms of age between women and men. They were asked to complete a questionnaire packet consisting of demographic items, measures of marital relations, communication styles, and psychological well-being. The participants either returned the completed questionnaires directly or sent them back by post. The study was anonymous.

Measures

The following three questionnaires were administered: The Well-Matched Marriage Questionnaire, The Marital Communication Questionnaire, and The Psychological Well-being Scale. All of them were Polish versions.

Marital relations. To assess the quality of marital relations the Well-Matched Marriage Questionnaire was used (Plopa, 2008). It consists of 32 items, to which people respond on a 5-point Likert scale ranging from 1 (I strongly agree) to 5 (I strongly disagree). The questionnaire enables the assessment of the quality of marital relations in four dimensions: (1) Intimacy – this represents a high level of satisfaction with being in close relations with the spouse ("I like the nature of my partner", "Our contacts with my partner have become deeper over recent years, and we feel closer to each other"); (2) Self-realization – this denotes the level of satisfaction with marriage, which comes from fulfilling one's potential, values, and goals ("On a basis of my marital experiences I think that we can find the fulfilment of our life only in marriage"; "The birth of children deepens and strengthens our love"); (3) Similarity –

this represents the level of partners' compatibility in reaching goals related to their marriage and family ("Having free time we try to be together", "Acting together and achieving common plans bring me satisfaction"); (4) Disappointment this characterizes the feelings of existential failures, which are a consequence of marriage ("Sometimes I would like to go back to my parents' home and remain there", "I regret my independence and freedom from the premarital stage"). A total score can then be computed by summing the four scale scores. The Cronbach alpha coefficients for scales range from .81 to .89.

Communication styles in marriage. The Marital Communication Questionnaire (Kaźmierczak & Plopa, 2008) measures communication styles displayed by partners in marriage. The questionnaire consists of 30 items, to which people respond on a 5-point Likert scale ranging from 1 (never, i.e., my partner never behaves like that) to 5 (always, i.e., my partner always behaves like that). It contains three scales: (1) Support – this reflects showing the partner respect and interest, and active participation in solving his/her problems ("My partner is interested in my successes and problems", "My partner cares for me"); (2) Engagement – this refers to creating an atmosphere of mutual closeness and understanding between partners by showing one's feelings, highlighting the uniqueness of the spouse, and preventing marital conflicts ("My partner confesses to me the feelings he\she has towards me", "My partner organizes outings (e.g., to the cinema, restaurant) or trips"); (3) Depreciation – this includes aggressive behaviour towards the partner, desire to dominate and control him/her, and the lack of respect for his/her dignity ("My partner criticizes me", "My partner behaves arrogantly and harshly towards me").

The questionnaire can be used to examine both partners' communication styles. The Cronbach alpha coefficients were respectively: Support α = .88, Engagement α = .77 and Depreciation α = .86.

Psychological Well-being. The Psychological Well-being Scale is a 42-item questionnaire that evaluates the level of individuals' development and self-realization (Ryff and Keyes, 1995). It comprises six scales: (1) Autonomy – this describes such qualities as self-determination, independence, and the regulation of behavior from within ("I am not afraid to voice my opinions, even when they are in opposition to the opinions of most people"); (2) Environmental

Mastery – this denotes a sense of mastery and competence in managing the environment and controlling a complex array of external activities ("In general, I feel I am in charge of the situation in which I live"); (3) Personal Growth – this is concerned with the self-realization of the individual and involves a continual process of developing one's potential ("When I think about it, I haven't really improved much as a person over the years"); (4) Positive Relations with Others – this reflects having warm, satisfying, and trusting relationships with others ("Most people see me as loving and affectionate"); (5) Purpose in Life – this encompasses an attitude of having goals in life and a sense of directedness ("I have a sense of direction and purpose in life"); and (6) Self-acceptance – this is a kind of self-evaluation that is long-term and involves awareness, and acceptance of, both personal strengths and weaknesses ("When I look at the story of my life, I am pleased with how things have turned out"). Each scale consists of seven items, with a mix of positive and negative items. Participants respond to the items on a 6-point Likert scale ranging from 1 (I strongly disagree) to 7 (I strongly agree). A total PWB score can be calculated by adding all the six dimensions. The Polish version was adapted by Krok (2009).

RESULTS

In the first step of statistical analyses correlations between marital relations and psychological well-being were calculated for wives and husband separately as shown in table 1.

The results revealed that the total marital relations were positively related to the total psychological well-being in wives and husbands. As regards particular dimensions of marital relations, intimacy, self-realization, and similarity positively correlated with both the total psychological well-being and most of its dimensions in wives and husbands. The only difference was found between self-realization and personal growth – the correlation was significant for husbands, but not for wives. In contrast, disappointment was negatively associated with both the total psychological well-being and most of its dimensions.

Table 1. Correlations among marital relations and psychological well-being

Psychological well-being	Marital relations									
	Wives					Husbands				
	Int	Self	Sim	Dis	Total	Int	Self	Sim	Dis	Total
Autonomy	.15	.12	.19*	-.31***	.25**	.15	.05	.27**	-.12	.18
Environmental mastery	.24**	.28**	.27**	-.39***	.38***	.25**	.22*	.36***	-.32***	.36***
Personal growth	.28**	.18	.37***	-.39***	.38***	.29**	.35***	.31***	-.23*	.36***
Positive relations with others	.25**	.19*	.38***	-.27**	.34***	.27**	.33***	.23*	-.39***	.39***
Purpose in life	.34***	.28**	.37***	-.37***	.43***	.30***	.28**	.39***	-.38***	.42***
Self-acceptance	.23*	.20*	.31***	-.32***	.34***	.50***	.42***	.46***	-.34***	.53***
Total score	.31***	.26**	.39***	-.43***	.45***	.37***	.34***	.42***	-.37***	.47***

$***p < .001$; $**p < .01$; $*p < .05$.
Int – intimacy, Self – self-realization, Sim – similarity, Dis – disappointment.

There was a difference in the correlation between disappointment and autonomy – it was significant for wives, but not for husbands. The total psychological well-being was positively associated with autonomy only in wives.

Next, correlations between communication styles and psychological well-being were calculated for wives and husband separately (Table 2 and Table 3).

The correlational analysis demonstrated close associations between communication styles and psychological well-being in both groups. One's support and one's engagement were positively linked to both the total psychological well-being and all its dimensions with wives and husbands. In contrast, one's depreciation had negative associations with psychological well-being.

Table 2. Correlations among wives' communication styles and psychological well-being

Psychological well-being	Communication styles					
	OS	OE	OD	PS	PE	PD
Autonomy	.31***	.24**	-.13	.24**	.14	-.17
Environmental mastery	.28**	.26**	-.27**	.29**	.28**	-.22*
Personal growth	.39***	.41***	-.26**	.37***	.40***	-.21*
Positive relations with others	.25**	.24**	-.30**	.24**	.19*	-.19*
Purpose in life	.42***	.41***	-.24**	.36***	.39***	-.28**
Self-acceptance	.31***	.30**	-.21*	.30**	.23*	-.23*
Total score	.41***	.39***	-.29**	.37***	.34***	-.27**

OS – one's support, OE – one's engagement, OD – one's depreciation, PS – partner's support, PE – partner's engagement, PD – partner's depreciation..
***p < .001; **p < .01; *p < .05.

Table 3. Correlations among husbands' communication styles and psychological well-being

Psychological well-being	Communication styles					
	OS	OE	OD	PS	PE	PD
Autonomy	.27**	.34***	-.16	.19*	.32***	-.22*
Environmental mastery	.42***	.52***	-.37***	.29**	.39***	-.45***
Personal growth	.31***	.45***	-.30**	.15	.31***	-.26**
Positive relations with others	.42***	.49***	-.38***	.24**	.23*	-.34***
Purpose in life	.46***	.55***	-.29**	.29**	.37***	-.23*
Self-acceptance	.48***	.60***	-.37***	.32***	.41***	-.35***
Total score	.49***	.62***	-.39***	.31***	.43***	-.38***

OS – one's support, OE – one's engagement, OD – one's depreciation, PS – partner's support, PE – partner's engagement, PD – partner's depreciation.
***p < .001; **p < .01; *p < .05.

A similar pattern of relations was found between the partner's communication styles and psychological well-being. Partner's support and engagement were positively linked to psychological well-being, while partner's depreciation had negative associations. Yet, there were differences in some correlations among wives and husbands. While the correlation between partner's support and personal growth was significant in wives, it was insignificant in husbands. Conversely, there was an association between partner's engagement and autonomy in husbands, but not in wives. Next, tests of the difference in correlation between the relationships of communication styles with psychological well-being for wives and husbands were conducted. The only significant difference was found between the correlations of one's engagement with psychological well-being ($p < .05$). The correlation in the group of husbands was stronger than in the group of wives. In order to examine the relative contribution of marital relations and communication styles to psychological well-being, two-step hierarchical regression analyses were conducted for wives and husbands separately. Marital relations were entered into Step 1, and communication styles entered into Step 2. First, calculations were made for wives (Table 4).

Table 4. Hierarchical multiple regression analyses for wives' psychological well-being

Predictors	Model 1			Model 2		
	β	t	p	β	t	p
Intimacy	-.11	-.77	.444	-.24	-1.44	.152
Self-realization	.15	1.44	.154	.20	1.82	.071
Similarity	.21	1.57	.119	.13	.85	.397
Disappointment	-.34	-3.15	.002	-.29	-2.48	.015
One's support				.09	.53	.599
One's engagement				.27	1.97	.048
One's depreciation				-.09	-.81	.421
Partner's support				-.01	-.05	.961
Partner's engagement				-.02	-.15	.882
Partner's depreciation				-.002	-.01	.989
R^2	.23			.29		
ΔR^2				.06		
F	7.67***			3.93***		

***$p < .001$; **$p < .01$; *$p < .05$.

In the first step of hierarchical regression analyses for wives, marital relations as predictors accounted for an average portion of variance (23%) in psychological well-being as the regression equation was statistically insignificant ($F = 7.67$; $p < 0.001$). In the second step, after introducing communication styles variables, the proportion of explained variance increased to 29% and the regression equation remain significant ($F = 3.93$; $p < 0.001$). The change in variance was 6% ($\Delta R^2 = .06$). The results of beta weights indicated that in model 1 disappointment predicted lower levels of psychological well-being, whereas in model 2 disappointment predicted lower levels of psychological well-being and one's engagement predicted higher levels of psychological well-being.

Next, similar two-step hierarchical regression analyses were conducted for husbands (Table 5). Their results turned out to be significant.

**Table 5. Hierarchical multiple regression analyses for husbands'
psychological well-being**

Predictors	Model 1			Model 2		
	β	t	p	β	t	p
Intimacy	.004	.03	.974	.13	1.07	.288
Self-realization	.13	1.15	.252	.07	.86	.389
Similarity	.28	2.10	.038	.21	1.97	.049
Disappointment	-.21	-1.99	.049	.10	.97	.333
One's support				.57	3.20	.001
One's engagement				.28	2.34	.021
One's depreciation				-.03	-.28	.777
Partner's support				.80	4.35	.000
Partner's engagement				.26	2.03	.045
Partner's depreciation				-.23	-2.19	.031
R^2	.23			54		
ΔR^2				.31		
F	7.57***			11.22***		

***$p < .001$; **$p < .01$; *$p < .05$.

A hierarchical regression with marital relations in the first step predicted 23% of variance in husbands' psychological well-being ($F = 7.57$; $p < .001$). Adding communication styles in the second step significantly increased the variance accounted for to 54% ($F = 11.22$; $p <$

.001). The change in variance was 31% ($\Delta R^2 = .31$). In model 1, similarity predicted higher psychological well-being and disappointment predicted lower psychological well-being. In model 2, a set of variables: similarity, one's support, one's engagement, partner's support, and partner's engagement predicted higher levels of psychological well-being, while partner's depreciation predicted lower psychological well-being. The husbands' results thus differed from those obtained by wives.

DISCUSSION

This study investigated relationships between marital relations, communication styles, and psychological well-being. Specifically, the predictive strength of marital relations and communication styles on psychological well-being was tested both for wives and husbands, independently. Using hierarchical regression analyses, the current study enables us to understand more precisely interrelationships between different facets of the factors examined, especially the relative contribution of marital relations and communication styles to psychological well-being for wives and husbands, independently.

Under the assumption that marital relations are a beneficial resource for psychological well-being, marital relations reflecting positive attitudes towards the spouse were hypothesized to be significantly related to psychological well-being. Overall, the results supported the first hypothesis, with correlational analyses of the data showing that intimacy, self-realization, and similarity were positively related with both the total psychological well-being and most of its dimensions in wives and husbands. In contrast, disappointment was negatively associated with the total psychological well-being and most of its dimensions. The three dimensions of marital relations: intimacy, self-realization, and similarity reflect positive attitudes expressed by spouses towards each other, while the dimension of disappointment characterizes a negative approach conveyed by spouses (Plopa, 2008). Overall, these data are consistent with previous assertions in the literature that when spouses understand their partner's thoughts and feelings, and relate to each other in an affirming and constructive way, they tend to experience higher levels of well-being (Carr & Springer, 2010; Musick & Bumpass, 2012; Baker et al., 2013).

Yet, the current study expands the literature by demonstrating that the relationship of marital relations with dimensions of psychological well-being is conditional upon the quality of the marriage interactions. Constructive marital relations were positively related to spouses' personal development and self-realization, whereas dysfunctional relations showed negative associations. Having satisfaction with being in close relations with the spouse, fulfilling one's potential and goals, and the compatibility to reach marital goals enhances spouses' abilities to experience positive human functioning in the categories of value, purposeful engagement in life, and realization of personal talents (Krok, 2013; Ryff, 2014).

In contrast, experiencing the feelings of disappointment and failure in marriage may decrease spouses' personal development and self-realization. Thus, the psychological well-being perspective perceives marriage as a process of building mutually beneficial relations between spouses, which can enable them to develop their potential and discover personal characteristics.

The statistical analyses also revealed close associations between communication styles and psychological well-being in both groups of spouses. Both own and partner's support and engagement were positively linked to the total psychological well-being and all its dimensions in wives and husbands. On the contrary, both own and partner's depreciation was negatively related to psychological well-being.

These results verified the second hypothesis assuming that constructive communication styles used by spouses were beneficial to psychological well-being. Furthermore, the data showing that the spouses' support and engagement styles, which are regarded as positive and constructive in marital communication were positively related to psychological well-being is consistent with previous research on this topic (Uebelacker et al., 2003; Plopa, 2008).

It supports the notion that the ways in which spouses express thoughts and feelings are conducive to experiencing their happiness in terms of personal development and self-realization.

Extending the literature, the current study also demonstrates that there were slight differences between men and women in the relationship of communication styles with psychological well-being's dimensions. The relationship between their partner's support and personal growth was important for wives, but not for husbands. Conversely, the relationship between partner's engagement and autonomy played a significant role only for husbands, but not for wives. In addition, the connection between one's engagement and psychological well-being was stronger in husbands than in wives.

The results are likely to indicate a slightly different value of communication styles for men and women in building their personal happiness based on values and purpose. The data revealing gender differences in marital communication is congruent with prior studies (Krok, 2007; Plopa, 2008).

The central results in this study demonstrate that the total psychological well-being depends on the relative contribution of both marital relations and communication styles, which was proved in hierarchical regression analyses conducted for both groups of husbands and wives. The model which included both marital relations and communication styles better explained the total psychological well-being of spouses than the model only with marital relations as predictors. These results supported the third hypothesis which assumed that the total psychological well-being depended on the relative contribution of both marital relations and communication styles. They also confirm previous theoretical considerations emphasising the importance of having positive and satisfactory marital relations, and employing constructive communication strategies in order to enhance psychological well-being (Noller & Feeney, 2002; Baker et al., 2013; Carr et al., 2014). Expressing loving and caring attitudes in combination with mature and supportive communication styles among spouses appears beneficial to existential happiness which reflects personal development and self-realization.

Our analysis is also the first we know of to explore the relative contribution of marital relations and communication styles to psychological well-being conducted independently both for wives and husbands. Being based on hierarchical regression analyses, it offers several new insights into the complex associations between marital relations, communication styles, and psychological well-being (Williams, 2003; Baker et al., 2013). For wives, only disappointment predicted lower levels of psychological well-being and one's engagement predicted higher levels of psychological well-being. In contrast, for husbands, similarity, one's support, one's engagement, partner's support, and partner's engagement predicted higher levels of psychological well-being, while partner's depreciation predicted lower psychological well-being. These results not explored in previous studies reveal evident differences between women and men in the relative contribution of marital relations and communication styles to their psychological well-being. Thus, they allow us to confirm the fourth hypothesis that postulated such relationships. They are consistent with much of prior research that identified significant, though modest, gender differences on well-being (Robins, Caspi, & Moffitt, 2000; Williams, 2003).

Expanding the literature, these findings also shed new light on the multifaceted predictive role of marital relations and communication styles on psychological well-being. As regards psychological well-being, men tend to rely more substantially than women on communication styles by showing the partner respect and active participation in solving one's problems, and trying to create an atmosphere of mutual closeness and understanding. Men are also more likely to focus on compatibility in reaching goals related to their marriage and family than women.

The above findings are partially in contrast to some research reporting that women engage more in marital communication than men (Plopa, 2008). Though women may be more likely to engage in communication with their partners by expressing extensively their thoughts and feelings, men appear to rely more strongly on marital communication in order to enhance some qualities related to psychological well-being, i.e., personal development and self-realization. In such a context, the most useful model is likely to be one that focuses on how marital relations and communication influence interpersonal relationships between spouses, and on how these factors can contribute to the spouses' life satisfaction conceptualized in terms of values and purpose.

The different contribution of marital relations and communication styles to psychological well-being between men and women can be more precisely comprehended in the perspective of social support, which is generally regarded as one of the most important mechanisms in marital relationships strongly associated with well-being outcomes (Dehle, Larsen, & Landers, 2001; Soulsby & Bennett, 2015). Social support can be characterized as the perception and actuality that a person is cared for, has assistance available from other people, and is part of a supportive social network. It is also defined as the emotional, instrumental or tangible aid exchanged between members of the social network (Lakey, 2010).

In the context of marriage, spouses offer intimacy, empathy, and daily interactions, which can provide buffer and protection against the negative effects of stressful events. Spouses also connect their partners to larger networks of friends, relatives, and community that can be drawn on in times of need (Musick & Bumpass, 2012). There is strong evidence that social support directly influences psychological well-being (Andrews & Withey, 2012; Soulsby & Bennett, 2015). Marital relations and communication can be regarded as means of providing social support, thus the presence of a supportive partner can have beneficial effects on psychological well-being. In addition, the differences existing in gender expressions of marital relations and communication styles may result in the different levels of contribution to psychological well-being between women and men.

There are some limitations about this study that need to be reiterated. First, the current research is entirely cross-sectional and therefore it is difficult to establish causal relationships between marital relations, communication styles, and psychological well-being. The model positing that spouses with higher levels of psychological well-being would be characterized by more caring and responsible marital relations, and more constructive communication styles is likely to work well.

To make the findings more accurate future research should employ longitudinal or experimental models. Second, couples partaking in this research were not assessed in terms of potential marital conflicts or serious problems existing at the time of the research. The sequences of negative behavior that occur during conflict may generate strong marital distress and emotional tension, which in turn could distort the results (Siffert & Schwarz, 2011). More precise measurement of currently existing marital conflicts is needed if future research is to more objectively examine relations between marital quality, communication, and well-being. Third, this research did not provide data based on direct observations of marital transactions, and relied on self-reports of marital relations and communications styles. Future research would significantly profit from gathering such data using micro-analytical procedures and observational techniques.

In conclusion, the present study provides evidence in favor of the important role played by the quality of marital relations and communications styles in spouses' psychological well-being. The mode of constructing mutual interactions and expressing one's thoughts and feelings substantially accounts for potential variation in perceiving personal happiness in terms of values and purpose. Although partners are intertwined in close and dynamic relationships with one another, it is their own type of marital relations and communication that shapes their view of the relationship and influences their subjective experience of life satisfaction. The findings imply that though marital relations and communication styles evidently contribute to spouses' psychological well-being, there are differences between women and men in the level of the relative contribution. As a result, better understanding the individual and couple characteristics under which marriage is likely to improve psychological well-being is a significant challenge in future research on marital interactions.

REFERENCES

Andrews, F. M., & Withey, S. B. (2012). *Social indicators of well-being: Americans' perceptions of life quality*. New York: Springer Science & Business Media.

Baker, L. R., McNulty, J. K., Overall, N. C., Lambert, N. M., & Fincham, F. D. (2013). How do relationship maintenance behaviors affect individual well-being? A contextual perspective. *Social Psychological and Personality Science*, 4(3), 282–289.

Bernard, J. (1972). *The future of marriage*. New York: Bantam Books.

Carr, D., & Springer, K. W. (2010). Advances in families and health research in the 21st century. *Journal of Marriage and Family, 72*, 743–761.

Carr, D., Freedman, V. A., Cornman, J. C., & Schwarz, N. (2014). Happy marriage, happy life? Marital quality and subjective well-being in later life. *Journal of Marriage and Family*, 76(5), 930–948.

Christensen, A., & Shenk, J. L. (1991). Communication, conflict and psychological distance in nondistressed, clinic and divorcing couples. *Journal of Consulting and Clinical Psychology, 59*, 458–463.

Dehle, C., Larsen, D., & Landers, J. E. (2001). Social support in marriage. *American Journal of Family Therapy*, 29(4), 307–324.

Du Rocher Schudlich, T. D., Papp, L. M., & Cummings, E. M. (2011). Relations between spouses' depressive symptoms and marital conflict: a longitudinal investigation of the role of conflict resolution styles. *Journal of Family Psychology*, *25*(4), 531–540.

Ferree, M. M. (1990). Beyond separate spheres: Feminism and family research. *Journal of Marriage and the Family, 52*, 866–884.

Gove, W. R. (1972). The relationship between sex roles, marital status, and mental illness. *Social Forces, 51*, 34–44.

Guerrero, L. K., Andersen, P. A., & Afifi, W. A. (2013). *Close encounters: Communication in relationships*. Thousand Oaks: Sage Publications.

Horowitz, A. V., McLaughlin, J., & White, H. R. (1998). How the negative and positive aspects of partner relationships affect the mental health of young married people. *Journal of Health and Social Behavior, 39*, 124–136.

Kaźmierczak, M., & Plopa, M. (2008). *Kwestionariusz Komunikacji Małżeńskiej. Podręcznik* [The Marital Communication Questionnaire. The manual]. Warszawa: Vizja Press & IT.

Krok, D. (2007). Znaczenie komunikacji interpersonalnej w funkcjonowaniu rodziny [The significance of interpersonal communication in the functioning of family]. In B. Soiński (Ed.), Rodzina w świetle psychologii pastoralnej [Family in the perspective of pastoral psychology] (pp. 41–53). Łódź: ALW.

Krok, D. (2009). *Religijność a jakość życia w perspektywie mediatorów psychospołecznych* [Religiousness and quality of life in the perspective of psychosocial mediators]. Opole: Redakcja Wydawnictw WT UO.

Krok, D. (2013). The sanctification process as a way of strengthening marital bonds. In K. Glombik (Ed.), *Glaube und Moral theologische Argumentation in der gesellschaftlichen Debatte der Gegenwart* [Faith and moral theological argumentation in the public debate of the presence] (pp. 127–147). Opole: Redakcja Wydawnictw WT UO.

Krok, D. (2015). The mediating role of optimism in the relations between sense of coherence, subjective and psychological well-being among late adolescents. *Personality and Individual Differences, 85*, 134–139.

Lakey, B. (2010). Social support: Basic research and new strategies for intervention. In J.E. Maddux, J. P. Tangney (Eds.), *Social psychological foundations of clinical psychology* (pp. 177–194). New York: The Guilford Press.

McNulty, J. K., O'Mara, E. M., & Karney, B. R. (2008). Benevolent cognitions as a strategy of relationship maintenance: "Don't sweat the small stuff" but it's not all small stuff. *Journal of Personality and Social Psychology, 94*, 631–646.

Musick, K., & Bumpass, L. (2012). Reexamining the case for marriage: Union formation and changes in well-being. *Journal of Marriage and Family, 74*(1), 1–18.

Noller, P., & Feeney, J. A. (2002). Communication, relationship concerns, and satisfaction in early marriage. In A. L. Vangelisti, H. T. Reis, M. A. Fitzpatrick (Eds.), *Advances in personal relationships. Stability and change in relationships* (pp. 129–155). New York, NY: Cambridge University Press.

Ong, L. M., Visser, M. R., Lammes, F. B., & De Haes, J. C. (2000). Doctor–patient communication and cancer patients' quality of life and satisfaction. *Patient education and counseling, 41*(2), 145–156.

Plopa, M. (2005). *Psychologia rodziny* [Psychology of family]. Kraków: Oficyna Wydawnicza "Impuls".

Plopa, M. (2008). *Więzi w małżeństwie i rodzinie. Metody badań* [The relations in marriage and family. Research methods]. Kraków: Oficyna Wydawnicza "Impuls".

Robins, R. W., Caspi, A., & Moffitt, T. E. (2000). Two personalities, one relationship: Both partners' personality traits shape the quality of their relationship. *Journal of Personality and Social Psychology, 79*, 251–259.

Robles, T. F., Slatcher, R. B., Trombello, J. M., & McGinn, M. M. (2014). Marital quality and health: A meta-analytic review. *Psychological Bulletin, 140*(1), 140–187.

Ryff, C. D. (1989). Happiness is everything, or is it? Explorations on the meaning of psychological well-being. *Journal of Personality and Social Psychology, 57*, 1069–1081.

Ryff, C. D., & Keyes, C. L. M. (1995). The structure of well-being revisited. *Journal of Personality and Social Psychology, 69*, 719–727.

Ryff, C. D., & Singer, B. H. (2008). Know thyself and become what you are: A eudaimonic approach to psychological well-being. *Journal of Happiness Studies, 9,* 13–39

Ryff, C. D. (2014). Psychological well-being revisited: Advances in the science and practice of eudaimonia. *Psychotherapy and Psychosomatics, 83*(1), 10–28.

Segrin, C., & Flora, J. (2014). Marital communication. In Ch. R. Berger (Ed.), *Interpersonal communication* (pp. 443–466). Berlin and Boston: De Gruyter.

Siffert, A., & Schwarz, B. (2011). Spouses' demand and withdrawal during marital conflict in relation to their subjective well-being. *Journal of Social and Personal Relationships, 28*(2), 262–277.

Sirgy, M. J. (2012). *The psychology of quality of life: Hedonic well-being, life satisfaction, and eudaimonia* (Vol. 50). London and New York: Springer Science & Business Media.

Soulsby, L. K., & Bennett, K. M. (2015). Marriage and psychological wellbeing: The role of social support. *Psychology, 6*(11), 1349–1359.

Stewart, J. (2005). Komunikacja interpersonalna: kontakt między osobami [Interpersonal communication: contact between persons. In J. Stewart (Ed.), *Mosty zamiast murów. Podręcznik komunikacji interpersonalnej* [Bridges not walls. A book about interpersonal communication] (pp. 38–58). Warszawa: Wydawnictwo Naukowe PWN.

Strong, B., & Cohen, T. (2013). *The marriage and family experience: Intimate relationships in a changing society*. Belmont: Cengage Learning.

Uebelacker, L. A., Courtnage, E. S., & Whisman, M. A. (2003). Correlates of depression and marital dissatisfaction: Perceptions of marital communication style. *Journal of Social and Personal Relationships, 20*(6), 757–769.

Vanassche, S., Swicegood, G., & Matthijs, K. (2013). Marriage and children as a key to happiness? Cross-national differences in the effects of marital status and children on well-being. *Journal of Happiness Studies, 14*(2), 501–524.

Waite, L. J. (2000). Trends in men's and women's well-being in marriage. In L. Waite, C. Bachrach, M. Hindin, E. Thomson, A. Thornton (Eds.), *The ties that bind: Perspectives on marriage and cohabitation* (pp. 368–392). New York: Aldine de Gruyter.

Williams, K. (2003). Has the future of marriage arrived? A contemporary examination of gender, marriage, and psychological well-being. *Journal of Health and Social Behavior, 44*, 470–487.

Zapf, D. (2002). Emotion work and psychological well-being: A review of the literature and some conceptual considerations. *Human Resource Management Review, 12*(2), 237–268.

In: Psychological Well-Being   ISBN: 978-1-63484-354-6

Editor: Rafael Bowers   © 2016 Nova Science Publishers, Inc.

Chapter 9

PSYCHOLOGICAL HEALTH AMONG FRAIL OLDER ADULTS WITH CHRONIC PAIN IN THE COMMUNITY: DOES THE HEALTHY LIVING PROGRAM HELP?

Mimi M. Y. Tse[1,], RN, PhD, Rose Heung[2], MS, and Vanessa T. C. Wan[3], RN, MSc*

[1]Assistant Professor, School of Nursing,
The Hong Kong Polytechnic University, Kowloon, Hong Kong
[2]Clinical Associate, School of Nursing,
The Hong Kong Polytechnic University, Kowloon, Hong Kong
[3]Registered Nurse, MandG, Prince Margaret Hospital,
Kowloon, Hong Kong

ABSTRACT

Background. Populations are aging and an increasing number of people are suffering from disease and disability as part of the aging process. Pain is common in older adults, and affects both their physical and psychological functioning. However, the majority of older adults who experience pain do not seek the advice of health care professionals. Uncontrollable pain can lead to a spiral of inactivity and reduce the quality of life of older adults in the community. A self-managed health program may help to break through this spiral, thus reducing uncontrollable chronic pain among frail older adults and enabling them to live happier lives.

Method. Two community elderly centers agreed to host the Healthy Living Program (HLP). Fifty community dwelling older people from those two centers were invited to join the six-week HLP. The program covered the following topics: healthy eating habits, pain management, and information on drugs related to pain and chronic illness. The targeted participants were recruited from the community elderly centers by convenience sampling. In the study, psychological well-being among older adults was measured pre- and post- test using a subjective happiness scale. In addition, information on the participants' knowledge of healthy eating habits, fall prevention, and drugs was collected.

---

[*] E-mail: hsmtse@inet.polyu.edu.hk, Tel.: 852 2766 6541, Fax: 852 2364 9663.

Results. A slight increase was seen in the participants' scores on the happiness scale after the HLP, but the change was not statistically significant. Their pain scores decreased, and their pain interference scores showed a statistically significant decrease ($p < 0.05$). Finally, a significant improvement was noted in the participants' intake of protein, vegetables, and fruit and in their knowledge of drug management.

Conclusion. A health self-management program should be offered to elderly people, and nurses should encourage them to engage in it to enrich their knowledge of how to take care of themselves, increase their happiness, and enhance their quality of life. Older adults with good habits will then be able to enjoy longer and healthier lives in the community.

INTRODUCTION

Pain is considered one of the most common problems in older persons. During the normal aging process, nearly 50 to 80% of older persons suffer from chronic pain, mostly musculoskeletal pain, including osteoarthritis, back pain, joint pain, and bone pain (Pickering, 2005). Chronic pain is associated with physical, emotional, and social limitations (Breivik, Collett, Ventrafrida, Cohen and Gallagher, 2006). In fact, uncontrollable pain can lead to a spiral of inactivity and reduce the quality of life of older people in the community (Parmelee, 2005; Rudy and Lieber, 2005; Strong, 2002).

According to Cavalieri (2002), the impact of pain on individual function, activity, and relationships can be neglected or dismissed as an inevitable part of aging and, consequently, under-treated. Unfortunately, when combined with other effects of aging, pain can lead to a rapid decline in mobility and function in the elderly. Their consequent disengagement from meaningful activities, valued roles, and routines may result in depression and poor self-esteem (Craig and Mountain, 2006). Older people with chronic pain may end up in hostel care as their final home, as their condition worsens.

Health care professionals play an important role in helping older persons manage their pain. By reducing their suffering from pain, older people can enhance their physical mobility and psychosocial functioning, thus improving their quality of life and enabling them to live more happily in the community. For these reasons, a Healthy Living Program (HLP) was launched in community elderly centers.

Neighborhood Elderly Centers (NECs) in Hong Kong

According to Social Welfare Department in Hong Kong (2015), the Neighborhood Elderly Center (NEC) is a place that offers community support services at the neighborhood level. Specifically, it provides comprehensive services to enable elderly persons to remain in the community, lead healthy, respectable, and dignified lives, and make positive contributions to society. The scope of the services provided by NECs includes educational and developmental activities, the provision of information on community resources and referral services, volunteer development, carer support services, counseling services, reaching out and networking services, social and recreational activities, and so on. Therefore, an NEC is an ideal place for community dwelling older people to acquire health information under a peer support atmosphere.

The Concept of Self-Managed Health - Healthy Living Program (HLP)

Most approaches to managing the pain of older persons have involved pharmacological and non-pharmacological methods. However, elderly people are at risk of being under-treated for pain (Hanlon, Backonja, Weiner and Argoff, 2009), including community dwelling elderly people (Brown et al., 2011). Inadequate pain management among older people may due to possible impairments in their cognitive status leading to the under-reporting of pain, their pain beliefs, or their inadequate knowledge of pain management (Tse and Vong, 2012). Therefore, the participants in the HLP were taught about the use of pain-killers and drugs commonly used to manage chronic illnesses among older persons.

Currently, several studies on supporting older people with chronic pain have been open to the idea of self management (Lansbury, 2000; Kemp, Ersek and Turner, 2005), covering a wide range of techniques such as relaxation, coping strategies, exercise, adaptation to activities, and education about pain and its effects. According to Stewart, Schofield, Elliott, Torrance, and Leveille (2014), the aim is to get older adults to engage in pain management, to inform and support them in this endeavor so that they will improve in health and well-being, and to improve the use of health care resources.

In this study, an interactive healthy living program was provided to community-dwelling older adults, focusing on healthy eating habits, drug knowledge, and preventing falls. It can be foreseen that such a study can enhance the self-care abilities of the elderly.

METHODS

Design and Sample

A pre-post experimental design was used in the study. After ethical approval was obtained from the Ethics Committee of the Hong Kong Polytechnic University, two elderly centers under the auspices of the Pentecostal Church of Hong Kong were invited to participate in the study.

Fifty community dwelling older people, both males and females, were recruited from the elderly centers by convenience sampling. The criteria for inclusion in the study were that the participants had to be aged 60 or above; have a frailty score of >1, and to be able to communicate in Cantonese. Those suffering from cognitive impairment, blindness, or deafness were excluded from the study.

The Six-Week Healthy Living Program (HLP)

The aim of the HLP is to enhance the ability of community dwelling older people to care for themselves. It is hoped that by providing information on health and healthy habits, older adults can keep living healthy lives in the community, reduce their risk of falling, and arrest the deterioration in their health. Interactive teaching took place in each session of the HLP, which lasted 30-45 minutes. It included the use of PowerPoint slides, Q and A sessions, games, and puzzles. The participants were arranged into small groups to facilitate learning.

Procedure

The participating centers put up posters in their premises to invite members to participate. They also made announcements during their regular meetings and phone calls to remind their members about the HLP. The response was satisfactory. At baseline, background information on the older persons was collected, including their age, gender, marital status, level of education, living conditions, spouse and family relationships, exercise habits, medical history, and pain-related information. In addition, the participants' scores in the Body Mass Index (BMI), Fried Frailty Index, Brief Pain Inventory (BPI-T), Happiness Scale, and Mini Nutritional Assessment (MNA) instrument were measured at baseline and after they had completed the HLP. The intervention consisted of six consecutive weeks of HLP conducted in the community elderly centers. An identical program was provided in each center. As mentioned previously, in the HLP older persons were taught about nutrition and healthy diets, preventing falls, and drug management. An additional interview session with a dietitian was provided to those obese participants with a BMI score of ≥ 23.0. As an evaluation, after the HLP, all of the participants were asked to fill out an identical questionnaire to determine whether they noticed any changes after participating in the HLP.

Measures

Pain Status

Pain situations among the community dwelling older persons were measured using the Geriatric Pain Assessment instrument. Included were assessments of pain intensity using a verbal rating scale (0 to 10-point scale), the pattern and location of the pain, and the use of analgesic drugs and non-drug therapies, including their type, frequency, and method (American Geriatrics Society Panel, 2002). Also assessed was the interference of pain in the participants' activities of daily living, their emotions, mobility, social relationships, sleep quality, and interest in living.

Happiness

The Chinese version of the Subjective Happiness Scale (SHS) is a four-item questionnaire that is used to evaluate a person's happiness (Kashdan and Yuen, 2007; Lyubomirsky and Lepper, 1999). Two items ask the respondents to characterize themselves using both absolute ratings and ratings relative to peers, while the other two items offer brief descriptions of happy and unhappy individuals and ask the respondents about the extent to which each characterization describes them (Lyubomirsky and Lepper, 1999). The participants respond to each item on a seven-point Likert scale. The Cronbach's alpha is 0.79 to 0.94. The test-retest reliability ranges from 0.55 to 0.90. The total range of scores is 4 to 28, with higher total scores indicating greater happiness.

Body Mass Index (BMI) and the Mini Nutritional Assessment (MNA)

The Body mass index (BMI) is calculated as weight in kilograms divided by height in meters squared, and individuals are classified as underweight, normal, overweight, or obese according to pre-defined BMI cut-off points.

Table 1. Classification of BMI for Adult Asians by WHO

Classification	BMI (kg/m2)
Underweight	<18.5
Normal range	18.5-22.9
Overweight:	≥23
Pre-obese	23-24.9
Obese I	25-29.9
Obese II	≥30

The BMI is regarded as the most commonly used tool to measure obesity in epidemiological studies, and is easy to measure, highly reliable, and best correlated to body fat content (Bray, 2004). Regarding classifications of adult body weight, the World Health Organization (WHO) defines a BMI of 18.5-24.9kgm² as the optimal or normal range, and BMIs of ≥25 and ≥30kgm² as overweight and obese, respectively (WHO, 1998). As there is increasing evidence that the risk of co-morbidities in relation to BMI differs among different races, the WHO has issued guidelines on cut-off values to classify overweight and obese individuals in Asian populations (Table 1). In the study, the Mini Nutritional Assessment (MNA) was used to better understand the nutritional intake of the elderly participants, such as their consumption of protein, vegetables, and fruits (Guigoz, 2006).

Data Collection and Analysis

Ethical approval was obtained from the Hong Kong Polytechnic University and from the corresponding nursing homes prior to the commencement of the study. Written consent was obtained from each participant after they were given an explanation of the aim and procedure of the proposed study, as well as in information sheet. Data were collected at baseline, before the commencement of the HLP, and at Week 6 upon the completion of the HLP. Data collection was performed individually and in private to avoid the potential confounding effects of peer pressure. The data were analyzed using the statistical software SPSS (Version 20). Descriptive statistics (mean, standard deviation, frequency, and percentage) were computed to illustrate the characteristics of participants. A comparison of their baseline characteristics was conducted by analyzing the results of a Chi-square test for categorical variables and an independent sample t-test for continuous variables. A dependent paired samples t-test was used to differences in the within-group outcome variables before and after the intervention. A p-value of less than 0.05 was considered significant for all statistical tests.

RESULTS

Demographic Data

Fifty older people (4 males and 46 females) participated in the study. Their ages ranged from 65 to 90 or above, with a mean age of 77.0 ± 8.8.

Table 2. Demographic Data (N = 50)

	N (%)
Gender	
Male	4 (8.0)
Female	46 (92.0)
Age	77.0 ± 8.8
Marital Status	
Married	23 (46.0)
Widowed	27 (54.0)
Education Level	
No Formal Education	28 (57.1)
Primary Education	15 (30.6)
Secondary Education	5 (10.2)
Post Secondary or above	1 (2.0)
Previous Occupation	
Primary Industry	29 (58.0)
Secondary Industry	2 (4.0)
Tertiary Industry	11 (22.0)
Housework	8 (16.0)
Living Condition	
Live alone	19 (38.0)
Living with spouse only	11 (22.0)
Live with spouse and children	5 (10.0)
Live with children	15 (30.0)

Over half (57.1%) of the participants had not received any formal education. More than half of them (54.0%) were widows or widowers, 38% of them were living alone and taking care of themselves, 22% were living with their spouse, and only 40% were living with their children.

Physical Parameters

Pain Status

After the program, the participants' pain scores decreased from 3.3 ± 2.1 to 2.8 ± 2.5, but the decline was not statistically significant. However, their pain interference scores dropped from 19.7 ± 18.8 to 12.0 ± 16.7, and the p-value of <0.05 showed that the change was statistically significant.

Body Mass Index (BMI) and Mini Nutritional Assessment (MNA)

After the HLP, no statistically significant change in the participants' BMI scores was seen, and the p-value was >0.05. When the BMI distribution of the participants was reviewed, a statistically significant change was noted, with improvements observed in those who were in an underweight condition ($p < 0.05$). In addition, there was a statistically significant improvement in the intake of proteins, vegetables, and fruits after the HLP ($p < 0.05$).

Psychological Parameters

Happiness

After the HLP, there was a slight increase in the happiness scores of the community dwelling older adults, from 18.8 ± 5.0 to 19.7 ± 5.3, with a p-value of >0.05, indicating no statistical significance.

Table 3. Physical and psychological parameters

Physical parameters	Pre-test	Post-test	p-value
Pain status			
Pain scores	3.3 ± 2.1	2.8 ± 2.5	.173
Pain inference	19.7 ± 18.8	12.0 + 16.7	.006**
BMI			
BMI	23.0 ± 3.2	23.3 ± 3.3	.331
BMI Distribution			.008**
Underweight	5 (10.2)	4 (8.2)	
Normal range	21 (42.9)	18 (36.7)	
Pre-obese	12 (24.5)	13 (26.5)	
Obese I	11 (22.4)	13 (26.5)	
Obese II	0	1 (2.0)	
Nutrition status			
Adequate protein, vegetables and fruit intakes			.003**
Adequate	11 (22.0)	14 (28.0)	
Inadequate	39 (78.0)	36 (72.0)	
Psychological parameter			
Happiness	18.8 ± 5.0	19.7 ± 5.3	.254

Note: * p < .05 and ** p < .01 was considered as statistically significant.

Table 4. Knowledge Management

Knowledge Management	(Scores)	Pre-test	Post-test	p-value
Nutrition knowledge		8.0 ± 2.7	9.0 ± 2.7	.076
Fall prevention knowledge		4.1 ± 0.9	4.5 ± 0.6	.041*
Drug management		8.4 ± 1.5	7.9 ± 1.4	.028*

Note: * p < .05 and ** p < .01 was considered as statistically significant.

Knowledge Management

In the study, a significant improvement was seen in the area of falls (p < 0.05). The participants' fall prevention knowledge increased from 4.1 ± 0.9 to 4.5 ± 0.6 after the HLP (p = 0.041). No statistically significant change was seen in their nutritional knowledge (p > 0.05). However, their knowledge of drug management increased significantly from 8.4 ± 1.5 to 7.9 ± 1.4 (p < 0.05).

DISCUSSION

Our study recruited 50 older participants from two Neighborhood Elderly Centers in Hong Kong. These centers provided similar services to the elderly. The community dwelling older people in the study suffered from chronic pain, and their pain scores before the HLP were 3.3 ± 2.1. Their pain intensity was less than 4, which is considered a mild grade of pain. Chinese older people seldom quantify how much pain they are in. Smith (2002) reported that in Chinese culture the elderly have the common belief that "Pain occurs in every old person…"; "I can do nothing for it…"; "I have to tolerate my pain…"; "Pain must get worse and I have no way of preventing or managing it." Unfortunately, older people believe that resting and taking analgesic drugs and ointments are the best ways to relieve pain (Tse, Wan and Ho, 2010). Beliefs stimulate the development of adaptive/maladaptive pain behavior, which may influence older persons' motivation to engage in pain treatments and coping strategies, and thus have an impact on the effects of treatment. Indeed, uncontrollable chronic pain may affect their activities of daily living, emotions, mobility, social relationships, sleep quality, and interest in living, as shown in the pain interference scores of 19.7 ± 18.8 among older people with chronic pain.

In addition, older people whose pain condition is worsening may find their psychological status affected, as they show a decrease in self-care ability and an increase in their dependency on others, which may lower their level of happiness and life satisfaction (Tse, Leung andHo, 2012). Therefore, geriatric pain is becoming a major concern in a rapidly aging society, and greater attention is being devoted to its management.

Various articles have focused on non-pharmacological interventions to manage chronic pain in community dwelling older persons (Park and Hughes, 2012). Such interventions have included physical interventions (exercise, acupuncture, transcutaneous electric nerve stimulation, and qigong therapy) and psychosocial interventions (self-management educational interventions, cognitive behavioral therapy, mindfulness-based meditation, and music therapy).

According to a guide on the management of pain in older people published in 2013, the self management of pain covers a wide range of techniques that include relaxation, coping strategies, exercise, adaptation to activities, and education about pain and its effects, thus these programs may be of benefit if support is given for an extended period. Besides the negative effect of physical ability and mobility, Clark (1999) highlighted the view that pain is a complex experience and that physical, psychological, social, and spiritual components make up the total pain experience. In this regard, psychological well-being – being positive and happy – is important in pain management.

In our study involving the healthy living program, interactive classroom-based lessons were introduced in a community elderly center to increase the participants' knowledge about healthy eating habits, drugs related to controlling chronic illness and pain, and preventing falls, and thus to enhance the participants' ability to take care of themselves in daily life. After they had completed the HLP, an increase was seen in their consumption of fruits and vegetables, measured by the MNA, with a p-value of <0.05, indicating that the improvement was significant. As indicated in the fall prevention session, participation in exercise can reduce pain and also significantly reduce pain interference, which also enhances psychological well-being, as measured by the subjective happiness scale. Scores for the latter increased slightly after the completion of the HLP, from 18.8 ± 5.0 to 19.7 ± 5.3. Certainly, a self-management program such as the HLP should be offered and nurses should encourage older persons to take part in it. This will enhance the health knowledge of older people, potentially leading to changes in their behavior and to the achievement of a better quality of life. This will allow older people to remain healthier and happier with peer support in the community.

CONCLUSION

In conclusion, community dwelling older people suffer from various health problems, such as pain that affects their activities of daily living and thus their psychological health. The six-week HLP program was effective in relieving pain and improving certain psychological functions among older people in the community. By learning about nutrition, fall prevention, and drug management, it is likely that older persons can reduce their pain, have a more balanced diet, and improve their psychological well-being. This will result in a better quality of life and greater happiness for older people in the community in the longer run.

REFERENCES

American Geriatrics Society Panel on Persistent Pain in Older Persons (2002). The management of persistent pain in older persons. *Journal of the American Geriatrics Society*, 46: 635 - 651.

Bray, G. A. (2004). Classification and evaluation of the overweight patient. In G. A. Bray and C. Bouchard (eds.), Handbook of obesity: Clinical applications (2nd ed., pp.1-32). New York: Dekker.

Breivik, H., Collett, B., Ventafrida, V., Cohen R., Gallagher, D. (2006). Survey of chronic pain in Europe: prevalence, impact on daily life, and treatment. *Eur. J. Pain*, 10: 287-333.

Brown, S. T., Kirkpatrick, M. K., Swanson, M. S., McKenzie, I. L. (2011). Pain Experience of the Elderly. *Pain Management Nursing*, 2011, 12(4): 190 - 6.

Cavalieri, T. A. (2002). Pain management in the elderly. *Journal of the American Osteopathic Association*, 102(9): 481 - 5.

Clark, D. (1999). 'Total pain', disciplinary power and the body in the work of Cicely Saunders, 1958-1967. *Social Science and Medicine*, 49: 727 - 36.

Craig, C. and Mountain, G. (2006). Lifestyle matters: An occupational approach to healthy ageing. Speechmark, Bicester.

Guigoz, Y. (2006). The Mini-Nutritional Assessment (MNA®) Review of the Literature – What does it tell us? *J. Nutr. Health Aging*, 2006, 10: 466 - 487.

Hanlon, J. T., Backonja, M., Weiner, D., and Argoff, C. (2009). Evolving pharmacological management of persistent pain in older persons. *Pain Med.*, 2009; 10(6): 959 - 61.

Kashdan, T. B. and Yuen, M. (2007). Whether highly curious students thrive academically depends on the learning environment of their school: A study of Hong Kong adolescents. *Motivation and Emotion, 31:* 260 - 270.

Kemp, C. A., Ersek, M., and Turner J. A. (2005). A descriptive study of older adults with persistent pain: use and perceived effectiveness of pain management strategies. *BMC Geriatr.*, 2005; *5*: 12.

Lansbury, G. (2000). Chronic pain management: a qualitative study of elderly people's preferred coping strategies and barriers to management. *Disabil. Rehabil.,* 2000; 22: 2 - 14.

Lyubomirsky, S. and Lepper, H. (1999). A measure of subjective happiness: Preliminary reliability and construct validation. *Social Indicators Research*, 46: 137 - 155.

Park, J. and Hughes, A. K. (2012). Nonpharmacological approaches to the management of chronic pain in community-dwelling older adults: A review of empirical evidence. *Journal of the American Geriatrics Society*, 60: 555 - 568.

Parmelee, P. A. Measuring mood and psychosocial function associated with pain in later life. In S. J. Gibson and D. K. Weiner (eds.), Pain in older persons (pp. 175-202). Seattle: The International Association for the Study of Pain, 2005.

Pickering, G. Age differences in clinical pain states. In S. J. Gibson and D. K. Weiner (eds.), Pain in older persons (pp. 67-85). Seattle: The International Association for the Study of Pain, 2005.

Rudy, T. E. and Lieber, S. J. Functional assessment of older adults with chronic pain. In S. J. Gibson and D. K. Weiner (eds.), Pain in older persons (pp. 153-173). Seattle: The International Association for the Study of Pain, 2005.

Smith, A. H. (2002). Patient and perseverance. Chinese characteristics. Norwalk: EastBridge, 2002: 152 - 61.

Social Welfare Department (2015). Neighbourhood Elderly Centre [online]. Available from URL: http://www.swd.gov.hk/en/index/site_pubsvc/page_elderly/sub_csselderly/id_ neighbourhood/[Accessed 2015 Sept 6].

Stewart, C., Schofield, P., Elliott, A. M., Torrance, N., and Leveille, S. (2014). What do we mean by "older adults' persistent pain self-management"? A concept analysis. *Pain Medicine*, 2014, 15: 214 - 224.

Strong, J. (2002). Lifestyle management. In Strong, J., Unruh A. M., Wright A., et al. (eds.). Pain: a textbook for therapists. Churchill Livingstone, London.

Tse, M. Y. M., Leung, R. W. S., and Ho, S. S. K. (2012). Pain and psychological well-being of older persons living in nursing homes: an exploratory study in planning patient-centered intervention. *Journal of Advanced Nursing*, 68 (2): 312 - 321.

Tse, M. Y. M. and Vong, S. K. S. (2012). Pain beliefs and pain-related profiles of older persons living in nursing homes. *Journal of Pain Management*, 5(2): 141 - 152.

Tse, M. M. Y, Wan, V. T. K., and Ho, S. S. K. (2010). Profile of pain and use of pharmacological and non-pharmacological methods for relieving pain in older persons in nursing homes. *J. Pain Manag.*, 2010; 3(3): 309 - 17.

World Health Organization (1998). Prevention and Management of the Global Epidemic of Obesity. Report of the WHO Consultation on Obesity. WHO: Geneva.

INDEX

B

C

D

G

H

Q

R

S

T

U

V

RECEIVED

JAN 1 2 2017

GUELPH HUMBER LIBRARY
205 Humber College Blvd
Toronto, ON   M9W 5L7